Cooperstown's Back Door

Cooperstown's Back Door

*A History of Negro Leaguers
in the Baseball Hall of Fame*

Paul D. White

McFarland & Company, Inc., Publishers
Jefferson, North Carolina

ISBN (print) 978-1-4766-9354-5
ISBN (ebook) 978-1-4766-5421-8

LIBRARY OF CONGRESS AND BRITISH LIBRARY
CATALOGUING DATA ARE AVAILABLE

Library of Congress Control Number 2024031986

© 2024 Paul D. White. All rights reserved

*No part of this book may be reproduced or transmitted in any form
or by any means, electronic or mechanical, including photocopying
or recording, or by any information storage and retrieval system,
without permission in writing from the publisher.*

Front cover image: Satchel Paige in Los Angeles, 1933
(UCLA Library Special Collections)

Printed in the United States of America

*McFarland & Company, Inc., Publishers
Box 611, Jefferson, North Carolina 28640
www.mcfarlandpub.com*

For Sam, my Boy-o.
For Katie, my Boo.
For Katie, my Bonus.
And for Shelley, my Love.

Table of Contents

Preface	1
1. Why Cooperstown?	5
2. The White Men at the Top	17
3. Integration	29
4. Foot Dragging	50
5. Change	74
6. The Back Door	94
7. The First Wave	102
8. Back to Obscurity	110
9. The Second Wave	124
10. The Second Special Committee	135
11. Over It	148
12. Another Effort, More Hope	158
Epilogue	180
Acknowledgments	183
Chapter Notes	185
Bibliography	205
Index	223

Preface

THE BASEBALL HALL OF FAME in Cooperstown, New York, is built upon a lie told by a murderer. By the time of the Hall of Fame's founding in 1935, everyone involved in the project to create a national museum and hall of fame dedicated to baseball knew about both the lie and the murder, and simply didn't care. A tale needed to be told, and money needed to be made, and inconveniences like historical accuracy wouldn't stand in their way. Promoting a convenient myth was exactly what they needed.

Myth building is a critical component of the Negro Leagues history as well, by necessity rather than by choice. Statistics for the Negro Leagues weren't kept in a coordinated way. Schedules varied. Newspaper coverage was incomplete. Newsreels of game action were essentially nonexistent. That forces those who want to tell the history of the Negro Leagues to use word of mouth, and eyewitness accounts. Those are notoriously inaccurate and tend toward the exaggeration of the extremes. It's easy for myths to proliferate under those circumstances. Josh Gibson didn't actually hit a home run that didn't land until the next day, and Cool Papa Bell couldn't turn off the light switch and be in bed before it got dark, but those exaggerations are retold happily to convey the flavor or the Negro Leagues and their players where numbers and reports do not.

Unlike the Negro Leagues and those who study them, the National Baseball Hall of Fame and Museum, and Major League Baseball as well, had a choice. They didn't have to build myths, they chose to. To some degree, they still do.

The Hall of Fame is not, and never has been, in the business of documenting the true and complete history of baseball. The goal, rather, has always been to build a myth about the sport that the public wanted to hear. To tell them a story, one that was neat, and easy to understand. One that would make the largest possible number of people buy tickets to the Hall of Fame, and stay in local hotels, and eat at local restaurants.

That's a critical fact to understand, because it explains so many of the subsequent decisions made by Hall leadership over the nearly ninety years it has existed. Public opinion was always a critical, perhaps the critical, factor in deciding the directions in which the Hall ultimately grew.

At the time of its founding in the 1930s, there was no appetite with the public at large to recognize that Black people played baseball. They were excluded from the Major Leagues and had been for more than fifty years. Their own separate leagues went largely unattended and unreported outside of the Black community. White Major Leaguers knew the quality of those players from barnstorming tours and exhibition matches, and sang their praises when given the chance, but the public at large and the leadership of the White Major Leagues preferred to ignore them.

The Hall of Fame followed the same course. Desperate to build an attraction that would appeal to the masses, they contacted the minor leagues, and colleges, and high schools, all in an attempt to portray baseball's history in a way that people would pay to see. They even involved the Boy Scouts. What they did not do was talk to a single Black person, including representatives of the Negro Leagues. Telling the game's story accurately would mean documenting uncomfortable truths that White baseball fans didn't want to hear, and likely wouldn't pay for.

The Hall of Fame and the village of Cooperstown were desperate to tie the town and the game together, happily retelling the fiction that their famous local son, General Abner Doubleday, had invented the sport there. They knew it wasn't true, and the Hall of Fame now openly admits it was a myth, but at the time it was the accepted, simplified story that most Americans believed, so the Hall's founders and the town's leaders latched onto it.

In doing so, they chose to ignore a true baseball pioneer, who really did learn the game while living in Cooperstown. But that pioneer, Bud Fowler, happened to be Black. Including him in their story would have been truthful but messy, and, they feared, unwelcome by potential patrons.

Further driving the decision to whitewash the game's past was the Hall's critical need to be aligned with so-called "organized baseball," the White Major Leagues and their minor league partners. The Hall needed baseball's buy-in to be successful, not only as a source of the artifacts necessary to make any museum successful, but also for the free advertising that would come with having an organization as large and successful as the Major Leagues touting their museum as a destination.

Baseball in the 1930s was the preeminent sport in America,

Preface

unrivaled by any team sport and vying for fans' attention with only boxing and horse racing as serious competitors. The commissioner, Judge Kenesaw Mountain Landis, wielded enormous power, and had the will to use it. He could crush the Hall of Fame as a viable attraction with just one press release, particularly since the Baseball Writers Association of America, and *The Sporting News*, and other media outlets, depended so heavily upon baseball for their own livelihoods.

It was critical for the Hall to remain on Landis' good side, or at least to stay away from his bad side. And Judge Landis didn't want Black people in the Major Leagues. In fact, he didn't even want them playing exhibitions against Major Leaguers.

With this as the environment into which the Hall of Fame was born, there was little chance that its leaders would choose to paint an inclusive, accurate picture of the game's past. To succeed, they felt the Hall needed to reflect American public opinion, rather than be something that made the public reflect.

That remains true today. The Hall of Fame has evolved over time, and strides have been made during the almost ninety years it has existed. Different stories are now told, more inclusive ones that come closer to accurately portraying baseball's long history. But that evolution has come from continuing to reflect the view of most of the American public, which has been changed during the Hall's existence by war, prosperity, technology, and social justice reforms.

Any examination of the Hall's history reveals an obvious pattern. They design their museum displays, and write their rules for election, based upon what they feel will best conform to public opinion. Gradual societal shifts typically aren't enough to alter those rules and displays, but more consequential catalysts are. The involvement of Black soldiers and sailors in World War II, the Civil Rights movement, a popular baseball documentary, and the murder of George Floyd have all served to drive change in the public's expectations from the Hall of Fame, and led to changes in how baseball's past has been portrayed.

Those changes have allowed the story of Black baseball to finally be told in fuller form by the sport's ultimate repository of its history, and further evolutions will happen over time, as the public demands them. But the Hall's general mission of reflecting that public demand has not changed. And there's little reason to expect that it will.

CHAPTER 1

Why Cooperstown?

THERE IS NO EASY WAY TO GET TO Cooperstown, literally or figuratively.

The figurative part is known. The name of the village has become synonymous with its largest attraction, the National Baseball Hall of Fame and Museum, and it's the dream of tens of thousands of Major League players to someday be selected to have a plaque in the Hall of Fame that bears their name.

Getting that plaque is the hard part. Of course, it takes immense talent to play or manage baseball. Or administer it, or umpire it, or in some way display enough excellence in the game that Major League Baseball decides you're worthy of a job. Then you must do that job at the highest level, exceeding 95 percent or more of your peers, and you must do that for at least a decade, usually far more.

Then you wait at least five years after you retire (unless you die first) to be judged by a select group of journalists, 75 percent of whom must agree you deserve one of those plaques. If you're passed over the first time, you have to hope that at least 5 percent of the journalists voted for you, giving you up to nine more years to be elected. And if you're still passed over, you wait and hope an ever evolving and even more select secondary group agrees to reconsider your career and decide that those journalists had been too strict with you.

That's the figurative road to Cooperstown. It's not an easy one, and, if you were a Black or dark-skinned Latin player who wasn't allowed to play in the White Major Leagues, the difficulty level goes up several notches.

The literal road to Cooperstown is even harder.

The village has been described as remote. That's accurate. If you've ever seen Daniel Day-Lewis in *The Last of the Mohicans*, running up and down mountains in the forest, the region around Cooperstown is what the filmmakers were trying to depict. Granted, they exaggerated a bit and filmed in North Carolina to get the look they wanted, but the book the film is based upon uses central New York as its setting. The book's author, James Fenimore Cooper, was a member of the family after which the village is named.

Modern life has arrived in the region since the book was written, but only by degrees. The roads are paved, but still winding and limited to two lanes. There is cellular service, but the surrounding hills will generally limit the number of bars on your phone. You can't come to Cooperstown by air or rail, so you'll be driving into town, passing a surprising number of homes that proudly advertise their awareness of current events, namely the outcome of the 2020 presidential election, which they apparently feel needs a re-do. The village itself is still small, with less than 1,800 residents in the last census. They are spread out over the area, which remains wooded and hilly and still has a large amount of farmland. The central part of the town around the Hall of Fame is a quintessential American small town, with no building taller than four stories and angled parking spaces on each side of Main Street.

The Hall of Fame itself has no parking available to visitors. For that you must find a public lot somewhere in town, or park in one of the satellite lots outside of the main village and ride a small shuttle bus to the Hall of Fame. The front doors are right on Main Street, and there is no other public entrance. Walking around the building takes you into the employee's parking lot and down an alley to get back to Main Street. There is no space on the grounds to hold the induction ceremony each year, which has outgrown the available space. For that, they now use the grounds of the Clark Sports Center on the other side of the Susquehanna River, a little over a mile away.

It seems like an odd place to have a major national tourist attraction, at least one that doesn't have to be there. There is only one place to see Niagara Falls, or see where the Battle of Gettysburg was fought, but there are any number of places that could have been the home of a national museum about baseball. Everything about the village begs the question, why the hell is the Baseball Hall of Fame here?

The answer to that question is a tale of two Abners.

* * *

In the early 1900s, two of the more prominent figures in the early days of organized baseball, Albert Spalding and Henry Chadwick, disagreed over the origins of the sport.

Chadwick, an Englishman by birth, and the preeminent sportswriter of his day who was credited with inventing the box score, felt that the sport had evolved from the game of rounders, noting their similarities were too many to view them as unrelated.

Spalding, the sporting goods magnate and former player who

1. Why Cooperstown?

It's hard to get to Cooperstown, a small town in central New York that seems to be an odd place for a national tourist attraction (author's collection).

helped organize the National League, didn't care for that view. He felt that the sport was purely American in origin, "and no other game or country has any right to claim its parentage."[1] Regardless of whether you feel his views are best described as patriotic or xenophobic, the upshot was that Spalding stressed the differences between rounders and baseball rather than their similarities, and very badly wanted to prove that baseball was a unique American invention.

Both men having published articles outlining their respective positions, and neither feeling the need to compromise, in 1905 they agreed to the formation of a commission that would study the matter and reach some official conclusion. Both men agreed to accept whatever result the commission settled upon.

It appears that Chadwick took all of this as a bit of good fun, something between friends and colleagues that the public would enjoy. He later described the disagreement as "a joke between Albert and myself."[2] Chadwick worked for Spalding, as editor of his famous *Spalding Base Ball Guides*, which was also the venue in which both men had published their respective views of the game's origins. The public debate, and commission to investigate the two views, would raise interest in the sport and, quite likely, increase sales of the annual guide.

Spalding, on the other hand, took the matter far more seriously. He personally selected each of the members of the commission, including its leader, and sent them off on a quest to determine which of the two theories was correct. His strong preference was well known among the committee, and he would work over the two years of its existence to assure they reached the conclusion that he wanted.

The responsibility for that result fell upon the judgment of Abraham Mills, an attorney, executive for an elevator company, a one-time soldier who had served in U.S. Army during the Civil War, and was, most relevantly, former president of the National League. The Mills Commission, as it soon became known, solicited input from the public, any information that would allow the commission to explore the origins of the game and reach some sort of conclusion.

Then Mills and most of his fellow commissioners sat back and did almost nothing for two years. They were all busy people with careers in other fields. Morgan Bulkeley was a sitting U.S. Senator for Connecticut. Former players Al Reach and George Wright were distributors of sporting goods. Former National League president Nicholas Young worked in the Treasury Department. They weren't spending their days combing through letters and telegrams from baseball fans.

Henry Chadwick, who knew all along that baseball wasn't invented by a single person, in Cooperstown or anywhere else (New York Public Library Digital Collection).

1. Why Cooperstown?

One member of the committee was at least keeping track of what they received. James Sullivan, head of the Amateur Athletic Union, or AAU, collected "hundreds of interesting letters and documents," which he reviewed on behalf of the committee. Nothing in those documents pointed to any single origin of baseball, but they did, at least, provide "amazingly clearheaded reminiscences by aged ballplayers and scribes."[3]

The commission began their work in 1905 and spent two years seeking firm evidence that never arrived. The closest thing to it were personal recollections of early games being played in different places, one of which was provided by a retired mining engineer from Colorado named Abner Graves.

Albert Spalding, the man behind the country's acceptance of the Cooperstown myth (Library of Congress).

In response to a syndicated advertisement for information that Spalding published in several newspapers, Graves wrote a letter to the editor of the Akron *Beacon Journal* in which he claimed to have been present in Cooperstown, New York, in the spring of either 1839 or 1840 when a young man named Abner Doubleday made alterations to the rules of a more common game called town ball and labeled the new game "Base Ball." According to Graves, Doubleday had laid out the field, including four bases and a ring for the pitcher to stand in, and his rules called for 11 players on each side and the basics of how outs were made.

There was absolutely nothing to corroborate Graves' recollections. In fact, there were some disturbing problems with his version of events, the first being that Abner Doubleday was already a plebe at West Point in the spring of 1839 and was unlikely to have been given leave.[4] It's possible he could have been back in Cooperstown in a later year, but also unlikely since his family no longer lived there.[5] Then there's the problem that Doubleday would have been 20 years old or more in the timeframe specified by Graves, while Graves was anywhere from five to seven years old. It would have been unusual for an adult Army officer-in-making to be playmates with kids of that age.[6]

Compounding these issues was the fact that Doubleday was a well-known national figure from his service in the Civil War, as well as a friend of Mills for thirty years, yet there was no record that he ever mentioned the sport of baseball to Mills or anyone else. He left behind dozens of personal diaries, had written a variety of newspaper and magazine articles, and didn't discuss baseball in any of them.[7]

Graves himself was a troubling figure. He seems to have been involved in a variety of adventures in his youth, from being involved in the California Gold Rush in 1849,[8] to sailing around Cape Horn,[9] to serving as a Pony Express rider in 1852.[10] It would be difficult for the commission to verify some of that information, but at least the Pony Express claim could have been debunked easily, since it didn't exist in 1852.[11] While in California, Graves did, apparently, deliver mail on horseback for a couple of firms, including Wells Fargo, but that's not the same as the Pony Express.

It appears the commission wasn't interested in debunking anything regarding Graves' claim. In fact, Spalding was thrilled to receive Graves' letter from Sullivan. Even though he'd established the Mills Commission to be an objective third party, separate from the participants in the original dispute, Spalding decided to circumvent the impartial commission he had hand-picked. He responded directly to Graves, seeking additional details, which Graves seems to have happily provided in a follow-up letter directly to Spalding in November 1905. It didn't provide any further specifics, or anything remotely like corroboration, but Spalding took it as evidence, nonetheless.

The commission remain in operation for another two years, collecting more speculative correspondence and further interviews with old ballplayers, but nothing in the way of concrete proof of baseball's invention in Cooperstown or anywhere else. Some of that time was spent trying to find a link between the Doubleday story and the Knickerbocker Base Ball Club of New York, in the hope that the two competing origin theories may somehow be merged into one. No such link was ever found, but a decision of some sort from the commission was expected.

To that end, Mills released a report of the committee's findings on December 30, 1907, in which he listed the various possible origins of

1. Why Cooperstown?

the sport but disregarded all but the Doubleday story. While admitting that the commission was resting its conclusion upon the "circumstantial statement by a reputable gentleman" (meaning Graves), Mills wrote that "baseball had its origins in the United States" and that "according to the best evidence obtainable to date" the game "was devised by Abner Doubleday at Cooperstown, N.Y. in 1839."[12]

Spalding got the decision that he wanted and was happy to advertise it. In fact, he asked Chadwick to do the advertising for him, in the form of a book about the origins of baseball. Chadwick, seemingly bemused by the entire affair, agreed, even writing a note to Mills in which he said

Abner Doubleday. Once identified as the founder of baseball, the Hall now acknowledges that story was a myth (Library of Congress).

the commission's final report was "a masterly piece of special pleading which lets my dear old friend Albert escape a bad defeat."[13] Sadly, Chadwick died shortly after, and never wrote the book, which Spalding then took upon himself to produce. In 1911, he published *America's National Game*, which was dedicated to the memory of his friend, Henry Chadwick, and included his boastful claim that he could "prove that Base Ball is our National Game."[14] He made no mention of Graves or the role he played but did repeat the "reputable gentleman" segment of Mills' final report and wrote that he had nothing to add to it other than a lengthy biography of Abner Doubleday.[15]

The commission's finding was immediately questioned in many circles. A series of articles in *Collier's* by Will Irwin noted the problems with Doubleday's enrollment at West Point, and convincingly cited an instance of the game's being played even earlier than Graves had asserted.[16] Other writers did the same, and Mills, when asked in

1926 what conclusive evidence was used by the commission to reach their decision, candidly admitted, "None at all, as far as the actual origin of baseball is concerned." In fact, Mills reportedly felt "that he had been manipulated to boost one old friend (Doubleday) by another old friend.... Spalding."[17]

None of the questions mattered in the eyes of the public. The story of a Civil War general creating the country's most popular sport in his small hometown was too compelling to ignore. The Doubleday myth became the true story of baseball's origins as far as most Americans were concerned, exactly as Albert Spalding hoped it would.

As for Graves, he went back to his life in Colorado. In 1909 he married his second wife, a woman named Minnie Latham, when he was 75 and she was in her early thirties. They lived in a house that was in her name, and when Graves asked her to sell it and she refused, they had an argument that ended with Graves shooting her.[18] He was arrested and found to be suffering from debilitating emotional and physical stress, so he was admitted to the same hospital where she lay dying. She decided to forgive him for shooting her but rewrote her will to disinherit him anyway. For his part, he kept saying, "I hope she dies," as he lay in bed, and she ultimately did. Found criminally insane in court, he was committed to an asylum and died in 1926, the same year Mills admitted that his commission had no reason to believe his story about Abner Doubleday and the origins of baseball.[19]

Abraham Mills, a friend of Abner Doubleday's and former president of the National League, who was tabbed by Albert Spalding to determine the origins of baseball (New York Public Library Digital Collection).

* * *

Nearly thirty years after Graves first told his tale, and nearly ten years after he murdered his wife, an old baseball was found in a trunk on a farm near Fly Creek, New York, in the general vicinity of Cooperstown. The farm was supposedly owned by the Graves family, and the old baseball, packed away with correspondence from Abner himself, was reputed to be the baseball he played with as a child.[20]

Enter Stephen C. Clark, one of the heirs to a family fortune that stemmed from investment in the Singer Sewing Machine Company. The family had lengthy ties to Cooperstown because their grandmother was from there, and many of them had built summer homes in the area. They'd also invested a great deal of money in a variety of enterprises. The Otesaga Hotel was built by the Clarks and remains a lovely resort on the shores of Lake Otsego. The Alfred Corning Clark Gymnasium, the town's recreation center named for Stephen Clark's father, was another family investment, as was the money they put up to establish the local Mary Imogene Bassett Hospital, which remains the cornerstone institution of the area's Bassett Healthcare Network to this day.

The town's economy, for several decades, had been built upon two things: Tourism and beer. The tourism centered on the lake and surrounding mountains, a summer get-away for rich New Yorkers, while the beer centered on the local crop of hops. Both of those economic pillars were in dire condition by 1934. The Great Depression had reduced disposable income for most Americans to the point that they were unable to vacation at Lake Otsego or anywhere else. And the market for hops had crashed due to both Prohibition and a blight on the local crop.[21] With these staples of local economic life in jeopardy, something had to be done to prop up the town, and, by extension, all the various economic investments the Clark family had made in the area.

Stephen Clark, philanthropist, heir to the Singer Sewing Machine fortune, and founder of the Baseball Hall of Fame (courtesy of the Baseball Hall of Fame).

14   Cooperstown's Back Door

Clark was not operating with entirely selfish motives. He was a noted philanthropist, having donated significant money to the town and region, using much of his family fortune for the betterment of others. That included establishing scholarships, and converting family property into public museums, further stimulating the local economy.

By the time Graves' old baseball resurfaced, both Clark and the town's leaders were already trying to draw attention to the Doubleday story and create reasons for fans of the country's most popular sport to visit Cooperstown. In May 1934, Clark held meetings of his Clark Foundation in Cooperstown. During a break, one of his employees, Alexander Cleland, was strolling through the village and saw the renovations that were taking place at the local ballpark, Doubleday Field. A workman enthusiastically asked him what he thought of it and mentioned the excitement about the town's planned celebrations of baseball's 100th anniversary that were scheduled for 1939, the supposed centennial of Doubleday's invention.

The encounter caused Cleland to ponder whether Cooperstown's connection to baseball was precisely the fix needed for the town's sagging economy. He wrote up his thoughts and submitting a proposal to Clark, in which he suggested the development of a baseball museum. It was a very thorough proposal, stressing the historical connection between baseball and the village, suggesting the involvement of the Baseball Writers Association of America (BBWAA) in advertising the new venture, and the cooperation of the Major Leagues, including potential funding sources from World Series profits or the playing of an inter-league All-Star game.

Clark, a lover of both museums and history, was enthusiastic about the idea from the moment it was proposed, and gave Cleland approval to begin pursuing it, including tracking down memorabilia that might be displayed. At first, Cleland struggled to locate items of interest, so when the family that was living on the old Graves farm found that battered, ancient baseball and decided to sell it, Clark eagerly purchased it for five dollars. He had a custom case built for it, and put it on display, thinking it would become a centerpiece of the museum he and his foundation were now pursuing.

The fact that the baseball didn't fit the physical description given in Graves' letters didn't stop them. The fact that Graves' entire Doubleday origin story had been questioned for decades, or that the head of the commission that had blessed it had since called it into question, didn't stop them either. Nor did the fact that Graves, by this point, was a convicted murderer who had died in an insane asylum.

Clark, Cleland, the leaders of the village, and, ultimately, the

1. Why Cooperstown? 15

leadership of the Major Leagues, all had a business opportunity to pursue, and an entire region's economy to be boosted during a difficult time. If that opportunity happened to be based on a myth that had been widely accepted by the public despite being provably false, so be it.

* * *

Fort Plain, New York, is a town of about 2,000 people that sits 25 miles northeast of Cooperstown, in the same sort of valley, surrounded by the same hills and fields. In 1858, a Black man named John W. Jackson, Jr. was born there. His father, John Sr., has been described as "a fugitive hop-picker," which makes sense given the region's staple crop, but he'd become a barber by the time John Jr. was born.[22]

When the 1860 census was taken, the family had already moved to Cooperstown, where John Jr. attended Cooperstown Seminary, a private academy, and learned to play baseball. It was a fully integrated upbringing with mostly White classmates, as only 28 Black people lived in Cooperstown at the time.[23] By 1870, the family was no longer living there, but the best estimate is that John spent most of his early years in Cooperstown and developed a keen interest and skill in baseball.[24]

We know this because, by the time he was 14 years old, he was already playing baseball professionally with an otherwise all–White amateur team in New Castle, Pennsylvania, just across the state line from Youngstown, Ohio. Speculation is that his middle-class family likely didn't approve of his life as a ballplayer, causing him to use a different name. He still went by Bud, a nickname he was given because that's what he called other players, but he was now going by a new last name, Fowler.[25]

It was as Bud Fowler that he played for an amateur club in Chelsea, Massachusetts, in April 1878, when he was barely 20 years old. A local all-star team comprised of players from the area was picked to play an exhibition against the Boston Red Caps, defending champions of the National League. Fowler pitched for the amateurs, and surrendered just three hits and one run, leading them to a 2–1 victory. That caught the attention of another local team, the Lynn Live Oaks of the International Association, a minor league affiliated with the National League. A month after beating the Red Caps, Fowler was asked to fill in for the Live Oaks when one of their pitchers was injured. He did, pitching a 3–0 shutout against the London (Ontario) Tecumsehs, and pitching in two other games that he lost.[26]

By playing for the Lynn team, Bud Fowler of Cooperstown became the first Black player to integrate a minor league, as well as the first known Black professional baseball player.

One would imagine that a new museum located in Cooperstown and dedicated to the history of baseball might have a keen interest in documenting the historic accomplishments of a native son. They certainly took great pains to do so regarding Abner Doubleday, despite ample evidence that they shouldn't.

But the founders of the Hall of Fame had no use for the story of Bud Fowler, or any other Black ballplayer. They were in the business of reflecting society, and American society was deeply segregated in 1935. The fact that some of the best baseball in history had been played in leagues made entirely of Black players wasn't enough to overcome that segregation, and so it wouldn't be enough for the Hall of Fame, either.

Another reason for Cleland and the rest of the Hall's museum's founders to ignore Black baseball was because they needed the cooperation of the Major Leagues to make the museum a success, and the Major Leagues refused to allow Black players onto their teams. More importantly, the all-powerful commissioner of baseball, Judge Kenesaw Mountain Landis, was already showing signs of apathy toward the concept of a Hall of Fame. And the last place Cleland wanted to be was on Landis' bad side.

CHAPTER 2

The White Men at the Top

BASEBALL COMMISSIONER Kenesaw Mountain Landis was first contacted about a potential baseball museum in Cooperstown in May of 1935. At the time, Landis was synonymous with Major League baseball. With Babe Ruth recently retired, Landis was seen by many as the craggy, dour, face of the game. That's exactly what Landis wanted.

Landis had been overt in the exercise of the virtually limitless powers he'd been given by the owners, which included fierce protections of the color barrier that had been in place for nearly forty years when he assumed office. Even the game's biggest star, Babe Ruth, was not safe from Landis' reach or wrath. When he went on a barnstorming tour after the 1921 World Series, in violation of a rule that prohibited World Series participant from barnstorming. Landis was enraged, angrily asking "Who does that big monkey think he is?"[1] This was said amid speculation that Ruth was of partly Black ancestry, a rumor that teammates used to insult him, and that Ty Cobb once used as an excuse not to share a room with him.[2] He then suspended Ruth and fined him the amount of his World Series check.

The barnstorming rule Ruth had broken was intended to prevent the two World Series teams from touring the country and replicating the series, which would have damaged the value of the World Series itself. But another aspect of barnstorming bothered Landis as well. White ballclubs that went barnstorming during the offseason to earn extra money were routinely being beaten by teams made up of Black players. From the inception of the Negro National League in 1920, the same year Landis was appointed commissioner, through 1924, records show that Black teams had a 29–31–2 overall record against their White counterparts. They essentially played White teams to a draw, and that's just from the records we know. The White press of that time was often reluctant to report on losses by White teams to Black ones, so it's likely the record of the Black teams was even better.

This bothered Landis, as it was disproving the standard disclaimer offered by White owners, players, managers, and reporters when asked why no Black players were on Major League rosters. The response was usually that no Black players were good enough, but the barnstorming tours were showing that to be a lie. Rather than allow this to continue, Landis decreed that no Major League teams could go on barnstorming tours using their Major League uniforms or using the name of their Major League team. He further limited the number of players from the same team that could be included on any barnstorming roster, on the theory that the Major Leagues could claim that any losses weren't by full Major League squads. When Rube Foster, the legendary Black pitcher, manager, and founder of the Negro National League, complained to Landis about the limitations on games between White and Black teams, Landis gave him a blunt response. "Mr. Foster, when you beat our teams, it gives us a black eye."[3]

This was the climate in which Alexander Cleland was operating as he attempted to launch the new baseball museum. He knew the museum wouldn't be successful without the backing of the Major Leagues. There had never been a museum dedicated to baseball, or any effort to retain the game's artifacts, which would be necessary for any displays the museum intended to have. Former players, in many cases, kept their old uniforms, bats and gloves, but acquiring them would require the museum to reach out to each of them individually, and without anyone from baseball management to vouch for them. Cleland had already found it difficult to track down items that might be of interest to the public. Coordinating with the Major Leagues, not only in collecting artifacts but

Judge Kenesaw Mountain Landis, the first baseball commissioner. He oversaw baseball's continued segregation for his entire 24-year tenure (Library of Congress).

2. The White Men at the Top
19

also in the public relations necessary to make the new museum successful with baseball fans, was critical.

That meant getting the backing of Landis, a man whose singular opinion was all that mattered in baseball and had already proven to be close-minded in matters related to race overall and the integration of baseball specifically. Under the circumstances, there was little chance that Cleland or anyone else associated with the museum would take any stance for racial justice that would have been counter to the segregationist position taken by Landis and the Major Leagues. In fact, he'd have to go out of his way to stroke Landis' ego.

Considering this, Cleland decided to approach Landis very carefully. He started by simply providing the commissioner with materials about the planned museum in Abner Doubleday's hometown, and the hopes of opening it in time to coordinate with celebrations of baseball's centennial anniversary in 1939. The local committee, he wrote to Landis, felt that since Landis was already serving as the head of those centennial plans, he should also serve as the national chairman of the efforts to build the museum. Essentially, he decided his best bet to garner Landis' support was to flatter him.

Cleland was disappointed by Landis' response. At first, there was none. More than a month passed without hearing back from the commissioner, enough time that Cleland reached out to Landis' secretary to find out if his letter had reached him. When Landis finally did reply, he was noncommittal, and told Cleland that he would defer any response until he could discuss the matter at the winter meetings in December, after the season was over.

As distressing as this no doubt was, Cleland could have saved his worry, because he'd already made an even stronger ally than Landis would ever prove to be. In November 1934, as part of his attempt to gain approval from the Major Leagues, Cleland had also reached out to John Heydler, president of the National League. The league presidents still had a fair amount of influence at the time, and Heydler had not only approved of the original plan to build a museum and conduct some form of ceremony at Doubleday Field, but he had also passed along copies of Cleland's information to both Landis and American League president William Harridge, long before Cleland ever contacted Landis directly.

More importantly for Cleland's purposes, Heydler had appointed former sportswriter Ford Frick as the league's director of public relations earlier that year, and when he fell ill and was forced to resign his position shortly after Cleland contacted him, it was Frick that took Heydler's place as league president.

Frick absolutely loved the plans for a museum in Cooperstown.

He'd been to the village during his sportswriting days, and was familiar with its small town charm, something that resonated with him as a native of tiny Wawaka, Indiana. When he learned of Cleland's plans, he endorsed them enthusiastically, writing to Cleland that both he and Harridge were committed to providing help "in perpetuating the birthplace of baseball," and promised their "fullest cooperation in any project."

Within months, Frick had added an even more vital component, one that Cleland hadn't considered. When Cleland noted that the village was hoping to draw reporters to their project for publicity, and that an All-Star game of some kind was the proposed means doing that, Frick replied that the game wasn't practical since there was already an All-Star game that had just been established. Instead, he suggested they launch a Hall of Fame as part of the museum and enshrine the game's greatest players in it.

Frick later claimed that the idea for a hall of fame for baseball players occurred to him coincidentally a few days before meeting with Cleland, when he visited the Hall of Fame for Great Americans located at New York University. "I was much impressed," wrote Frick in his autobiography, "and had a notion that a Baseball Hall of Fame would be great for the game. Cleland's visit afforded the opportunity to try the idea out."[4]

Whatever the origins of the idea, passing it along to Cleland was the first step in cementing Frick's place as a critical figure in the game's history. The arc of his life was already remarkable even at that point. He'd started on a farm in Indiana, went to college, moved to Colorado to become a high school English teacher, and turned his hobby as a sports reporter into a full-time job. The work he did in Colorado got him sufficient notice to be offered a job by a paper in New York City, the *New York American*, where he also served as one of Babe Ruth's ghost writers and a radio announcer. A dozen years later, the National League public relations opportunity arose, and he found himself president of the oldest baseball league in the country before he turned forty.

Now he was the brainchild behind the institution that would serve as the ultimate honor for the game, a place where he would ultimately serve as chairman of the board of directors, be inducted as a member, and have a prestigious broadcasting award named for him even though "radio announcer" stands far down the list of his career accomplishments. To this day, two portraits occupy the rotunda outside the Hall of Fame's plaque gallery. One is of Stephen Clark, who funded the entire enterprise, as well as much of the economy of Cooperstown, and drove the idea of bringing a national baseball museum to the village. The other portrait is of Ford Frick.

2. The White Men at the Top

Ford Frick (holding hat), with American League president William Harridge. Frick was the new president of the National League when he suggested a Hall of Fame be built in Cooperstown (Library of Congress).

* * *

Frick taking the lead in coordinating the Major Leagues' participation in developing the museum and Hall of Fame, rather than Landis leading the effort himself, did nothing to remove the racial boundaries that Cleland and the Hall would have to follow. Frick's hands were far from clean regarding segregation and racial justice, and his views and words need to be looked at a bit more closely to understand the Hall of Fame's handling of the Negro Leagues during its first several decades. His deep interest in the Hall of Fame was a boon to those trying to start it, and an absolute disaster for Negro Leagues players who had to contend with his views and influence for the next forty years.

Before coming to New York as a sportswriter in 1922, Frick spent his entire life in two states: Indiana and Colorado. One thing those states had in common in the early part of the 20th century is that each was so heavily populated with members of the Ku Klux Klan that they elected governors who were openly members of that hate group or

22   Cooperstown's Back Door

were at least allied with them. Indiana, where both Frick and Landis were born and raised, had such a surge of Klan activity that it had been labeled "the epicenter of the national Klan movement" of the early part of the century.[5] That's not to imply that Frick was a member, or even sympathized with the KKK's cause, but it's inarguable that he was surrounded by anti–Black voices and sentiments during all the formative years of his life.

In his autobiography, Frick looked back at this same period with deep affection, fondly recalling with sentimentality the tune "Mammy" by Al Jolson, a song about a White man who had been nursed by a slave. Frick called this period "the golden age" of sports, listing several top athletes of the time, not one of whom was Black. Jack Johnson had been heavyweight champion during Frick's college years, but he wasn't mentioned. Rube Foster was an exceptional pitcher, manager, and founder of the Negro National League during this time, but Frick didn't mention him, either. Any number of great Black baseball players were in their prime during these years, including Oscar Charleston, Martin Dihigo, Dick Redding, and John Donaldson, to name just a few, yet Frick ignored their existence in this "golden age," despite their playing the sport Frick had made his career for more than fifty years.

Once in New York, Frick became a successful enough writer that he caught the attention of Babe Ruth's agent, Christy Walsh, and they reached an agreement for Frick to become one of a few ghost writers for Ruth, penning columns under his name. Frick and Ruth became friendly, and he was perfectly willing to compromise journalistic ethics to help his friend. In September 1925, Frick went so far as to write a column for Ruth in which he claimed to accept responsibility over failing to carry out a sign from his manager but didn't think he was being treated fairly by the team, while also writing a second column under his own byline in which he supported Ruth's claims and argued that the Yankees had a double standard that they applied to Ruth.

Frick would continue this pattern of favoritism, and of glorification of the past, segregated version of baseball, throughout his career. He would later entitle his 1973 autobiography *Games, Asterisks and People* in part because one of his most infamous acts as commissioner was to again put his thumb on the scale to protect his friend, Babe Ruth, making the decision that Roger Maris would have to break Ruth's single-season record of 60 home runs in the season's first 154 games, the same length season played when Ruth set the record, otherwise it wouldn't be considered the formal record. It would instead be listed separately in official baseball records, with a distinguishing mark of some sort, later assumed to be an asterisk, to distinguish it from Ruth's original record.

2. The White Men at the Top

Frick made no apology for this. He later told Jerome Holtzman, "What the dickens, I tried to protect the Babe because his record should stand until it's honestly beaten.... Now Hank Aaron's going for Babe's lifetime record of 714 home runs. Well, if he breaks it, he breaks it. But I'll never change my mind about Babe Ruth. Hell, Hank Aaron's already had two thousand more times at bat than Ruth had in his whole career. And the seasons are longer, you know, more games. He gets more opportunities."[6] Apparently, Aaron compiling his record against fully integrated competition, while also dealing with racism and death threats, were not circumstances worthy of Frick's consideration.

Furthering his personal biases, Frick was a staunch advocate for the Baseball Writers Association of America, the BBWAA, not only being the voting body for the Hall of Fame, but also having their own award and wing in the Hall where they are honored as members. This is not surprising coming from someone who still described himself during this retirement years as "a newspaperman at heart,"[7] and it fit perfectly with the preferences of Clark, Cleland, and others to have the press heavily involved for publicity reasons. As with the Major Leagues, the BBWAA during this time was not integrated. As Wendell Smith of the *Pittsburgh Courier* later said, "The baseball writers, at that time, were very conservative.... As an organization they didn't do much to advance our cause. When I applied for membership, I was turned down. They said I wasn't eligible because I wasn't covering day to day, that it wasn't my daily assignment. I made my appeal on the basis that if the sports editor for the *Daily Worker*, a Communist paper, was qualified, so was I."[8] This is the organization chosen by the Hall of Fame to determine its membership.

During his years in New York, Frick served as the first president of the New York chapter of the BBWAA. Every year, at the chapter's annual dinner, a minstrel show would be the evening's primary entertainment. Dan Daniel of *The Sporting News* found it hilarious. "I'm still laughing," he wrote of the 1933 event.[9] Frick was an enthusiastic participant in the show, donning blackface and telling jokes.[10] Upon being named director of publicity for the National League in 1934, it was reported that Frick would now be able to tell his jokes as end man of the minstrel show directly to league president John Heydler.[11]

Frick was mostly silent on the issue of race throughout Judge Landis' days, making him complicit in the ongoing segregation of baseball. When he did make a statement, it was always in support of Landis' argument that no formal color barrier existed. "I state unequivocally that there is no discrimination against Negroes or anybody else per se, in the National League. And you can quote me on that."[12] He would claim instead that integration wasn't possible due to societal issues, claiming that "the complex social barometer of this country makes it impossible for the Negro player to crash the big leagues," saying in essence that White players and fans wouldn't stand for Black players in the Major Leagues.[13] Time did nothing to alter Frick's views on the subject. He claimed again in his autobiography, "Contrary to common belief, baseball never had any rule prohibiting the employment of black players. What baseball operators had done, through the years, was bow abjectly to what they thought was overwhelming public opinion."[14]

He was very clear in his view that the purpose of those who owned the responsibility for preserving and growing the game, a group that included the commissioner, league presidents, owners, players, and writers, was to focus strictly on the positive. In the introduction to his autobiography, he bluntly stated, "This is not a controversial book.... You may feel I have overstepped reality in my praise of an individual, or in describing the thrill of some dramatic event— or that I have been overly enthusiastic in my defense of baseball, and baseball's rules and practices. I plead 'guilty,' proudly and without excuse. It was intentional.... This is a book written by a 'lucky' fan, for fans everywhere. I hope it is a happy book."[15] That all proved to be true. Frick largely ignores most controversies from his tenure in the game, and those he does mention are treated as minor disturbances in an otherwise uninterrupted half-century of joyous baseball experiences. There isn't a lot of reality in the memoir.

Wendell Smith became the first Black member of the Baseball Writers Association of America the same year the Jackie Robinson reached the major leagues (courtesy of the Baseball Hall of Famse).

2. The White Men at the Top

As so, when the Hall of Fame was approaching its grand opening to coincide with the centennial of an event that never happened, Frick intervened to prevent the embarrassment of the baseball establishment. A relative of Alexander Cartwright came forward, claiming that his relative, and not Abner Doubleday, was the true inventor of the game and should be honored as such. He noted that the Doubleday creation myth was fiction, and made it clear he wanted Cartwright properly recognized if the Hall of Fame wanted to avoid a public controversy. Seeking assistance in how to handle this potential calamity, Cleland contacted Frick, former public relations specialist, and Frick immediately went to work. He told Cleland that the Hall's intention was to honor the game, not any individual, signaling that baseball officials were content to back away from the Doubleday myth somewhat even before the new Hall of Fame building opened.

The Hall's Centennial Commission, of which Frick was a member, quickly voted to elect Cartwright to the Hall in 1938, and an announcement was made that a day would be held in Cartwright's honor the following year as part of the centennial celebrations. Abner Doubleday was not chosen for induction, either then or at any time since.

As for Black players, teams, or fans, Frick admitted there were no plans to include any Negro Leagues representation in the centennial celebration, and he wasn't open to the idea. "Organized baseball is celebrating in its own particular way," Frick told the *Pittsburgh Courier*. "However, we would be willing to give the Negro leagues suggestions as how to develop a similar celebration program."[16]

As with the Major Leagues, Ford Frick felt that any celebration of baseball's faux centennial should be segregated, too.

* * *

With a former sportswriter leading baseball's effort, and with the museum's founders openly wishing for publicity that would help them be successful, it's no surprise that the BBWAA would be given outsized influence in the affairs of the Hall of Fame. That influence is unchanged as of this writing, 87 years later.

As we've seen, the BBWAA was not a progressive organization at that time, and while it has grown and evolved with time, it's fair to note that progress has been slow. The BBWAA didn't elect a Black president to lead the organization until LaVelle E. Neal III was elected for the 2014 term, 105 years after the BBWAA was founded. The writers literally didn't elect a Black leader until six years after the United States had.

When Jerome Holtzman interviewed sportswriters for his book, *No Cheering in the Press Box*, many of their attitudes toward race relations and social justice were laid bare. Marshall Hunt, after describing Ruth as "the big baboon," gushed about evenings he and Ruth would sometimes spend at "some of those fine old Southern homes—mansions, plenty of help.... The host, coming from an old-time family, would ... have Negroes in hose, dressed just as they were at the end of or before the Civil War. And a big show in the kitchen, waiters, all sorts of attendants...."[17]

Fred Lieb, past president of the BBWAA, said, "I've been somewhat amused this past summer reading about the trouble Hank Aaron was running into chasing Ruth's record. Aaron said—and it came out in the papers—that the fans were writing him abusive letters, calling him 'n_____,' and he said that Babe Ruth was never confronted with anything like that." He then goes on to outline how Ruth's "Negroid features" had caused him to be taunted by teammates and opponents at times, as if this somehow equates to the repeated death threats Aaron received, which "somewhat amused" him.[18]

Fred Russell couldn't understand how the playing of "Dixie" could be viewed as offensive by anyone, calling it a "stirring tune."[19] Gene Kessler felt that Joe Louis "did more to help the colored people than any other athlete because he handled himself so well," going on to explain that outspoken Black boxers like Jack Johnson or Muhammad Ali were too "arrogant" or had too much "braggadocio" to be helpful to their race.[20] Jim Schlemmer proudly stopped attending the soap box derby when girls were allowed to participate and felt women sportswriters should be banned from the press box. "Women just don't belong there, any more than I belong at some tea party. They should be home doing the laundry and baking cookies."[21]

One of the leading figures among baseball writers at that time was J.G. Taylor Spink, owner and editor of *The Sporting News*, known as "The Bible of Baseball," for the influence it wielded within the game. Under Spink's leadership, *The Sporting News* virtually ignored Black baseball, particularly prior to the 1940s. When Black players were mentioned, unflattering racist stereotypes or backhanded compliments in the paper's coverage were common, often by Spink himself.

In describing a game played by Rube Foster's Chicago American Giants, Spink expressed surprise at the quality of play, expecting "the old happy-go-lucky high score game," and instead finding that the players demonstrated "remarkably good conduct."[22] In a column he wrote in 1934, Spink included as a note of trivia that "There have been three negroes in minor leagues, but only one in the majors, and he did not last more than a couple of days ... [Frank] Grant played second for Buffalo in the National League in 1887." He added that John McGraw had tried to

2. The White Men at the Top

J.G. Taylor Spink, owner and editor of *The Sporting News*, dedicated considerable space in "The Bible of Baseball" to opposing integration (courtesy of the Baseball Hall of Fame).

sign Grant to play for the Baltimore Orioles at the turn of the century, "but other clubs hollered." The trivia was wrong on several counts—Buffalo was no longer in the National League in 1887, Grant never played for a Major League team, while Fleet Walker did, and he lasted far more than "a couple of days"—but also stopped short of offering anything beyond the brief note about clubs "hollering" to explain why so few Black players had reached the majors.[23]

The reporters Spink employed were no better, using the same sort of racist stereotypes to describe Black players as well as Jews, or other ethnic immigrants. Edgar G. Brands had a regular column in *The Sporting News* entitled "Between Innings," and regularly included racist tropes he apparently found humorous. His column from June 18, 1931, in which he mocked the speech of Negro Leagues player Bob Murphy, was typical.

> "The fust Columbus n_____ what comes up hits de fust ball I pitches for a home run. De next time dat n_____ come up he hit one out'en de park. The third time dat n_____ comes up dey tuck him of in a ca-art. Wasn't no n_____ gonna get three home runs offen me in one game."[24]

The pidgin grammar is original to the article, and typical of the newspaper's representation of Black players. The four instances of the n-word have been sanitized above from the full version that appeared in the article. The following year, Brands used his platform in Spinks' paper to label Black people "pickaninnies," while describing how White players in Wilmington, North Carolina, had developed the racist habit of rubbing a Black person's head for good luck to break batting slumps.[25] In the October 16, 1919, issue, in an editorial about gambling on the 1919 World Series, then-editor Earl Obenshain wrote, "Because a lot of dirty, long-nosed, thick-lipped and strong-smelling gamblers butted into the World Series—an American event by the way—and some of said gamblers got crossed, stories were peddled that there was something wrong with the games that were played."[26]

Racist tropes were so common to Spink that he even inserted them in pieces that had nothing to do with any racial or ethnic minorities. In his 1947 biography of Landis, Spink described the antipathy with which Landis viewed Branch Rickey: "From the start, the Commissioner regarded him as the colored boy in the baseball farm's wood pile, even though Rickey's acumen and ability as an organizer had converted a lowly second division team into one of the top clubs of the National League."[27]

At the time of the Hall's founding, the views expressed by Spink and others in his family paper were common among the American population and the members of the BBWAA. Even if the leadership of the Hall of Fame objected to those views, there was little they could do about it. They needed baseball writers to get the word out about their new venture, and openly catered to them in exchange for that publicity. When the BBWAA was suggested as the voting body for Hall of Fame members, there's no record that anyone associated with the Hall of Fame objected.

And when the National Baseball Centennial Commission was formed in 1939 as part of baseball's centennial celebrations, among the prominent Americans appointed to it with the likes of universally respected Americans like General John J. Pershing were Charles J. Doyle, president of the BBWAA, and J.G. Taylor Spink, owner and editor of The Bible of Baseball.

CHAPTER 3

Integration

BEFORE THE DOORS OF THE NEW Hall of Fame building were officially opened, a pattern was already established that wouldn't be broken for 36 years: No Black person would be elected without ten years of playing time in the Major Leagues.

This was an entirely arbitrary decision, just as the decision to exclude Black players from the Major Leagues had been. There was no magic to the ten-year rule, and in fact it made some sense to be lenient about it particularly regarding players from the 19th century, when careers were often much shorter. In those cases, however, the rule often didn't prevent induction, as a creative path would be found to bring the player into the Hall. Candy Cummings, supposed inventor of the curveball, was inducted as a pioneer instead of as a player, since his career lasted only six years. Officially, George Wright's career lasted just seven seasons, not 12 as one will often see in online sources, because his first five years as a player were in the National Association which is not an official Major League. No matter, he was brought in as a pioneer, too.

The same trick was applied to Albert Spalding, who was the premier pitcher in the early days of the Major Leagues, leading his league in victories six consecutive seasons and surpassing fifty in two different seasons. But his career was also short, just seven years, and further truncated by the unofficial status of the National Association, so he, too, was elected as a pioneer/executive. In later years, the Hall would waive the ten-year rule to allow Addie Joss to be elected, feeling that his untimely death from tubercular meningitis after only nine seasons in the Major Leagues had artificially shortened what was already a Hall of Fame career.

These avenues around the ten-year rule were available to include great Black players as well if the Hall of Fame and its various election bodies had chosen to apply them, as they frequently did in favor of White people. But, regarding anyone associated with the Negro Leagues, the Hall of Fame decided to forego these alternate paths to induction for almost four decades.

The man known as baseball's first statistician, Henry Chadwick, was part of the third class in 1938, but the man called Black baseball's first historian, Sol White,[1] was passed over. Catcher Roger Bresnahan was part of the Hall's seventh class, elected in 1945, and was credited with being the first catcher to wear shin guards. The reality was that Cooperstown's own Bud Fowler pioneered the use of shin guards twenty years earlier, but he, too, was passed over by the Hall of Fame.[2] The founder of the American League, Ban Johnson, and co-founder of the National League, none other than Albert Spalding again, were members of the Hall of Fame classes of 1937 and 1939, respectively, while Andrew "Rube" Foster, founder of the Negro National League, was ignored.

The choice to exclude Black people from the Hall of Fame did not stem from ignorance of the quality of the play in the Negro Leagues and its predecessors. By the time of the Hall's founding, stories of the excellence of the Negro Leagues and their individual players were commonplace. Many of the most talented, respected, highest-profile figures in the Major Leagues were openly praising Black players. John Henry "Pop" Lloyd had been described for years as "the Black Honus Wagner," and when Wagner was asked about the nickname, Lloyd's reputation in the game was of such high quality that Wagner, one of the five original Hall inductees, claimed he was honored by the comparison.[3] Josh Gibson won the Triple Crown of the Negro National League in the same year the Hall elected its first class, 1936, and had already drawn the nickname "The Black Babe Ruth,"[4] while Ruth himself was open in his praise of the Black players he played against. He once noted that "Cannonball Dick Redding could have graced the roster of any big-league club."[5] Barnstorming tours between Negro Leagues teams and teams made up of White Major Leaguers had been taking place for decades. Dizzy Dean, after a tour pitching against Satchel Paige, told the press, "Satchel's a better pitcher than I ever hope to be."[6] When Joe DiMaggio managed an infield single against Paige in a 1936 exhibition game, the only hit he ever recorded against him, he declared Paige was "the best and fastest pitcher I ever faced."[7]

In the same year, 1936, that Gibson was being labeled the Black Babe Ruth and DiMaggio was calling Satchel Paige the best pitcher he ever saw, Ty Cobb was elected to the Hall of Fame as part of its first class, The Original Five. Cobb's attitudes toward Black people are well known. Though the degree of his racism has been disputed in recent years, it's inarguable that he held racist views and frequently acted on them.[8] He also was suspected of throwing games, betting on games, and possibly even a murder. He, along with Tris Speaker, were thrown out of baseball by American League president Ban Johnson in 1926 for

3. Integration

Ty Cobb continues to hold the place of honor in the Hall's display of the first five men elected, despite rumors he belonged to the KKK and widespread reports of his bigotry toward Black people (Library of Congress).

gambling allegations but were reinstated by Judge Landis.[9] None of this deterred voters, and Cobb was elected with the highest percentage in the first class, 98.2 percent, a record that would stand for 56 years. The plaques of The Original Five remain the centerpiece of the Hall's plaque gallery to this day. Cobb's plaque hangs in the center, the place of honor. Speaker, Cobb's partner in betting on and possibly fixing games, and a suspected member of the Ku Klux Klan,[10] was elected the next year.

It wasn't just the legends of Black baseball that drew rave reviews from White counterparts. Lesser known players were also praised. Former Major Leaguer Al Moore, who played with Frankie Frisch when he was in his prime, said of Philadelphia Stars second baseman Pat Patterson that he "knows his way around the keystone as well as any second baseman in the majors."[11] The playing style of aging outfielder Fats Jenkins of the New York Black Yankees was compared to Joe DiMaggio by former Pirate Eppie Barnes, saying, "his big league ability is obvious to those who have seen him in action."[12] Former Red Sox shortstop Red Kellet said of Baltimore Elite Giants shortstop Wild Bill Wright that he may have missed his calling because "He could give Jesse Owens a good race."[13] And, of course, Giants manager John McGraw thought so highly of second baseman Charlie Grant that he tried to sign him in 1901 by pretending that he was of Native descent instead of Black, but the ruse was discovered before Grant could play a game.[14]

With the talent level this obvious, calls to elect Black players to the Hall of Fame were being made almost from the moment the Hall was established. The *Chicago Defender*, an historical Black newspaper, ran a series of articles in early 1939 seeking the public's input into which Black players were worthy of the Hall of Fame, specifically profiling John Henry Lloyd, Rube Foster, and others. Jimmy Powers used his column in the *New York Daily News* to highlight the accomplishments of several Black players. He noted that Smoky Joe Williams once beat Christy Mathewson in an exhibition, and listed several Black players he felt were worthy of Hall of Fame consideration, including Williams, Dick Redding, and José Méndez. Another article in the *Daily News* noted that singer and former football star Paul Robeson had picked a group of players he felt belonged in the Hall of Fame, including Williams, Lloyd, Redding, Méndez, and Spottswood Poles.[15] In a January 1940, article in the *Pittsburgh Courier*, Cumberland Posey, owner of the famed Homestead Grays, identified what he felt were the greatest Negro Leagues teams of all time, and wrote that "the so-called 'Hall of Fame' in Cooperstown, N.Y., has missed its calling if some of these names are not listed on its walls."[16] In 1939, Edwin Henderson published *The Negro in Sports*, a book recounting the accomplishments of a variety of great Black athletes while also outlining their struggle to be allowed to play. He included a list of Black baseball players who were worthy of the Hall of Fame, including Josh Gibson, Biz Mackey, Smokey Joe Williams, and Cannonball Dick Redding. Eleven of the 20 he listed were ultimately elected, decades later.[17]

All these testimonials fell upon deaf ears. In fact, while all of this was happening, overt racists were being elected to the Hall of Fame with great fanfare and celebration, as we've seen. That trend continued in 1939, when the Hall elected their fourth class. Along with Cummings and Spalding, the Old-Timers Committee elected Cap Anson. Another reputed member of the Ku Klux Klan, Anson was the driving force behind the Major Leagues being segregated in the 1880s, having threatened to pull his team from the field rather than play against a team that fielded a Black player. Both Frick and Landis, an unabashed fan of Anson's when he was growing up as a fan of Anson's Chicago White Stockings, were on the three-man committee that elected him.

The decision by Hall of Fame leadership to intertwine their institution with the White Major Leagues meant that there was no hope that those same leaders would begin admitting Black players when baseball leadership was refusing to integrate their leagues. Many people were actively trying to erase that color line, but it was being actively enforced by Landis, Frick, and others.

Whenever the subject was raised, Landis, Frick and other leaders of baseball would pretend no such line existed. They would stress that any owner was free to sign any Black player, without restriction. Reasons provided for why that hadn't happened for decades typically fell into three categories:

> Black players aren't good enough to play in the Major League.
> Black players wouldn't be accepted by White players or managers.
> Society at large wouldn't accept integrated baseball, and many
> White fans would stop coming to games.

The first two of these reasons were, of course, false. As noted, Black players were obviously good enough to compete, or even excel, in the Major Leagues. Barnstorming tours proved that point, repeatedly, and the White players who needed those barnstorming tours to earn extra money in the offseason were more than happy to note that their Black opponents were every bit as good as White Major Leaguers. Babe Ruth was the best player in baseball, as well as the most recognized and most popular. He played against Black teams all the time, and happily sang the praises of his opponents. In 1933, he told the *Pittsburgh Courier* that "Cannonball Dick Redding could have graced the roster of any big-league club," and further noted that "the colorfulness of Negroes in baseball and their sparkling brilliancy on the field would have a tendency to increase attendance at games. The [All-Star] game in Chicago should bring out a lot of white people who are anxious to see the kind of ball that colored performers play."[18] The players themselves would have eagerly pounced on any opportunity offered. As Bob Kendrick of the Negro Leagues Baseball Museum in Kansas City, Missouri, noted, "They just wanted the chance to prove they could play this game as well as anybody else."[19]

The issue of whether White players and managers would accept Black teammates was debunked often, but no more effectively that in a series of articles Wendell Smith wrote in the *Pittsburgh Courier* in 1939 that were inspired by the response Ford Frick gave when asked about the color line.

"Many baseball fans are of the opinion that major league baseball does not want Negro players, but that is not true," Frick told Smith in February of that year. "We have always been interested in Negro players but have not used them because we feel that the general public has not been educated to the point where they will accept them on the same standard as they do the white player."[20] In other words, don't blame us, blame those ignorant, unaccepting fans of ours.

With Frick on the record that the fans needed to be educated, Smith set out to do exactly that. Over the course of the 1939 baseball season, he interviewed dozens of players and managers from the Pirates and the various National League teams that visited Pittsburgh, asking them directly if they knew of Black players good enough to play in the Major Leagues and if they would be accepted. Their responses were unequivocal. The response from Pirates manager, and future Hall of Famer, Pie Traynor was representative of the views expressed; Yes, "plenty of Negro players" would have been good enough to play in the White Major Leagues, and yes, "I would certainly use a Negro payer who had the ability."[21]

The statements Smith collected and published invalidated the first two excuses baseball representatives usually offered. The players were clearly good enough and would be accepted onto Major League rosters. Their own players and managers were on record saying exactly that.

Smith's series also served to attack the final excuse, that White fans weren't ready for integrated baseball and would not pay to watch it. This reason comes closer to the truth of why integration persisted, but it had little to do with the views of the actual fans. Barnstorming tours had proven for decades that there was a market for games played with both Black and White players on the field. Ruth, the game's biggest attraction, felt White fans would be drawn to the style of play he'd witnessed Black teams demonstrate. At a minimum, the barnstorming successes proved that a Major League team composed only of Black players would be a draw to fans, even if integrated rosters may not.

That's the solution some advocated, including Satchel Paige. Paige had been criticized for expressing the view that he wasn't in favor of integration as it had been proposed and took the opportunity of the 1942 East-West game to explain himself. Taking the microphone mid-game, he told the crowd that he did favor integration of the Major Leagues but preferred that a full team of Black players be admitted to one of the Major Leagues, rather than stripping away only the most talented individual players. He felt that would hurt Black-owned businesses, specifically the Negro Leagues teams that would lose their star attractions.[22] On this point, sadly, later events would prove him right.

It's unlikely fans would have rejected Black players, and there's no record of fans expressing any intention of boycotting the Major Leagues in droves if Black players started appearing on their favorite teams' rosters. Ruth's comments about Black ballplayers being an attendance draw were proven correct by Brooklyn fans in 1947, and fans throughout the National League that year whenever Jackie Robinson and the Dodgers came to their city. In fact, there's little record the fans were asked their opinions of integration at all. The White leadership was simply assuming it to be true, and they did so because of their own underlying fear of integration: Losing money.

Baseball owners, then as now, were protecting their financial interests first, and concerns about social justice were far down the list of their priorities, if they made the list at all. Frick's original comments to Smith hinted at this reason. "The big leagues are in the same position as newspapers," he said. "We cannot do anything we want to until public opinion is ready for it."[23] As an independent, privately-owned cooperative of businesses, of course the leagues could have done whatever they wanted. Frick wasn't claiming that the league didn't have the power or control necessary to integrate their rosters. He was claiming that they couldn't do so without the racist elements of the American public punishing them for it financially. Casey Stengel, manager of the Boston Bees, was blunter in his interview with Wendell Smith. "Sometimes I wonder if it would be profitable to admit Negroes in the majors. I wonder if the Negro fans would follow them to the extent where their presence on a big league team would be justified."[24]

Adrian "Cap" Anson was one of the first 19th-century ballplayers elected to the Hall of Fame despite his role in forcing the major leagues to be segregated (Library of Congress).

Years later, Frick also gave a more honest assessment of owners' motives. "They were afraid of upsetting the status quo, afraid of alienating the white clientele that largely supported the professional game."[25]

All the theories offered by baseball leadership as reasons why integration should be avoided had one thing in common: Racism. That commonality was not far removed from the arguments. It was one question away, if anyone in the media dared ask it.

Why?

Black players aren't good enough to play in the Major Leagues? Why?

White players and managers wouldn't accept them? Why?

Fans would stop coming to games? Why?

There certainly would have been some temporizing responses offered at first, like Frick's attempt to say the public wasn't sufficiently educated when queried by Wendell Smith, but any persistent line of inquiry would have ultimately reached the truth if the interview subject had been honest enough to answers truthfully. Many White Americans, from the owners of teams down to patrons of the game and back up to the commissioner's office, held racist views of Black people, and therefore didn't want to associate with them. It really is that simple. It's the Occam's Razor of baseball segregation, and no alternate theories offered by Landis, Frick, J.G. Taylor Spink, or anyone else defending the practice ring true.

Wendell Smith knew this and said it plainly when others wouldn't. In December 1938, he openly compared the leadership of the White Major Leagues to Adolf Hitler when he learned that those leaders intended to send a letter to Hitler demanding he halt his barbaric treatment of Jews. Smith viewed that as hypocritical and said so. "They play the same game as Hitler. They discriminate, segregate and hold down a minor race, just as he does. While Hitler cripples the Jews, the great leaders of our national pastime refuse to recognize our black players."[26]

Very few White sportswriters joined with Smith and other Black journalists in taking baseball to task for its stance on segregation. Smith noted that Warren Brown of the *Chicago Herald-Examiner* and *Chicago American*, Dave Egan of the *Boston Record*, Dan Parker of the New York *Daily Mirror*, Jimmy Powers of the *New York Daily News*, and Shirley Povich of the *Washington Post* were among those who used their columns to question Landis and other baseball leaders.[27]

Easily the staunchest advocate in the White press to end the color line was Lester Rodney, sports editor of the *Daily Worker*. In 1937, Rodney published more than fifty articles about segregation in baseball, and nearly doubled that number in 1938.[28]

3. Integration   37

Smith took further steps to force baseball officials to respond. He wrote to the commissioner in 1939, asking if he, Paul Robeson, and *Pittsburgh Courier* editor Ira Lewis could address the owners at one of their upcoming meetings. They were allowed to speak, and did so for about twenty minutes, advocating for the talented Black players who were being denied the chance to prove they were good enough to play in the Major Leagues.[29] Ford Frick, in describing the meeting later, noted that Landis wouldn't allow discussion on the subject to proceed, not only because public opinion wouldn't support integration, but also because of the technical matter that the issue hadn't been placed on the agenda properly. "Judge Landis, the then Commissioner, declared that public opinion would be against such a move. He ruled out any discussion on the ground that the question had not been properly noticed on the agenda, as required under the rules. Formal effort to bring the subject before the meeting was stopped by the judge's ruling—but the idea persisted in the minds of some of the officials."[30]

Supposedly one of the owners suggested an open discussion but, if that occurred, it didn't happen when Smith was still in the room. He later wrote that "the reaction, frankly, was silence. We went in, made the presentation, came out and the meeting continued." Smith and his cohorts sent a letter to Landis later, thanking him for allowing them to address the owners, but no reply was ever sent to them.[31]

The ongoing refusal of Landis to address the issue of segregation, coupled with the onset of World War II, prompted Lester Rodney to launch a campaign in 1942 called "Can You Read, Judge Landis?" Trade unions across the country were solicited to contact Landis directly, calling for an end to baseball's segregation policy on the grounds of equality and fairness, as well as patriotism during time of war. Several large unions passed resolutions to that effect and forwarded them to Landis. A petition calling for an end to the color line was signed by more than a million people and was sent to Landis' office. The campaign distributed leaflets to theaters in New York in advance of the debut of the film *Pride of the Yankees* about Lou Gehrig. They included a quote from Gehrig: "I have seen and played against many Negro players who could easily be stars in the big leagues. I could name just a few of them like Satchel Paige, Buck Leonard, Josh Gibson, and Barney Brown who should be in the majors. I am all for it, 100%."[32]

Rodney continued the campaign by sending an open letter to Landis on May 2, 1942, under the headline "Time for Stalling Is Over, Judge Landis." In it, he noted that Black servicemen were included in the growing casualty lists that were being reported, and that Landis no longer had any excuse to remain silent on the issue of segregation, claiming that it was actively hurting the war effort. He followed this up with additional open letters, taunting him with headlines asking, "Can You Hear, Judge Landis?" and "Can You Talk, Judge Landis?"[33]

None of this moved Landis to act, but it finally did motivate him to issue a statement in July 1942. He was further persuaded it was necessary to say something in response to a comment from the Dodgers' manager, Leo Durocher, in which he alleged that Landis was the main obstacle that prevented the team from signing Black players.[34]

"There is no rule in organized baseball prohibiting their participation to my knowledge. If Durocher, or any other manager, or all of them want to sign one or 25 Negro players, it is all right with me. That is the business of the manager and the club owners. The business of the Commissioner is to interpret the rules and enforce them."[35]

J.G. Taylor Spink at *The Sporting News* eagerly gave his support to the accuracy of this statement by Landis, adding that no rule against White and Black teams being integrated was needed since each group preferred to draw talent from their own race and hadn't extended any invitations to players of other races. He also note "leaders of both groups know their crowd psychology and do not care to run the risk of damaging their own game." He went on to ponder the possible tragedies that might arise if a player of one race threw at a batter or spiked a member of the opposite race. Spink felt that the only people seeking to integrate the game was "agitators" who were trying to "thrust themselves into the limelight," and speculated that Satchel Paige and other Black stars may not have "blossomed forth" as they had if they'd done so on integrated teams in front of integrated fans. "It is doubtful if the road would have been so easy."

Yes, he actually wrote that the stars of Black baseball had a comparatively easier experience than if they'd been allowed to play in integrated leagues. He concluded by noting while some Black people wouldn't agree with him, they weren't considering the issue broadly enough to consider the overall good of race relations. "They ought to concede their own people are now protected and that nothing is served by allowing agitators to make an issue of a question on which both sides would prefer to be let alone."[36]

Spink wasn't alone among prominent White sportswriters in expressing overt disapproval of integration. Gordon Cobbledick of the Cleveland *Plain Dealer* wrote that Black players being allowed into the Major League could cause "social problems." He warned of there being "hell to pay" if a Black player let it get under his skin when a Southern White pitcher "threw a little too close to him," fell into a slump, and was benched as a result. Cobbledick envisioned the *Daily Worker* labeling

3. Integration

such a situation discrimination, causing fans of different races to suddenly dislike each other when they "formerly got along amicably."[37]

More commonly, Landis' statement was largely taken for what it was, an overt passing of the buck to team owners. Having the issue thrown into their laps by the commissioner, most team leaders refrained from commenting any further. An Associated Press article the next day contained quotes from just two members of baseball management. James Gallagher, general manager of the Cubs, said that none of the team's scouts had ever recommended a Black player, and that he thought the country would be better off if people stopped "stirring up racial hatred." William Benswanger, president of the Pirates, agreed with Landis that there was no agreement of any kind to ban Black players.[38] Benswanger added that he would be conducting tryouts to three Black players "in the near future," news which his manager, Frankie Frisch, received with a decided lack of enthusiasm. "I'm just the manager, and must do what I'm told."[39]

This was not the first time that Benswanger had spoken of signing Black players. Being in Pittsburgh, he had a first-hand view of two great Negro Leagues franchises, the Pittsburgh Crawfords and Homestead Grays, with the Grays renting Forbes Field from the Pirates for many of their home games. He'd seen them play enough to know that Black players were easily talented enough to play in the Major Leagues and admitted as much to the *Pittsburgh Courier*.[40] He went further, claiming to have made several attempts to purchase Grays standout Josh Gibson, only to be turned down by Grays owner Cumberland Posey. Wendell Smith doubted the story was true, feeling that Benswanger was "baseball's number one phony."[41]

Benswanger's promised tryouts never happened. Almost as soon as he'd mentioned the possibility of tryouts, Benswanger began to back away from the idea. While there was a "thundering roar of approval" from Black fans when the news broke, and an outpouring of letters and telegrams in support of them, Benswanger also received some "scathing denunciations," and was leery of being associated with an effort that was being spearheaded by reporters from the *Daily Worker*, a communist newspaper. "So far as colored boys playing in the major and minor leagues are concerned, I reiterate that I think they should be allowed to play, but I certainly resent any Communist paper telling us how to proceed."[42] This was a reference to the *Daily Worker* having already identified three players they viewed as being can't-miss prospects that should be worked out by Major League clubs: pitcher Dave Barnhill, infielder Sammy Hughes, and a 20-year-old catcher from Philadelphia named Roy Campanella.[43]

40 Cooperstown's Back Door

Put off by the connection to communists, Benswanger said the Pirates would scout Black players themselves, in cooperation with local sportswriters, both Black and White. That never happened. As the weeks passed, he began to avoid taking the calls of Rodney, Wendell Smith, and other reporters, hoping they would eventually stop asking him. The best Rodney got ultimately was a return call from Benswanger's secretary, telling him the tryout was off, without any further explanation.[44]

This wasn't the first aborted tryout of the 1942 season. During spring training for the White Sox in Pasadena, California, a Black journalist named Herman Hill showed up at their camp on March 18 with two Black players in tow. One was Nate Moreland, a pitcher who had been a teammate of Campanella with the Baltimore Elite Giants in 1940, before pitching for the Alijadores de Tampico in the Mexican League the year before. The other player was a local multi-sport athlete, better known as a football player with UCLA, Jackie Robinson. Jimmy Dykes, manager of the White Sox, treated them rudely, refusing to pose for photos with them, while claiming that he had no power to sign Black players. "It's strictly up to the club owners and Judge Landis," he claimed. "Go after them!"[45] This didn't sit well with Landis, who apparently brought Dykes in to see him about his comments and told him to "keep his trap closed about the incident."[46]

While all of this was happening on the integration front, the Hall of Fame was blissfully ignoring the controversy. In 1942, they finally elected someone else for the first time in three years. Their fifth class had only one inductee, Rogers Hornsby. He was reportedly also a member of the Ku Klux Klan,[47] a man so angry at baseball and the world that the final book he wrote was entitled *My War with Baseball*, in which he boasted of his ability and willingness to cheat during this playing days. His co-author, Bill Surface, wrote of Hornsby, "[H]e was a compulsive horse player and a conniver for financial gain on an embarrassingly small scale. His apparent prejudices against Jews and Negroes were shocking but, on examination, turned out to be simply two items in a long accounting against the world."[48] Hall of Fame voters, like Hornsby's employers during his playing days, were able to look past all his bigoted, unsportsmanlike behaviors and elect him anyway, while the keepers of the sport still enforced barriers to simple participation for those against whom Hornsby was bigoted.

In January 1942, as the United States' role in World War II expanded, Landis reached out to President Roosevelt, asking him if he wanted baseball to be suspended for the duration of the war. In response, Roosevelt sent what is now known as his Green Light Letter, in which he

3. Integration

encouraged Landis to keep playing games to boost morale for the troops overseas and for civilians at home.[49] The license to keep fielding teams was welcome, but as the needs of the military grew and increasing numbers of Major League players entered military service, the shortage of players with Major League ability became acute.

By 1944, more than 60 percent of the players who had been in opening day lineups in 1941 were no longer playing baseball.[50] The minor leagues were similarly decimated, with more than 4,000 players entering the military during the war. Over 150 players made their Major League debut in 1944, the most in any season between the expansion years of 1915 and 1969.[51] Chuck Hostetler made his debut for the Tigers five months shy of his 41st birthday, and wasn't bad, hitting .298. Joe Nuxhall famously debuted at the age of just 15 for the Reds, though he didn't fare as well, being tagged for five runs in less than one inning. Pete Gray got more than 250 plate appearances for the Browns despite having only one arm. Bert Shepard pitched a game for the Senators despite having one leg.[52] Teams even bent their standards regarding race, by signing players from Cuba and other Latin American locations with complexions that previously may have been a shade or two too dark for their tastes, illustrating the unprecedented level of desperation for baseball owners to find players.

And yet they still would not sign Black players. The military, like baseball, was not yet integrated, and there were limits on the number of Black men who could serve and the roles they were allowed to have in each service. While a million or more Black men ably and proudly served, including many ballplayers, the Negro Leagues were less impacted by the ongoing talent drain than were the White Major and Minor Leagues. They were an obvious solution to the talent problems owners were facing, and it was this situation that prompted Leo Durocher to make his comment about his desire to sign Black players if he wasn't prohibited by Landis and ownership. And yet, despite the loss of most of their players and a desire by at least some of their managers to replace them with Black players, despite President Roosevelt's having issued Executive Order 8802 barring racial discrimination from war industries, Landis did nothing but issue his statement that threw the matter back at team owners, none of whom were willing to act to erase the color line.

If Bill Veeck is to be believed, Landis and Frick went even further than simply encouraging current owners to maintain the color line. They also worked to bar any prospective owners, like Veeck, who might want to sign Black players.

In late 1942, Gerry Nugent, owner of the Philadelphia Phillies, was deeply in debt. The team was terrible, having lost at least 100 games and finished last in the National League for five consecutive seasons. Nugent wanted out and put the team on the market. Veeck, son of long-time Cubs president Bill Veeck, Sr., was already the owner of the minor league Milwaukee Brewers, and saw the Phillies sale as an opportunity to own a Major League club. Beyond that, he saw a unique opportunity to immediately be competitive.

According to Veeck, he was working with Black sportswriter Doc Young and Abe Saperstein, most famously known as the founder and owner of the Harlem Globetrotters basketball team but also the owner of several Negro Leagues baseball teams at different times, to assemble a team of Black players to sign with the Phillies once he took over. He would then use this all-star squad to destroy the depleted National League competition.[53] He reached an agreement with Nugent on a price, and was ready to close the deal, but "out of my long respect for Judge Landis, I felt he was entitled to prior notification of what I intended to do."[54]

Shortly after letting Landis known his plans, Veeck was contacted by Ford Frick, advised that the Phillies had been turned over to the National League office, and any agreement he had with Nugent was no longer valid. The club was then sold to William Cox, owner of a lumber company and former president of the American Football League, which shuttered when the war began. According to Veeck, Frick sold the team to Cox "for about half what I had been willing to pay."[55] Frick never commented on Veeck's allegations, even his most damning charge, that "Frick was bragging all over the baseball world—strictly off the record, of course—about how he had stopped me from contaminating the league."[56] Even in his own autobiography years later, Frick was silent on the issue, never mentioning Veeck at all.

There are some holes in Veeck's story, including misidentifying the year when all of this supposedly happened, and mixing up the names of A.S. "Doc" Young and Fay Young, a different Black sportswriter. This has led some to conclude that the story isn't true, with some going to far as to allege that Veeck made it up in advance of the publication of his autobiography in 1962.[57] More recent research corroborates some of what Veeck claimed. Both Saperstein and Fay Young told versions of the same story, as did Doc Young, and other writers. There is documentation of Veeck's telling this story as early as 1946, just three years after the events in question.[58]

Whether the exact details of Veeck's story are true or not, it's telling that it was accepted as fact for decades, striking those who heard it as being entirely plausible, given the people involved and the level of

3. *Integration*   43

commitment to enforcing the color line they had displayed. It's also indisputable that Frick did, in fact, sell the team on Nugent's behalf to Cox, who lasted less than one year in the game before he was banned for life by Landis for gambling on Phillies games. In November 1943, the same day Cox was banned, the team was sold to Bob Carpenter. He and his son, who took over the team in 1949, hired Herb Pennock to be their general manager and Ben Chapman to be their field manager. Both men were heavily involved in efforts to boycott games against the Dodgers[59] and verbally abuse Jackie Robinson when he entered the league in 1947.[60] Under Carpenter's ownership, the Phillies would become the last National League team to integrate, a decade after the color line finally fell.

The first key step in that line finally falling took place in November 1944, when Kenesaw Mountain Landis died. Two weeks later, a special committee at the Hall of Fame voted to induct Landis as a member. He was the sole member of the Hall of Fame's sixth class despite being someone who "spent his 24-year tenure upholding the game's color line."[61] Ironically, earlier that same year, it was Landis who had introduced what has become known as the "character clause" to Hall of Fame voting procedures, requiring voters to consider not only a players' career on the field, but also that player's "integrity, sportsmanship, [and] character."[62]

The names of various prominent figures were offered as candidates to be Landis' replacement, but they were tied up in more important jobs with the war still ongoing, so the position was offered to Albert "Happy" Chandler, then serving as a U.S. Senator from Kentucky, a segregated state for which he had served as governor before his election to the Senate. Because of his home state, it was presumed by many that Chandler's view on upholding the color line would fall very much in line with those of Landis. J.G. Taylor Spink went so far as to forward Chandler a copy of his 1942 editorial in which he argued against integration, with a cover note saying he "took care of the situation."[63]

But Chandler wasn't what he seemed. There's little doubt that he held some racist, bigoted views, and later examination of his actions calls into question whether he advocated for integration or simply didn't get in the way of it. Regardless, he clearly wasn't an opponent in the way Landis was. He was a politician and had taken note of the changes in the country brought on by the war. As noted, more than a million Black men served in the armed forces, and President Roosevelt had banned racial discrimination by the Federal government, unions, and all war-related industries.[64] The Double V Campaign had been launched by the *Pittsburgh Courier,* noting that the "V for Victory" slogan being used to promote the war effort against the tyranny of the Axis powers didn't go far enough, and called for a second victory over injustice and discrimination within the United States.[65] Taking all of this in, Chandler made his views on the issue known to the *Courier's* Ric Roberts early in his tenure. "If a black boy can make it on Okinawa and Guadalcanal, hell, he can make it in baseball." Then he added, even more clearly, "I don't believe in barring Negroes from baseball just because they are Negroes."[66]

Chandler was going to be asked to prove the truth of those statements early in his tenure, in part because of a Jewish city councilman in Boston. Isadore Muchnick, seeking to force baseball to address their ban on Black players, wrote to both the Braves and the Red Sox before the 1944 season, advising them that unless they began to consider signing Black players, he would use his position to block the city council waiver the teams needed to continue playing games on Sundays.[67] Muchnick's motivation for this action was later portrayed as opportunistic. He was said to be "representing a predominantly black district,"[68] and Wendell Smith later claimed that he had given Muchnick the idea once he noted that he "was running for reelection in a predominantly Negro area and was having quite a hard time getting reelected."[69] Neither of these assertions is true. Muchnick's district was 99 percent White, and he ran unopposed in two elections.[70] The truth is that he simply noted an injustice and was one of the few White public officials at that time who used his position to correct it.[71]

Both Boston teams stalled when Muchnick contacted them. Eddie Collins, general manager of the Red Sox, replied to him that "We have never had a single request for a try-out by a colored applicant."[72] Muchnick released that response publicly, and was contacted by Smith, who advised him that Black players would welcome the opportunity to play in the Major Leagues, and that Collins' claim was wrong. By the time this had transpired, the 1944 season had begun, so Muchnick temporarily set the issue aside.[73]

Conditions before the next season were entirely different. Landis was now dead, and Chandler was on record not only claiming that the color line was wrong but had also noted the injustice of Black men fighting for freedom around the world without being able to have it at home. Muchnick contacted the teams again, and Collins once again made his claim that the team had "never had a request for a try-out by a colored applicant.... It is beyond my understanding how anyone can insinuate or believe that 'all ballplayers regardless of race color or creed, have not been treated in the American Way' so far as having equal opportunity to play for the Red Sox."[74]

3. *Integration*   **45**

While Muchnick was renewing his pressure, sportswriter Sam Lacy of the *Baltimore Afro-American* was conducting his own campaign. He wrote to the Red Sox, Braves, and Yankees, suggesting that a chief scout be hired by the Major Leagues to identify Black players who were able and willing to play in the White Major Leagues. In his letter to Collins, he mentioned the Sunday baseball ban that Muchnick had threatened the year before.[75]

Pressured on multiple fronts, and with a different commissioner possessed of more modern attitudes toward race now leading the sport, Collins replied to both Muchnick and Lacy, promising to hold a tryout for any worthy players who expressed an interest.[76] Wendell Smith advised Muchnick that he would identify three qualified prospects from the Negro Leagues and arrange to have them come to Boston. The three players he settled on were Sam Jethroe, outfielder with the Cleveland Buckeyes, Marvin Williams, second baseman of the Philadelphia Stars, and Jackie Robinson, former football star at UCLA who had recently signed to play shortstop for the Kansas City Monarchs.[77]

After some delays caused by the death of President Roosevelt, the tryout was finally held at Fenway Park on Monday, April 16, 1945. Neither Collins nor manager Joe Cronin attended, and none of the Red Sox players were present either. Two Red Sox coaches, Hugh Duffy and Larry Woodall, conducted the workout, with Duffy later reporting that he was impressed. "Pretty good ball players," he said to the few reporters who were present. He also reportedly told the players they looked good.[78]

One of the reporters present was Clif Keane of the *Boston Globe*, who later claimed, "I distinctly remember during the workouts somebody yelling 'Get those n_____s off the field.' In those days, people used that word a lot. But I can't recall who yelled it. People used to say it was Collins. But I don't really know."[79]

For his part, Robinson never claimed to have heard that slur used. He did, however, say, "We knew we were wasting our time. It was April 1945. Nobody was serious then about black players in the majors, except maybe a few politicians.... They said we'd hear from them. We knew we were getting the brushoff. We didn't wait around to work out with the Braves. It would have been the same story."[80]

The Red Sox, of course, didn't sign the players. Under the ownership of Tom Yawkey and management of Collins and Cronin, who would succeed Collins as general manager in 1947, the Red Sox didn't sign a Black player until 1959, the last Major League team to do so. According to Cronin, he advised the players that their only farm club that had roster openings was in Louisville, Kentucky, a location he didn't think they would want to be assigned given the status of race relations there.

46 Cooperstown's Back Door

"Besides, this was after the season had started and we didn't sign players off tryouts in those days to play in the big leagues. I was in no position to offer them a job. The general manager did the hiring and there was an unwritten rule at that time against hiring black players. I was just the manager."[81]

There are at least three excuses offered by Cronin, at least two of which weren't true. The Red Sox had three minor league affiliates in 1945, not one. Two of them, Louisville and Roanoke, were in segregated states, but the third was in Scranton, Pennsylvania. The starting second baseman, shortstop, and two of the three starting outfielders for Scranton that year never made the Major Leagues, so it's not as if Williams, Robinson, and Jethroe would have been blocked by better talent. As for mid-season signings, two months after the tryout the Red Sox signed 38-year-old Dolph Camilli to be their new first baseman despite never seeing him play. Camilli hadn't played in the Major Leagues in two years and had just been fired as manager of the Oakland Oaks of the Pacific Coast League. The Red Sox came to contract terms with him over the phone from his home in California. The announcement of the signing was made by Cronin, not Collins, implying that it was Collins that closed the deal. During the announcement, Cronin admitted that Camilli wasn't even in shape to play.[82] But at least Cronin did acknowledge the "unwritten rule" against signing Black players, contrary to Landis' and Frick's repeated assertions.

Collins was already a member of the Hall of Fame when these events took place, having been elected in 1939. Cronin joined him as a Hall of Famer in 1956. In 1980, four years after his death, Yawkey was also elected.

A month before the tryout, as part of his letter-writing campaign to Major League officials, Sam Lacy "persuaded major league baseball to study the possibility of integrating the major leagues." Just a week after the Fenway tryout, on April 24, 1945, Lacy spoke to a meeting of the owners, after which they formed a committee that was grandly labeled the Major League Committee on Baseball Integration. Its members were the Dodgers' Branch Rickey, Larry MacPhail of the Yankees, a Black magistrate from Philadelphia named Joseph H. Rainey, and Lacy.[83]

Nothing ever came of that committee, which never met, but both Rickey and MacPhail continued to play roles in integrating baseball. Rickey's is well-documented, and he would take center stage six months later with his signing of Jackie Robinson in October of 1945.

MacPhail's role isn't as well-known but is revealing of the nature of the last-ditch opposition to integration that many baseball leaders attempted. After the signing of Robinson, a steering committee was formed to investigate a variety of issues facing baseball. The committee's members were MacPhail; Yawkey; Sam Breadon of the Cardinals; Phil Wrigley of the Cubs; and the two league presidents, William Harridge of the American League, and Ford Frick of the National League. The "race question" was one of the issues the committee addressed in the report of their findings and recommendations that they issued in the summer of 1946.[84]

That section of the report, authored by MacPhail, included the standard empty ownership position that baseball was open to all American boys, and that no race, color or religion was considered as disqualifying,[85] but then noted the various financial reason why the committee felt it would be bad business to integrate. MacPhail noted that the Yankee organization brought in $100,000 of annual income from renting Yankee Stadium to their minor league affiliates, and that integration would threaten that income. He paid some lip service to the notion that Negro Leagues teams had an investment interest in their players as well which integration would destroy, seemingly acknowledging that Major League teams wouldn't fairly compensate Negro Leagues teams when signing their best players. But his primary point was centered upon economic impact on Major League clubs if they signed Black players. "I will not jeopardize my income nor their investment."

MacPhail continued later in the report: "A situation might be presented, if Negroes participate in Major League games, in which the preponderance of Negro attendance in parks such as Yankee Stadium, the Polo Grounds and Comiskey Park could conceivably threaten the value of the Major League franchises owned by these clubs."[86] Jeff Obermeyer of the Society for American Baseball Research has noted that MacPhail's conclusions about integration possibly being damaging to teams actually contradicted another part of the same report, in which the committee noted that they were aware that fans wanted to see the best players, regardless of race, and that attendance therefore wasn't likely going to be adversely impacted by integration. That wasn't sufficient to offset the financial concerns of baseball executives, however. As Obermeyer notes, "Racism, in the minds of most of the major-league owners at the time, was good for business."[87]

All the committee's members signed the report, attesting that they agreed with the conclusions and recommendations it contained.[88] Branch Rickey later claimed that a vote was held among the owners on whether they agreed with the report's recommendations, with Frick making certain that all the owners were aware of what they were signing. Rickey claimed he was the only person to vote against adopting the report. The report was intended as an internal memo only, and Rickey asserted that Frick was careful to pick up all copies of the report after the meeting, to ensure that it wouldn't leak publicly. "After we read them they were collected. Frick checked off the names to see that he had all the copies."[89] Several owners later denied the report ever existed,[90] but that was proved false when a copy of the report was found among Happy Chandler's papers.[91] The language of the report is unambiguous. The steering committee warned that even one club breaking ranks and signing a Black player "may exert tremendous pressures upon the whole structure of professional baseball, and could conceivably result in lessening the value of several major league franchises."[92]

Throughout 1945 and 1946—as Chandler was taking over the leadership of baseball, Rickey was signing Robinson, and owners were documenting their reasons why full integration was a bad idea—the Hall of Fame was pressing forward. They elected two straight classes with double-digit inductees, nearly doubling the number of existing members. Among the new members elected in 1945 were Hugh Duffy, the Red Sox coach who had led the sham tryout at Fenway Park earlier in the year, and Roger Bresnahan, who was credited with being the first player to wear shin guards when that honor actually belonged to a Black man, Bud Fowler. The 1946 class included Joe Tinker, Johnny Evers, and Frank Chance, mostly because a famous poem had been written about them.

Obviously, none of the 21 inductees in those two years were Black.

The 1946 class did, however, include Clark Griffith, who had been a pitcher for twenty years at the turn of the century before becoming a manager and, ultimately, owner of the Washington Senators.[93] While he owned the team, the stands at Griffith Stadium were segregated, with Black patrons required to sit in the right field pavilion. They supported the team anyway, in part because Griffith rented the stadium to the Homestead Grays for half of their home games. The finest Black players in the country were routinely playing in Griffith's ballpark, and he knew it. As early as 1937, he told Sam Lacy of the *Washington Tribune* that "the time is not far off when colored players will take their places beside those of other races in the Major Leagues. However I am not so sure that time has arrived yet."[94]

In 1943, Griffith called Buck Leonard and Josh Gibson into a meeting and asked them directly if they wanted to play for the Senators. They both said they did, but Griffith refused to sign them anyway. He'd expressed to Lacy that integrating the Major Leagues would kill the Negro Leagues, a point that would later prove to be correct, and Griffith relied on income from the Homestead Grays too much. Signing Leonard and Gibson would have made his team better, but it would have made his finances suffer, so he did nothing.[95]

He was rewarded with a plaque in Cooperstown in 1946. It wasn't until 1954 that the Senators finally fielded a Black player, Carlos Paula. Griffith died a year later, leaving the ownership and day-to-day management of the team to his adopted son, Calvin. Six years later, Calvin Griffith moved the Senators to Minnesota, later saying that he did so because "I found out you only had 15,000 blacks here. Black people don't go to ball games, but they'll fill up a rassling ring and put up such a chant it'll scare you to death. It's unbelievable. We came here because you've got good, hardworking, White people here."[96]

CHAPTER 4

Foot Dragging

NO MAGICAL WAVE OF RACIAL JUSTICE swept across baseball once Jackie Robinson was promoted to the Dodgers in 1947. Opponents of integration didn't change their minds and realize the errors of their past thinking. They fought integration, or, at the very least, didn't accept it. What did happen was that the various excuses used in the past were suddenly gone.

Black players weren't good enough? Well, Jackie Robinson led the league in steals, batted .297, finished fifth in MVP voting and won the inaugural Rookie of the Year Award, which now bears his name.

White players and managers wouldn't accept them? Mostly this proved false, as various players and managers had told Wendell Smith and others over the years. In some cases, there was resistance, but that proved easy enough to fix. Branch Rickey simply traded away the opponents or ordered them benched. When pitcher Kirby Higbie, from South Carolina, voiced that he didn't want to play with Robinson or any other Black player, he went from being a two-time All-Star and valued member of the pitching staff on the eventual pennant winners, to being traded to the worst team in the league and out of baseball within three years.

Even Ford Frick had a hand in stopping dissent. Rumors reached his office that a group of players on the Cardinals intended to boycott games if the Dodgers brought Robinson with them to play in St. Louis. Both Frick and Cardinals owner Sam Breadon later downplayed the likelihood of an actual strike by the players happening,[1] and the players rumored to be involved denied that any serious discussion of a strike took place,[2] but Frick did apparently make it clear that any player who refused to take the field would be suspended.[3] Whether this was for reasons of fairness and social justice, or to keep from disrupting business, is unknown.

As for the warnings that White fans would stay away for fear of mingling with new Black fans in the stands, these also proved to be false. Attendance in the National League jumped nearly 17 percent over the 1946 season. Only one National League team, the Phillies—the same team Bill Veeck was denied purchasing during the war and was now the most openly antagonistic toward Robinson—saw a drop in attendance. All other teams saw increased ticket sales, boosted by visits from the Dodgers. The American League had its own integration story unfolding. Veeck, now the new owner in Cleveland, signed Larry Doby in July. He kept him on the roster for the rest of the season, but Doby didn't play much, and wasn't good when he did. While the Indians saw an enormous 44 percent surge in attendance, the league overall didn't see any real change. Overall attendance was down slightly, about 1 percent. Even the eventual World Series–winning Yankees saw a small drop in attendance.

Robinson's personal battles that season are well-documented. Herb Pennock, the Phillies general manager, reportedly called Rickey in advance of the first Dodger series in Philadelphia and said, "[You] just can't bring the n_____ here with the rest of your team, Branch. We're just not ready for that sort of thing yet."[4] A threatened boycott was abandoned when Rickey advised that they would gladly accept the forfeit. The Phillies manager, Ben Chapman, so famously rode Robinson with racist epithets that commissioner Chandler had to warn the team to stop the harassment.[5] Several members of the Cardinals, including Joe Medwick and Enos Slaughter, spiked Robinson as he fielded throws at first base. Cardinals' catcher Joe Garagiola also spiked him, and when Robinson said something to him the next time he came to the plate, Garagiola used a racist slur in response.[6]

None of this behavior fazed the Hall of Fame and its electors. When Pennock died of a cerebral hemorrhage the following January, the voters took pity on him, overlooked the racist behavior of his team toward Robinson, and voted him into the Hall of Fame. Medwick followed him in 1968, and Slaughter in 1985. Garagiola's career didn't warrant consideration for the Hall of Fame, but his use of a racist slur against the century's first Black player didn't stop the Hall of Fame from honoring Garagiola with the Ford C. Frick Award for broadcasting in 1991.

The BBWAA, and some of its most famous members, also took steps to delay full acceptance of integration in baseball. J.G. Taylor Spink took the opportunity of the rumored boycott by the Cardinals to write another editorial in *The Sporting News* in which he made it clear that "*The Sporting News* has not changed its views as expressed in 1942." He went on to quote much of that original 1942 editorial in which he had criticized the notion of integration, concluding with the demeaning story of how heavyweight boxing champion Joe Louis once served a pork chop lunch in his home to a group of sportswriters before excusing himself to eat separately in the kitchen.[7] In that same issue, Spink printed a guest column by Gordon Cobbledick of the Cleveland *Plain Dealer* in which Cobbledick defended the actions of Ben Chapman and the rest of the Phillies team, even though veteran players felt it was beyond the pale.[8]

Even Dixie Walker, the Alabama-born right fielder for the Dodgers who asked Rickey for a trade rather than play with a Black man, told Chapman that his treatment of Robinson had crossed a line.[9] Cobbledick dismissed that view, saying that Chapman's offensive language was "a legitimate baseball weapon." Noting that bench jockeying was standard practice, and that all rookies were subjected to it until they proved they could take it, Cobbledick chalked up Chapman's actions as more of the same. "He believed it was his duty as manager of the Dodgers' opponents to ascertain whether Robinson's play could be affected by verbal abuse." In Cobbledick's view, treating Chapman's racism differently than other forms of gamesmanship was a double standard.[10]

Once the Indians signed Larry Doby, *The Sporting News* printed an anonymous editorial, quoting an anonymous all-star player, arguing that it appeared White players were now the ones being discriminated against. His principal problem was that Black players were not being required to spend several years in the minor leagues, something White players nearly always did. "I fought my way through the minors for five years. I rode buses all night for three of those five years, so that I could get a chance in the majors. If we are to have Negroes in the majors, let them go through the long preparation the white player is forced to undergo. Let us not discriminate against the white player because he is white." The anonymous editor added only, "*The Sporting News* believes that this summarization is worthy of consideration."[11]

A year later, when Veeck signed 40-something Satchel Paige, Spink opened one of his ink barrels at the Bible of Baseball and condemned the move as nothing more than a publicity stunt. With a nod toward the changing times that he was about to rail against, Spink laid out a disclaimer about the motivations of *The Sporting News* in the criticism he was about to level at Veeck. First he made it clear that it would be unfair for anyone to oppose another person's path to success in life solely because of their race, and that any criticism of the signing of Paige that might appear in *The Sporting News* had nothing to do with Paige being Black. In fact, he claimed that "no man at all familiar with the editorial policy of *The Sporting News*, and its reaction to the strivings of the Negro to gain a place in the major leagues, will question the motives of this paper."[12]

4. Foot Dragging

53

Spink then spent a paragraph giving a selective partial history of the actions of *The Sporting News* and its publishers, meaning himself, about furthering the cause of Black baseball players. It was classic cherry-picking, in addition to clearly being a preamble to the word "But." He was too good a writer to use that conjunction, but that didn't stop him from launching into his expected screed against Veeck. "*The Sporting News* [again, meaning Spink himself] believes that Veeck has gone too far in his quest for publicity, and that he has done his league's position absolutely no good insofar as public reaction is concerned." He noted that reports about Paige's age varied from 39 to as old as 50, and that signing a 50-year-old White player wouldn't have served the purpose of enhanced publicity that Veeck was apparently trying to achieve. Spink noted that a "rookie" of Paige's advanced years reflected poorly on the Major Leagues overall, as it would "demean the standards of baseball in the big circuits. Further complicating the situation is the suspicion that if Satchel were white, he would not have drawn a second thought from Veeck."[13]

Spink finishes his complaint with an appeal to American League president William Harridge to refuse to approve Paige's contract.[14]

Paige was actually 41 years old, not 39 or 50. Nine other pitchers played that season at the age of 39 or older. Rip Sewell, two months older than Paige, won 13 games for an all–White Pirates team that was only five-and-a-half games out of first place at the time Spink wrote his complaint about Veeck and Paige. Dutch Leonard spent the entire season in the rotation of the unintegrated Phillies and led the league in losses. Spink didn't bother to write anything about the Pirates' or Phillies' decisions to keep these older players in their pitching rotations. When the still-segregated Red Sox, who would finish the regular season in a tie for first place with Veeck's Indians, only to lose a one-game playoff, signed 43-year-old Earl Caldwell two weeks after Paige signed, Spink wrote nothing. The only mention made in *The Sporting News* about the transaction was, "The Sox admitted pitching inadequacy when they bought ancient Earl Caldwell of the White Sox."[15] There was no opining about demeaning the standards of baseball, or of Caldwell's contract being disapproved by the league office.

Spink's bigotry certainly wasn't representative of all members of the BBWAA, but the organization remained somewhat conservative overall. It continued to have prominent members like Cobbledick, former BBWAA president, and others who wrote in opposition to integration. Bob Cooke of the *New York Herald Tribune* went so far as to complain that Robinson's signing would "run the white people out of baseball." His theory, attributed to an anthropologist, was that Black

54   Cooperstown's Back Door

people had longer heel bones, which genetically made them faster than White people. Cooke felt that was unfair, an advantage that White people couldn't overcome. "The Negroes have the legs. It starts with Robinson but it doesn't end with Robinson.... They are going to take over our game."[16] Pete Norton, sports editor of the *Tampa Tribune*, made it clear that the custom of segregation in the South shouldn't be questioned, writing, "there can be no good reason to break down the traditions of this section of the country," going on to note that the practice of banning "mixed sports contests" was in place "to avoid unpleasant incidents, and has been found, over a period of 82 years, to be the sensible way to eliminate any possible trouble."[17] Norton didn't bother to note the type of trouble segregation eliminated and didn't speculate about the root cause of why that trouble may arise.

The BBWAA itself did finally demonstrate some progress by admitting Wendell Smith as the first Black member in 1947, followed the next year by Sam Lacy. However, simultaneously to those admissions, the BBWAA also instituted the rule that a writer had to be a member of the BBWAA for ten years before they would be eligible to vote on ballots for the Hall of Fame. That rule continues today, but in 1947 it had the effect of making Smith, Lacy, and any other Black writers the BBWAA admitted to its ranks wait a decade for the privilege that they had been denied due to their race.[18]

Generally, the writers didn't seem to know quite know how to write about the situation. Arthur Daley of the *New York Times* proved this in back-to-back columns that appeared on the day of Robinson's first game and the following day. Before the game, Daley wrote about the "precedent-shattering implications of Robbie's promotion," and of the pressure on Robinson, who could not be viewed as "an ordinary rookie," noting that he "almost has to be another DiMaggio in making good from the opening whistle." He recognized that it wasn't a fair situation before noting that Robinson was a pioneer, and "pioneers never had it easy."[19] The very next day, when summarizing the game, Daley ignored his own build-up to the history being made and waited until his tenth paragraph before labeling it "quite uneventful." He went on to use the standard tropes about well-behaved Black people, praising Robinson because he "minds his own business," and "makes no effort to push himself. He speaks quietly and intelligently when spoken to."[20] In general, the writers acted like nothing momentous was happening unless events, like the Cardinals' rumored boycott, forced them to recognize the issues that came along with integration.[21]

The BBWAA didn't seem to let race impact their voting on annual awards. The first national Rookie of the Year Award was given in 1947,

4. Foot Dragging 55

and the BBWAA voted to give it to Robinson. It was not an obvious choice, though the award has since been re-named for him. Only one award was given in both Major Leagues at the time, and Ferris Fain of the Philadelphia Athletics arguably had as good a year as Robinson. Pitcher Larry Jansen of the Giants won 21 games with a 3.16 ERA, and likely had a more valuable year than any other rookie. Yet the BBWAA voted it for Robinson anyway. That became common practice. The award was split to have one for each league starting 1949, after which a Black player won one of the awards for five straight years. During the 1950s, a Black player was Rookie of the Year in seven of the decade's ten seasons. Voting for the Most Valuable Player followed a similar pattern, with a Black player winning one of the awards in eight seasons of the 1950s. The voting for the Cy Young Award was different, in part because there was only one award to give each year until 1967, and partly because teams were slower to sign Black pitchers than hitters. Even so, the first Cy Young ever awarded went to a Black pitcher, Don Newcombe, in 1956.

The Hall of Fame during this time was still following their standard practice of following the lead of public opinion in general and the leadership of baseball in particular. The general population certainly seemed to be accepting of Black players in the Major Leagues. There was no quantifiable backlash among White fans at the ticket booths. Initially, crowds in Brooklyn were smaller, and predominantly Black.[22] Opening Day wasn't a sellout, confirming the fears many baseball executives had expressed about White fans not supporting an integrated team. That dissipated as soon as Robinson established himself and the team was successful. Attendance for the Dodgers and the entire league went up, just as it had in 1946 as the war had ended and the best players had returned to play. If anything, attendance seemed to be firmly tied to conditions in the economy at large as opposed to the racial makeup of the teams. Attendance surged immediately after the war, fell back during economic recessions in 1949 and 1953, then climbed steadily for the rest of the 1950s during more prosperous times. There would always be prejudice that Black players experienced as individuals, but that didn't have an impact on the business of baseball, or its popularity.

Baseball leadership, however, was another story. By the end of the 1940s, only three teams had joined the Dodgers in signing Black players; Bill Veeck's Cleveland Indians, Richard Muckerman's St. Louis Browns, and Horace Stoneham's New York Giants. They were very slowly followed by four more teams—the Braves, White Sox, Athletics and Cubs—that were struggling in the standings and hoping an infusion of talented Black players would make them competitive. It was obvious at that point that teams which had integrated were enjoying more success. Through 1953, only half of the 16 Major League teams had integrated, yet only one World Series, in 1950, featured two teams that remained segregated. The Yankees in 1953 were the last segregated team to win a pennant.[23]

With no obvious impact on ticket sales, and clear success on the field for Black players individually and for the teams that signed them, it's difficult to identify valid reasons for the other eight teams to be so slow in signing Black players. Among the teams that were the slowest to sign Black players, the common thread appears to be racism.

The Pittsburgh Pirates, whose ownership had flirted with the idea of tryouts for Black players while Judge Landis was still alive, only to back away, didn't have a Black player until 1954. The three other teams to integrate in 1954 were all associated with the South: the Cincinnati Reds, just across the river from segregated Kentucky, the St. Louis Cardinals, located in a state that had a star in the Confederate flag and with a roster that apparently had a sizable contingent of racists, and the Washington Senators, owned by the Griffith family, which would ultimately move the team to Minnesota largely because the state had a large percentage of White residents. The worst offenders in harassing Robinson, the Phillies, didn't integrate until 1957. The Tigers were owned by Walter Briggs, a man described by Wendell Smith as "very prejudiced. He's the major league combination of Simon Legree and Adolf Hitler."[24]

Briggs died in 1952, his son sold the team in 1956, and only then, in 1958, did the Tigers sign a Black player. Tom Yawkey's Red Sox, which had already passed on a chance to sign Robinson and other Black players in 1945, didn't sign any until 1959, the last team to do so. The promotion of Pumpsie Green only happened after longtime general manager Joe Cronin moved on to become American League president earlier that year, and openly racist manager Pinky Higgins, who once vowed, "There'll be no n_____s on this ball club as long as I have anything to say about it,"[25] was fired midseason.

The only other holdout team was the New York Yankees. Wildly successful for 25 years by the time Jackie Robinson broke the color line, and leading the league in attendance virtually every season, the club had no sense of urgency to integrate. They seemed to win the pennant every year without the benefit of any Black players, a fact noted by Jackie Robinson in 1952. "It seems to me the Yankee front office has used racial prejudice in its dealings with Negro ball players. I may be wrong, but the Yankees will have to prove it to me."[26] Yankee general manager George Weiss defended the club, saying, "It has always been our hope that one of these shall prove good enough to make it with the Yankees. But we

4. Foot Dragging

do not intend under any circumstance to bring one up just for exploitation."[27] It was another three years before the Yankees finally integrated, promoting Elston Howard to the Major League roster in 1955. Yankee manager Casey Stengel, who had once been punched by Cuban pitcher Dolf Luque over alleged racist insults,[28] commented on the signing, "When I finally get me a n____, I got one who can't run."[29]

With much of the leadership of baseball dragging their feet in integrating their teams, and with their primary voting body, the BBWAA, also being slow to integrate and placing voting barriers before its new Black members, the Hall of Fame moved with its usual deliberate speed on the issue. Election after election passed without a review of Black players, managers, or executives who could have been elected, at least as Pioneers, at any point. Meanwhile, individuals who had been tacit or vocal opponents of integration continued to be elected, their past behavior apparently posing no problems to the Hall of Fame or its electors.

Frankie Frisch, who, as manager of the Pirates, had distanced himself from the possibility of his ownership signing Black players, was elected in 1947. Pennock, as noted, joined him in 1948. Al Simmons, who had been mercilessly hard on Willard Brown in his brief stint on the St. Louis Browns,[30] was elected in 1953. Joe Cronin, who presided over the segregated Red Sox for nearly two decades, was elected in 1956.

Whether the Hall of Fame was pleased with this or not is unknown. For the most part during this time, they were more interested in simply having anyone elected, preferably people who were alive to accept the honor. After the initial classes of inductees, the Hall of Fame largely went dormant during the years of World War II. There was no voting held in 1940 or 1941. They elected Rogers Hornsby in 1942, cranky old racist that he was, and no one else. In 1943, they had no election again. In 1944 there was no election for modern players, but the Old Timers Committee did elect Landis, who was, of course, dead. In 1945, the BBWAA finally voted again for the first time in three years but didn't elect anyone.

At this point, the leadership of the Hall of Fame feared the lack of new inductees was going to kill public interest.[31] Tourism of any kind was already limited by travel restrictions during the war, and the lack of ceremonies to induct new members gave baseball fans one less reason to come to Cooperstown. In 1945, with the war ending, the hope was that a new class would be elected, and an appropriate induction ceremony held, jumpstarting postwar visitation. But when the BBWAA voted in January 1945, they didn't give 75 percent of the vote to anyone, leaving the Hall of Fame without any reason to hold a ceremony.

The leadership of the Hall, including founder Stephen Clark, who

58 Cooperstown's Back Door

served on both an expanded version of the Old Timers Committee as well as a permanent committee of trustees, decided that action was needed. First, they elected ten men through the Old Timers Committee, nine players and a manager, but since their purview was limited to those whose careers took place before 1900, only two of the ten were still living. On top of that, they changed the voting rules to require the BBWAA to hold a vote every year instead of every three, including the introduction of a nominating vote for the first time. They felt that part of the problem was that the ballot wasn't limited, allowing voters to write down any ten eligible players, with the result being that votes were spread out across too many viable candidates. In the new dual voting process would, the first vote would continue to be open, but would serve only to produce a top 20 that would then be voted on a second time, each writer voting for five of the 20.[32]

In the first year, 1946, nothing changed. The new nominating vote narrowed the list to 20, and then the follow-up vote failed to produce a candidate with 75 percent. Not content to have another year with no inductees, the Old Timers Committee crammed 11 men into the Hall. Five of them were living, including Clark Griffith, who was still firmly committed to dragging his feet in signing Black players because he was too busy profiting from rentals of his stadium to Negro Leagues teams.

It's important to note that Stephen Clark, founder, trustee, and president of the Hall of Fame, was on the committee that felt Griffith and those like him should be members. It was Clark that was setting the standard for the institution to follow. It was he and Landis who had instituted the so-called "character clause" that forced the writers to consider a player's personal traits in addition to his performance on the field.[33] With Landis dead, Clark alone was in position to direct how that clause should be interpreted by the writers when they voted. He could have specifically directed them to take things like racism, or Klan membership, into account, but he never did. Clark wanted members elected and ceremonies held. The Hall of Fame couldn't be a thriving attraction to Cooperstown if it never elected anyone or held any celebrations people could attend. And so, like the leaders of baseball, even if Clark's personal preference had been to take a stand against racism or injustice, he set that aside in favor of what would help the Hall of Fame the most financially. If that meant honoring the Clark Griffiths and Herb Pennocks of the baseball world, so be it. Clark was not about to rock the boat.

Beginning in 1951, Clark had a definite ally in the commissioner's chair, strongly aligned to the proposition that baseball peace should be maintained. Happy Chandler's tenure as commissioner ended before his first term had even expired. Ever the politician, Chandler campaigned for an extension of his contract more than two years before it was set to expire. He chose the owners' winter meetings in December 1949 as the place to make the request, having spoken openly about having earned the extension, as if the votes of the public or the players mattered. They did not. Chandler had made enemies among many of the owners, for a variety of reasons. He'd also angered the membership of the BBWAA over a decision he made to appoint what many of the writers felt was an unqualified member of their profession to be the official scorer for the 1949 World Series. The group was upset enough to "overwhelmingly" pass a resolution asking him to exercise more care in the future when naming scorers.[34] His request for an extension was tabled until the following year, though Chandler was given a salary bump of $15,000 to appease him.[35]

It didn't work. When the subject came up again in December 1950, and the owners again didn't extend Chandler's deal, he became upset. He asked for reconsideration of the issue in March 1951, but when it was again rejected, Chandler resigned, serving as a lame duck until July.[36] Chandler made claims later in life that he'd been forced out because of his stance on integration, but that appears to be a bit of retroactive reputation-building on his part. He claimed at the time of Robinson's death in 1972, "I never regretted my decision to let Robinson play, but it probably cost me my job."[37] That conflicted with his own statements at the time of his resignation, when he noted that his decision to void the Yankees' attempted sale of Dick Wakefield to the White Sox likely cost him the support he needed to get the necessary three-quarters majority to approve his next term.[38]

In his place, the owners elected Ford Frick the new commissioner. It was a job he later claimed that he didn't want,[39] but it shouldn't have surprised anyone. After six years of changes and disagreement overseen by Chandler, the owners wanted peace. They wanted a commissioner wouldn't be considered a "player's commissioner," as Chandler had been.[40] What the owners wanted was someone who wouldn't rock the boat.

That was Frick, a man so committed to the glory days of baseball that he seriously suggested legalizing the spitball again, 25 years after it had been outlawed, to cut down on the number of home runs being hit.[41] When a minor league affiliate of the Washington Senators announced their intention of signing a woman to pitch for them, Frick quickly issued a ruling that said such a move would be a "travesty," and banned all clubs from signing women, any violation of which would be "subject to severe penalties."[42] He was "adored by baseball's owners," largely because he was gifted at keeping conflicts to a minimum.[43] He'd carried the same water as Landis whenever integration was discussed, refusing to admit any formal or informal color barrier existed.

When Alexander Cartwright's family began to complain in advance of baseball's big centennial celebration that their ancestor wasn't being given the credit he deserved for developing the game, it was Frick who coordinated their appeasement and voted to put Cartwright into the Hall of Fame. When the report from the owner's steering committee included a section that outlined how integration would hurt them financially, it was Frick who went around the room picking up copies of the report so they wouldn't leak to the media. After Robinson joined the Dodgers, for their first series played at Polo Grounds in Harlem against the Giants, Frick and others feared that the largely Black crowd would become unruly. His proposed resolution for that was to suggest to the Dodgers that maybe Robinson should "sprain an ankle and miss a few games."[44] The team should move more slowly during their integration experiment, in his view, rather than risk a public reaction that might be embarrassing to baseball.

Now Frick was commissioner, in an even more visible position to calm whatever waters the owners wanted calmed. He had fewer powers available to him than Landis had enjoyed, the result of a pair of restrictions the owners had implemented after Landis died. No longer could the commissioner use the "best interests of baseball" as a reason to overturn any policy approved by the owners, and owners could now sue the commissioner if they felt the need to do so.[45] Neither restriction was likely to impact Frick's preferred approach to the role. He was focused very firmly on keeping the game as unchanged and noncontroversial as possible. Before even taking office in September 1951, Frick was called before Congress to testify about baseball's ongoing anti-trust exemption and the reserve clause. He was already protective of the owners' interests and rigorously defended the reserve clause, stating that "In 16 years, I have never heard a single player complain about the reserve clause. I never heard of one who didn't think it sensible and necessary to his own welfare."[46]

It was this sort of willingness by Frick to maintain the status quo that made him an attractive commissioner to the owners. They wanted someone, unlike Chandler, who would quietly keep everything and everyone on the same non-controversial page. They wanted someone who would do his best to keep controversies to a minimum. For instance, early in Robinson's first season with the Dodgers, while Frick was still president of the National League, there were concerns that the first series played against the Giants at the Polo Grounds in Harlem might lead to conflict. Harlem had a large Black population, and it was feared that unruly behavior in the stands might break out.

Frick's response to this possibility could have been bold, and public. It could have grabbed headlines. He could have issued a public statement urging calm from all involved or backing Robinson's right to play. He could have bent to the preference of some owners by using the possible unrest as a reason to order the Dodgers to leave Robinson at home, providing proof to the theory that the public wasn't ready to handle integration in baseball. Courses of that sort would be both bold and controversial, and Frick possessed neither of those traits. Instead, he privately suggested to Frick that "it might be unwise to press 'too hard' by putting the black man in the very first series up there in such a highly inflammable black environment. How about leaving him home in Brooklyn for a few days with a 'sprained ankle'?"[47]

Frick's method for handling Robinson, once he became more emboldened to defend himself on the field and play the more aggressive style he preferred, was representative of the type of leadership the owners preferred. That style was attracting attention, like yet another anonymous editorial in *The Sporting News*, with the headline "Stop, Look and Listen, Jackie," noting the several "rhubarbs" Robinson had been involved in, particularly with umpires, and advised him to "reflect on those high attitudes which have served him so well, to adopt a more moderate course."[48] So, when Robinson had a collision with the Giants' Sal Maglie during a game in April 1951, setting off an argument and resulting in complaints to the league office about Robinson's style, Frick quietly went to the Dodgers and told them to "keep Robinson in line"; otherwise, he would have to step in.[49] There was no similar stepping in by Frick when, for instance, Russ Meyer of the Phillies called Robinson a "n_____ m_____f_____" after a similar collision on the field.[50]

Before going too far in questioning Frick's motives, we should recognize that most of the people involved in integrating baseball were complex individuals who had a variety of issues they were dealing with beyond race relations. While it's true that Frick came from a time and place where racism was the norm, we also have no conclusive evidence that he was personally a bigoted man. Many of his actions and words suggest the opposite was true. When interviewed by Wendell Smith in 1939, Frick recalled that when he was a member of the basketball team at DePauw University, the team stopped in a restaurant to eat before a game in Richmond, Indiana. One of his teammates, Noble Sissle, was Black, and the owner of the restaurant refused to serve him. "Angry, we all got up and walked out," according to Frick.[51]

When the Cardinals were rumored to be discussing a strike, Frick at least advised their ownership that the players needed to reconsider, and possibly threatened to suspend them if they didn't play. Frick included a full chapter about breaking the color line in his autobiography, noting that the inclusion of Black players was a necessary move, without which "baseball would never have been able to break its provincial, nineteenth-century boundaries, and become truly national in scope and interest." He hailed Rickey's signing of Jackie Robinson as "his greatest accomplishment, his finest hour."[52] Robinson later wrote that Frick's support of his free speech rights played an important part in his success.[53] In fact, Frick's stance on integration may have sunk his first chance at being commissioner. He was among the early candidates to replace Landis when he died,[54] but reportedly had expressed to a Black reporter several years earlier that he did not understand why baseball owners objected to signing Black players, a stance that reportedly eliminated him from consideration at the time.[55]

Frick became commissioner at a time when Congress was pressing baseball about its antitrust exemption. The sport was being criticized for not having any teams west of St. Louis. Television rights were a new consideration that required his attention, along with burgeoning attempts among the players to organize a labor union. Handling all these issues to the satisfaction of the owners that employed him took much of Frick's attention, so keeping the controversy over baseball's slow integration process to a minimum was in his best interests regardless of whatever his personal views about integration may have been.

About a year after Frick assumed his new role as commissioner, Robinson appeared on the television show *Youth Wants to Know* in November 1952, and said he thought that "the Yankee management is prejudiced. There isn't a single Negro on the team and very few in the entire Yankee farm system."[56] The Yankees responded publicly, and filed a complaint with Frick, who decided to try to placate both parties. On one hand, he apparently expressed that he wanted Robinson to "soft-pedal some of his remarks" moving forward to avoid public controversies when possible. At the same time, he noted that he had no intention of talking to Robinson or anyone else with the Dodgers about the specifics of Robinson's views about the Yankees because "baseball still has the right of free speech."[57] Robinson later claimed that Frick encouraged him to continue speaking his mind. "Whenever you believe enough in something to sound off about it," Frick reportedly told him. "Whenever you feel strongly that you've got to come out swinging, I sincerely hope you'll swing the real heavy bat and not the fungo."[58]

That became the norm of Frick's time as commissioner. He overtly defended the interests of the owners that employed him, and used his prior public relations experience and time spent as a sportswriter to massage media coverage of the game to keep controversies to a minimum. He was not, in any way, a crusader for social justice or anything else. He said that overtly in another of Robinson's books. "Baseball's function is not to lead crusades, not to settle sociological problems, not to become involved in any sort of controversial racial or religious question."[59] One does suspect, though, that had it suited the owners' interest to crusade a bit, Frick would have done so.

Frick was not the only person whose actions should be viewed with some level of complexity. For instance, though Joe Medwick was one of the Cardinals that spiked Robinson during his first season, there was no speculation at the time from the Dodgers, Robinson, or the press that it was intentional.[60] Medwick had played against Black players in the past, most famously as part of Dizzy Dean's tour in 1934,[61] without any known negative incidents. During an earlier series against Brooklyn in June of that year, Medwick took it upon himself to offer Robinson hitting advice, telling him he was too tight at the plate. "Loosen up and hit that ball," he said. "If you do, you'll burn up this league, Jack."[62]

During the same June series, Joe Garagiola was noted to have casually "talked shop" with Robinson.[63] For decades after he allegedly used a racist slur against Robinson in an argument on the field, Garagiola insisted it wasn't true. A popular broadcaster whose work was loved by fans and respected enough to be honored with the Ford C. Frick Award in 1991, he was devastated when the incident with Robinson was highlighted in a children's book that his grandchildren read, prompting them to ask him why he hated Jackie Robinson. "He said something to me. I said, 'Why don't you just hit,'" Garagiola said in an interview years later, his voice breaking. "I've lived with this thing unfairly. It was a little bit of jockeying to break his concentration, that's all.... It wasn't even an argument.... You just don't know the grief and aggravation this has caused."[64]

In 2014, Garagiola was the recipient of the Hall of Fame's Buck O'Neil Lifetime Achievement Award, an award that is intended to honor those "whose extraordinary efforts enhanced baseball's positive impact on society, broadened the game's appeal, and whose character, integrity and dignity are comparable to the qualities exhibited by O'Neil."[65] He was chosen because of his work in not only raising money for the Baseball Assistance Team, but also for pushing that organization to not only assist former players who had fallen on hard times, but also former Negro Leaguers, umpires, and women from the All-American Girls Professional Baseball League.[66]

Robinson's teammate, Dixie Walker, a native of Alabama, was among the Dodgers who advised Branch Rickey before the season that they didn't want to play with a Black man. Walker, in fact, was alleged to be the ringleader. He later denied leading any coordinated effort,[67] but admitted that he'd told Rickey he had reservations about playing with Robinson. Rickey took that seriously enough that he tried to arrange a trade, but Walker was the team's best hitter and Rickey couldn't get the right return.[68] He decided instead to keep him on the roster, gambling that Walker was a good enough professional that he would ultimately do what was best for the team. That's exactly what Walker did. Though Robinson later said that Walker was the only man on the roster with whom he had no real relationship, that was Robinson's preference.[69] Walker was professional with him, offering batting advice at times,[70] and defending him when Chapman and the Phillies hurling their worst racist insults at him.[71] He gave credit to Robinson in later years, but also at the time, saying "No other player on this club, with the possible exception of Bruce Edwards, has done more to put the Dodgers up in the race than Robinson has. He is everything that Branch Rickey said he was when he came up from Montreal."[72]

Even the image of Jackie Robinson is more complicated and conflicted than the one ordinarily painted of him. He is of course worthy of all the praise he's received for re-integrating baseball, for his performance on the field, and for using his influence to advocate for civil rights. At the same time, he was clearly a difficult person to get along with, and not always consistent in his support of other Black players and activists. After the 1949 season, he took a group of Black players on a barnstorming tour but had arranged the finances in such a way that he was likely going to receive as much as four times more than the money guaranteed to the others. That included stars like his teammates Roy Campanella and Don Newcombe, and Larry Doby of the Indians. When they confronted him, Robinson was unapologetic. "If you guys feel I should have made your deal for you, I am in favor of calling off this tour right now."[73] The disagreement was the first of many that caused the easygoing Campanella to eventually end his friendship with him.

Robinson also denigrated the style of play in the Negro Leagues, claiming it was "more exhibition baseball," and that Negro Leaguers would need time in the minors before they would be ready for the Major Leagues.[74] His testimony in 1949 before the House Un-American Activities Committee was deeply divisive in the Black community. While he used the opportunity to criticize Jim Crow policies that unfairly targeted Black people, he also failed to defend activist Paul Robeson against false charges that he had said Black Americans wouldn't go to

4. Foot Dragging

war to defend the country against Soviet aggression,[75] prompting one report to label Robinson a "stooge" of the right-wing politicians running the committee.[76] Robinson's later support of certain conservative politicians, including Richard Nixon, caused many in the Black community, including Malcolm X, to feel he had betrayed them.[77] This was not, of course, the majority view of Robinson. He rightly remains mostly revered for his actions. But he had his enigmatic qualities, as many of the principal participants in baseball's integration saga did.

Among the most enigmatic was a player that Robinson played against during his barnstorming days, and to whom he would be inextricably linked, Bob Feller. Like many stars of the 1930s and '40s, Feller regularly played baseball in barnstorming tours across the country after the season was over. Salaries at the time, even for stars, weren't sufficient to keep them from having to find jobs during the offseason, and many made baseball that job. Feller was among them, beginning in his very first offseason, before he had even reached his 18th birthday.

In October 1936, Satchel Paige arrived in Des Moines, Iowa, to play against a team of local White players, including Feller. It would be a night game, played just up the road from Feller's family farm in Van Meter. Paige was only 29 years old, at the height of his pitching abilities, coming off a year with the Pittsburgh Crawfords in which he led the Negro National League in strikeouts and shutouts, leading the team to the pennant. Feller had played against Black players in the past at the field his father Bill had constructed on their property, Oak View Park, and was only a week removed from pitching the final game of his first Major League season in Cleveland. The first batter he faced was Cool Papa Bell, the lightning fast outfielder and Paige's teammate in Pittsburgh. Feller retired him, then faced Sammy Hughes, who had batted .319 for the Washington Elite Giants and led the league in triples. He singled, the only player to reach base against Feller in three innings of work.[78]

Five years later, they faced each other again. In three exhibition games played in October 1941, the two great pitchers dueled to a virtual draw. When asked later about Feller, Paige was complimentary, saying, "that there boy is just about the best."[79] When Feller was asked about Paige, he was less complimentary, paying backhanded compliments while denigrating Paige's work ethic. He acknowledged that Paige had a great fastball, but claimed that he didn't think Paige consistently wanted to put in his best effort, while also noting that he didn't know of many Black ballplayers good enough to play in the Major League. "I've seen just about all of them, and there are only a few who I think could make good up there.... [Paige] can still throw a fast ball that smokes—when he wants to. His biggest trouble is that he doesn't want to really bear down often enough. I wouldn't say that he'd be great in the major leagues if he were up there."[80]

These were elite players Feller faced, at the peaks of their careers. And yet, in 1946, when asked again if he'd ever faced any Black players who could play in the Major Leagues, Feller's view hadn't changed. In fact, it was even more harsh. He said he hadn't faced a single player that was Major League caliber, other than "Maybe Paige when he was young."[81]

Feller's comments about Black players' abilities are obviously wrong and seem to demonstrate either a complete lack of scouting ability by Feller, which is highly unlikely, or prejudice of some kind on his part. Before judging either his scouting abilities or possible bigotry, though, we must first recognize an incontrovertible truth about Bob Feller. In addition to being an outstanding pitcher and a patriotic American who interrupted his career to serve his country, and in addition to being the only pitcher to throw an Opening Day no-hitter, setting a strike-out record when he was just 17 years old, and being featured in advertisements across the country, Bob Feller was also kind of a blowhard.

It takes a blowhard to routinely refer to a museum dedicated to his career, designed by his son, filled with his personal mementos, as "my museum," as if he built it personally.[82] It takes a blowhard to gripe so much about his war service depriving him of even better career statistics that he felt compelled to carry a folded sheet of paper around in his pocket everywhere he went, with the title "What if there had been no war," on which was a projection of what his career numbers could have been.[83] When asked about Lou Gehrig's famous "Luckiest Man" speech, it takes a blowhard to reply, "He's wrong. I am. I'm still alive."[84] And it takes a blowhard to think, let alone say, despite having a plaque in the Hall of Fame and a museum in his hometown, "If I don't promote myself, who will?"[85]

Bob Feller had an opinion about everything, particularly if it involved baseball, and he seemed to have something in his nature that compelled him to express those opinions as bluntly as possible. His sister, Marguerite, once said of him, "He let you know where he stood. And I said about him before, there were two sides of it: his side and the wrong side."[86] Many of those opinions involved standards. Standards for what makes a hero. "Don't get this wrong: Heroes don't come home from wars, survivors come home from wars. I'm a survivor."[87] Standards for what a good tourist attraction should be. He felt the Field of Dreams field in his native Iowa, for instance, was "a waste of time."[88] Standards for what makes a good father. His dad, Bill Feller, was that standard.

"[H]e had great common sense and insight. He knew human beings very, very well. He was honest. He paid cash for everything. He worked hard for 40 years. He never took a vacation for over 40 years. My father was a very successful Iowa farmer. He didn't give me money, he gave me time."[89] His standards for a good ballplayer were firmly entrenched in the time in which he played. As Joe Posnanski has written of him, "He was president/CEO and chairman of the 'In my day, ballplayers were ballplayers' conglomerate."[90]

When it came to Black ballplayers, Feller believed they were substandard for the Major Leagues. Despite pitching against Satchel Paige and Cool Papa Bell when they were in their prime, and despite barnstorming with Paige and others after the 1941 and 1945 seasons, he didn't see them as being good enough to play with White players. On October 2, 1945, Feller faced off against Paige again, this time with a team of Black all-stars led by Chet Brewer. Playing shortstop for Brewer's squad was Jackie Robinson, who had already signed with the Dodgers though it hadn't been announced yet. In the eyes of reporters, Feller's past tours against Black players and this single game against Robinson made him somewhat of an expert, one of the few White Major League pitchers to have faced him. After Robinson's contract with Rickey was announced, they asked Feller what they thought of him.[91] He said Robinson was "a typical football player—they're all alike. They're tied up in the shoulders—can't hit an inside pitch to save their necks." He went on to say that while he thought Robinson seemed like a smart guy of high character, "I can't see any chance at all for Robinson. And I'll say this— if he were a white man I doubt if they'd even consider him as big league material."[92]

A year later, Feller doubled down. He'd spent the offseason after the 1946 season barnstorming with Paige again, and again facing top-notch Black players. By this time, Robinson had already performed brilliantly for the Dodgers' top farm team in Montreal, leading the International League with a .349 batting average and 113 runs scored. The Royals won the league title, and Robinson was named league MVP. But when Feller was asked if he thought Black players could succeed in the Major Leagues, his reply was typically blunt. "Haven't seen one— not one. Maybe Paige when he was young. When you name him, you're done. Some are good hitters, some can field pretty good. Most of them are fast. But I have seen none who combine the qualities of a big league ball player."

"Not even Jackie Robinson?" asked reporter Steve George of *The Sporting News*. "Not even Jackie Robinson," Feller replied.[93]

Feller's tours against a team of excellent Black players undoubtedly helped further the cause of integration in baseball as it demonstrated the skills of Black players against top-notch Major Leaguers. Buck O'Neil, who was part of Paige's team on the 1946 tour, said that since Robinson had already proven himself in the minor leagues, and other teams may have been scouting Black players as a result, "this tour was an event that could have a real effect on big-league integration...[W]e could at least prove ourselves against big-leaguers in these games."[94] Many of the Black players did exactly that. Hank Thompson, among others, reportedly hit well against Feller the entire tour,[95] and Paige regularly outpitched him. Yet Feller remained dismissive of the same talent he had just gone out of his way to display to the American public. He made an enormous amount of money from the tour, something he was very concerned about, having missed several lucrative seasons during the war, but seemed to have no appreciation for the opponents who made that windfall possible. In fact, in at least one instance, Feller paid Paige based on net receipts of the tour instead of gross receipts as called for in their contract. Even after Paige confronted him about it, Feller still didn't pay, forcing Paige to file suit against him to get the money he was owed.[96]

One year later, Feller found himself teammates with a Black player, Larry Doby, the first Black player in the American League. Though his barnstorming tours had positioned him to be more familiar and comfortable with Black players than most Major Leaguers, Feller did nothing to ease Doby's transition to the White Major Leagues. He wasn't unfriendly, or hostile. He didn't refuse to shake hands with him, as some in the Cleveland clubhouse reportedly did, but he also didn't use his vast influence as the biggest star on the team and somewhat of an expert on Black players to make sure Doby was accepted. "Feller was sort of in his own world," Doby later said, "really only concerned with what affected Bob." Feller said he "paid very little attention" to Doby when he was introduced. "Shook hands, said hello, welcome to the wigwam or some comment such as that and went about my own business."[97]

Midway through the 1948 season, Paige joined Feller and Doby in Cleveland, and again Feller was preoccupied with his own issues. He was being booed throughout the league, not only because he was struggling more than usual on the mound, but because he had become wildly unpopular among fans and his peers after he skipped the All-Star Game. Since the proceeds from that game went to the players' pension fund, Feller's popularity around the league plummeted. The players' views were neatly summed up by Junior Stephens, shortstop of the Red Sox. "When he was on his own tour, Feller pitched about three innings every day. He was getting a lot of dough for himself. Now that all players

4. Foot Dragging

benefit from the All-Star game, Bob should have made sure that he'd be here."[98]

After the Indians won the World Series that year, Feller was sitting by himself in the clubhouse during the celebration. He'd not only been shunned by players and booed by fans around the league that year, but had pitched poorly during the Series, and seemed to want to remain separate from the party. It was Doby who saw him and came over, even though Feller had done little to help Doby with his transition to the Major Leagues. Doby knew what it felt like to be isolated, even by some of the same players who were now celebrating after refusing to shake his hand the year before, so he went over to Feller and offered him his hand. "There were a lot of things—apology, brief happiness, and earnest congratulations—in Feller's eyes at that moment. He in turn reached out with an eager hand which once fired the fastest pitch in baseball and lighted that somber corner with his smile. Nobody else could spare the time."[99]

Whatever was in Feller's eyes at that moment, and whatever he'd seen from Paige and Doby during the season, it did nothing to change his views about Black players. "[T]here are few Negro ball players who can make the grade," he said in an article in *Ebony* magazine after the season. And, in true Feller fashion, he simply couldn't stop there. "[B]aseball today has no politics in playing. There is no discrimination against anybody, foreign-born or Negro. Either you have it or you don't. If players have the ability, they'll make the grade. I think that more clubs will open to Negroes in the coming years—once there is more available talent."[100]

With views this hardened, Feller appeared to be an unlikely candidate to be the first star player to advocate for Negro Leagues players to be inducted into the Hall of Fame, yet that's exactly what he did.

In 1962, Feller had been retired for five years and would be eligible for the Hall of Fame for the first time. Ironically, so would Jackie Robinson. Due mostly to the extreme backlog of players to consider, as well as eligibility and balloting rules that shifted every few years, no player had yet been elected in their first year of eligibility. In fact, the BBWAA had shown an unwillingness to reach a consensus on which players to elect. After electing 12 players in just four years of the 1930s, the BBWAA elected only eight players during the entire 1940s. This was in part due to the war, and because the Hall of Fame allowed the BBWAA not to hold an election every year, but also because there seemed to a belief among enough writers that an extreme standard for entry had to be applied. The 20 players the writers elected during this time were outnumbered by the 24 players elected by the Old Timers Committee, while the previous Centennial Committee had added 13 managers, executives, and pioneers. By the dawn of the 1950s, the membership of the Hall of Fame was largely populated by dead people who had played or managed decades before any of the museum's potential customers had been born.

This changed in the 1950s, largely at the Hall of Fame's behest. They had mandated that the BBWAA hold a vote every year and clarified the eligibility rules. Two players who had played as recently as the mid–1940s were elected in 1951, Jimmie Foxx and Mel Ott. Two more were elected in 1952, and again in 1953. A total of 15 players were elected by the BBWAA from 1951 to 1956, almost double the number from the 1940s.

And then, nothing.

After yet another shift in the rules, no election was held by the BBWAA in 1957. In 1958, no one got even 52 percent of the votes cast. Again, no election for the writers was held in 1959. In 1960, no one cracked 55 percent of the votes. In 1961, there no election held again.

Entrance into the Hall of Fame for modern players, which looked so promising in the early part of the decade, came to a screeching halt in the last half of the 1950s, and didn't show any signs of changing as the 1960s began.

This was the climate under which Bob Feller and Jackie Robinson became eligible for Hall of Fame consideration for the first time. Chances were not high that they

Jackie Robinson was the first Black man to be elected to the Hall of Fame, in 1962. Ironically, he was elected the same year as Bob Feller, who had claimed he'd never seen a Black player who could make it in the major league, "Including Robinson" (Smithsonian Institution).

would break the streak of election failures. Robinson didn't think he'd be elected, feeling that he'd had an adversarial relationship with enough writers that it would prevent him from getting enough votes.[101]

This may have been the reason why Feller decided to work with writer Ed Linn on an article that was published in *The Saturday Evening Post* in January 1962. Given the characteristically direct title "The Trouble with the Hall of Fame," the article contained Feller's views on where the Hall of Fame and its voters had gone wrong. "There seems to be a growing belief that modern ballplayers should be judged by more severe standards than the old-timers in order not to 'cheapen' the Hall of Fame," Feller wrote. "I don't want to see the Hall of Fame cheapened any more than anybody else does. But I don't want to see it become a wax museum either. The present system works against the modern ballplayer and particularly against the modern pitcher—who, with the changes in baseball during the past three decades, has been having a tough enough time getting in anyway."[102]

Feller's point in the piece is as obvious as the title. Worried about his own chances for induction, he calls for the voters to put the "modern ballplayer" into the proper perspective, especially when pitching is considered. He goes on in that vein for a few more paragraphs, making cases for some players he felt had been overlooked, which led to a couple of surprises. The first was his assertion that Satchel Paige should be elected to the Hall of Fame. "I believe very strongly ... that there should be a niche for Satchel Paige. To be sure, his major-league record doesn't qualify him, but that was only because the old color line kept him out of the majors for so many years." He went on to say that he was in a better position than anyone to make that judgment about Paige because of all the barnstorming they had done together. Feller was using the same experiences that had caused him in the past to claim that Paige may not have been Major League material to now justify a place for Paige in the Hall of Fame. In fact, he suggested that if Jackie Robinson wasn't elected when the results of the 1962 BBWAA election were announced, a special committee should be appointed "to get Satch in as the first Negro in the Hall of Fame."[103]

It's impossible to know what changed Feller's mind on this subject. He was not the sort of person that did that often and didn't offer explanation or apologies when he did. The only justification he provided was that the famed double play combination of Joe Tinker, Johnny Evers and Frank Chance had been elected based on a poem, with no qualifications as players, and therefore a precedent had been set for someone like Paige, whose Major League career wouldn't have qualified him.[104] Note that he didn't say Paige should be a full member of the Hall. He said there should be a "niche," or "corner," for him, and that he'd largely be elected "because he has become a legend," implying that he didn't necessarily endorse Paige's Negro League credentials as being worthy of full membership. He also stuck to his previous claims that Paige was backed by "relatively untrained Negro players" on those barnstorming tours, failing once again to acknowledge that many of those players, like Cool Papa Bell and Willard Brown, would have been Major League stars if given real opportunities.

While Feller noted that both he and Robinson were on the ballot that year, and that Robinson had a very good chance of being elected, he stopped short of endorsing Robinson's election. He recognized the irony that they came up for consideration at the same time given his prior prediction that Robinson wouldn't do well in the Major Leagues, and said it pained him to admit that prediction, but he didn't apologize for it, or note in any way that he felt Robinson's career was worthy of the honor.[105]

A player of Feller's stature making a case for a player from the Negro Leagues to be elected to the Hall of Fame should have been major news among baseball writers, but it was barely mentioned. His advocacy for Paige wasn't ignored by writers, but they did little more than note it and move on. Willis "Sec" Taylor wrote in the *Des Moines Register*, "Feller says Satchel Paige should be in the Hall in a special niche, although his big league record does not qualify him, but only because the color line prevented his playing for many years."[106] Jim Murray, in his nationally syndicated column, wrote, "Bobby is not even particularly enthusiastic about Jackie Robinson passing through the portals with him. He thinks Satchel Paige should be the first Negro to get to Cooperstown. For one big reason: Satch is a pitcher. And Bobby is partial to pitchers."[107]

Some writers did make cases for Paige. Without mentioning Feller's article, Ed Nichols in *The Daily Times* of Salisbury, Maryland, asserted that Paige should be elected, and raised the names of other Negro Leagues stars as well. "Long before Jackie Robinson pulled on a pair of spiked shoes, the Negro Leagues produced some great ball players.... [F]oremost among them was Leroy Paige, a man many feel was one of the greatest pitchers who ever lived.... If truly earned fame is the measuring stick, as it should be, then Satch belongs in the Hall of Fame."[108] Syndicated columnist Walter L. Johns of the Central Press Association also advocated for Paige's election, without mentioning Feller's article.[109] Over a year after Feller's article, David Condon used his much larger platform in the *Chicago Tribune* to argue for Paige's election. "Satchel Paige's color kept him out of the majors until Bill Veeck had the guts to bring him up in 1948.... Let baseball not compound the injustice done Paige, one of the most skilled of all pitchers, and permit his color to keep him out of the Hall of Fame."[110] Few others, outside of the Black news media, took up Paige's cause.

It's possible that writers viewed it as another in the long list of opinions Feller liked to talk about, and as such could safely be ignored. It's also possible that they didn't take it seriously because, later in the article, he also endorsed the election of relatively obscure pitchers George Blaeholder, "who invented the slider," and Firpo Marberry, "the first of the great relief pitchers."[111] For whatever reason, Feller's new stance, unexpected and noble as it may have been, didn't carry much weight, either in the media or with the Hall of Fame. A change in the way Negro Leagues players would be thought of would require something else, from someone more respected in baseball circles.

It was going to take Ted Williams. Right on the front steps of the Hall of Fame.

CHAPTER 5

Change

HIS FRIENDS SAID they'd never seen him so nervous. A record crowd was expected, one that forced the ceremony to be moved, from the usual setting on the front steps of the National Baseball Hall of Fame and Museum, to Cooper Park behind the building. Even with that logistical move, the crowd overflowed to the street in front of the building anyway.[1] But, after a 21-year career in the Major Leagues, playing in front of tens of thousands of fans each game, it's doubtful the crowd size was the root of his nerves.

It certainly wasn't the dress code either, as he refused to comply with tradition and wore one of his casual polo shirts under a sport coat. As usual, he refused to wear a necktie, though he did make the concession of buttoning his shirt's top button.[2]

The presence of baseball luminaries, like the new Commissioner of Baseball, likely didn't heighten his nerves either. In fact, he kicked off his comments that day by making fun of Commissioner William Eckert's former role as a Lieutenant General in the Air Force, noting that both he and Eckert had been pilots, and that no "matter what you might have heard, there were many times when the Air Force went out first … and the Marines had to go out and hit the targets they missed." As expected, the adoring throng of fans burst into laughter.[3]

So, no, it wasn't the brass, or the crowd, or the pressure to wear a tie, that made Ted Williams nervous that day. It was the speech.

Never a confident public speaker, but also deeply aware of the importance of the occasion, Williams knew this was not something he could do off-the-cuff. Famed baseball writer and analyst Bill James once wrote that Williams "spoke memorably without notes" that day,[4] but that's not right. The truth is that he worked on his speech at the hotel in Cooperstown for a couple of days. He used hotel stationery to capture what he planned to say, passing on a chance the day before the ceremony to watch a Red Sox farm team play so he could work on his speech instead. That night, he left a dinner with family and friends early so he could continue working on it alone in his room.[5]

74

The next day, July 25, 1966, Williams delivered a brief but eloquent speech in front of a crowd estimated at ten thousand. He spoke for just six minutes, reading from his hotel stationery notes, thanking coaches, managers, and the writers who voted for him. He spoke of the value of hard work, and the humility and pride he felt at being included among the game's greats. Then Williams touched on Willie Mays' recent home run that moved him past Williams on the all-time list. He applauded the achievement and exhorted him to go hit even more, noting that it was the nature of baseball to have new great players pass former greats.

Ted Williams threw considerable stardom and influence behind the idea of inducting players from the Negro Leagues into the Hall of Fame, and he used his acceptance speech to do it (courtesy of the Baseball Hall of Fame).

"Baseball gives every American boy a chance to excel. Not just to be as good as someone else but to be better than someone else. This is the nature of man and the name of the game.... And I hope that someday, the names of Satchel Paige and Josh Gibson in some way can be added as a symbol of the great Negro players that are not here only because they were not given a chance."[6]

Williams left no applause break after that line, and likely didn't need one. A random clap can be heard far in the background, dying out after a couple of seconds,[7] but none of the baseball dignitaries seated near him offered any reaction at all to this ground-breaking statement by the man who had openly sought to become—and many feel succeeded in becoming—the greatest hitter in the history of the sport.

The sentiment Williams expressed that day was one he'd held most of his life. As a kid in San Diego, he had saved his money so he could afford a ticket to see Satchel Paige pitch in an exhibition game.[8] Once

Paige finally made the big leagues, Williams had almost no luck against him, managing just two singles and two walks in 11 plate appearances. He struck out just once, but in such frustrating fashion that he broke the bat upon returning to the dugout. (That bat—with what the Hall of Fame claims are Paige and Williams' signatures—is now part of the Hall's collection.)[9]

It wasn't just Paige that Ted Williams admired and treated with fairness. When the Red Sox became the last team in baseball to integrate by calling up infielder Pumpsie Green in 1959, Williams went out of his way to treat him as an equal, with Green becoming Williams' preferred warm-up partner before games.[10] He'd gone out of his way to give money to former Negro Leaguer Ted "Double Duty" Radcliffe when he learned he was having financial trouble, and had intervened with a hotel in Florida that refused to give John "Blue Moon" Odom a room because of the color of his skin.[11]

Praising Willie Mays for passing him was simply an extension of Williams' view that hard work should be all that mattered in baseball. It was, to him, the fair thing. Calling for Negro Leagues players to be eligible for baseball's highest honor during his own induction speech was likewise simply an extension of that point of view. "Nobody encouraged me on this," he later told Bob Costas. "I thought this thing alone.... I'd seen Satchel Paige, and I'd seen Josh Gibson, and I'd heard about Buck Leonard, and I'd heard about some of the other great Black athletes, and it just came out that day I wrote in my speech that I hoped someday that the great Black players of the past, who only because of their color never had a chance to play in the big leagues [would be elected]."[12]

The silence that day from the leaders of the Hall of Fame and Major League Baseball soon extended to their actions. At the time Williams made the comment, just one Black man, Jackie Robinson, was a member of the Hall of Fame. He had barely been elected, surpassing the 120 necessary votes by just four in the election of 1962. Except for Native American Charles Bender, there were no Native American, Latino, Japanese, or other minority players in the Hall. Nothing about that situation changed for the next three years, until finally Roy Campanella was inducted in 1969. Campanella became the first, and, until Barry Bonds and his PED allegations, the only three-time MVP who had to wait as long as seven years after he was first eligible before finally being elected to the Hall of Fame.

The media reaction to Williams' speech, however, was different. The publicist for the Los Angeles Angels, George Goodale, told reporters that he felt every Major League team should be brought to the Hall of Fame and have a recording of Williams' speech played for them.[13]

According to reports in the *Boston Globe* the next day, those who had attended the ceremony in prior years felt his speech "was the best acceptance that they had heard."[14]

The rest of the media in Boston were less complimentary, and less focused on Williams' message of inclusion for Negro Leagues players. Jerry Nason, columnist for the *Boston Globe*, acknowledged that Williams may have a point about Black players, while using the same column to argue, "If Paige not being in Cooperstown makes it a 'Hall of Shame' it has to be equally so for Addie Joss, whose skin was white and whose pitching was heroic."[15] To Nason, Joss' dying of tuberculosis before he played the tenth season that would have made him eligible for the Hall was a special circumstance the Hall should consider. "If ever the victim of an injustice needed Ted Williams to speak up for him it is Addie Joss."[16] Nason apparently felt that having a short career due to tuberculosis was a bigger injustice than having no Major League career at all simply because of the color of your skin.

At least Nason granted Williams' point. His rivals in other Boston papers largely ignored it, choosing instead to focused on a perceived slight to one of their former colleagues. When Williams was handed his plaque before his speech, a member of the crowd yelled out, "What would Dave Egan think of this?" Egan, who had died in 1958, was a writer in Boston for most of Williams' career, and the two had a long-running feud.[17] After hearing the remark, Williams was reported to have said, "F___ Dave Egan," while standing too far from the microphone for anyone to have heard him clearly.[18] Some reporters later claimed they never heard the remark at all, but the *Boston Traveler* and the *Boston Herald* each ran pieces that focused on the supposed remark, claiming it had "stunned the crowd of 10,000" when, in fact, virtually no one heard it at all, and those who did couldn't confirm what Williams had said.[19]

Williams denied saying it, and Red Sox owner Tom Yawkey called the *Traveler* columnist, Tim Horgan, into his office, where he played an audio recording of the entire event for him. The reported remark couldn't be heard, and Yawkey demanded a "page-one retraction" while making a veiled threat that the newspaper's affiliated radio station could lose the lucrative Red Sox broadcast rights unless such an apology was made. The newspaper and Horgan caved in and printed the retraction, with the *Herald* following soon after.[20]

Such was the state of the Boston sports media that a groundbreaking civil rights statement by the best hitter in the history of baseball was largely ignored in favor of a lament about a tubercular dead White player from the turn of the century and a possibly imagined insult to a dead White reporter.

Outside of Boston, Williams' statement drew more commentary and support from columnists than had Bob Feller's argument for Paige's election four years earlier. Most major newspapers ran a story from one of the news services, the AP or UPI, and both of those stories mentioned Williams' call for the inclusion of Negro Leagues players. Many papers edited that statement out of the version they published, but most did not. Several prominent columnists also took up Williams' cause. Shirley Povich, of the *Washington Post*, called Williams' plea for inclusion of Negro Leagues players "magnificent."[21] Dick Young, writing in *The Sporting News*, supported Williams' statement at the end of his weekly column. He noted that the leaders of the Hall of Fame had done the right thing in changing the rules to allow Casey Stengel to be eligible immediately. "Now let's follow it up by taking Ted Williams' cue; let's find a way to honor such immortals of Negro baseball as Josh Gibson and Satchel Paige. The Hall of Fame is dedicated to all of baseball's greats, and such men certainly belong in that category."[22]

One of the more enthusiastic supporters in the media was Bud Burns, of the *Nashville Tennessean*. He called it the "best suggestion I've heard in a long time" and went on to chastise the Hall of Fame for not being more inclusive overall, arguing that not only Negro Leagues players should be eligible, but also players who distinguished themselves in the minor leagues, and active players as well.[23] An editorial in the *New York Post*, which was reprinted in other papers, called it "the slugger's finest moment."[24] Dave Condon again used his column in the *Chicago Tribune* to argue for Paige's election, and Gibson's as well.[25]

The greatest attention was paid by Black sportswriters, publishing in newspapers targeted at Black readers. Ric Roberts of the *Pittsburgh Courier* was effusive in praising Williams, calling it his "finest hour," and wondering if future generations would recognize Williams as "a great man, a more sentimental gentleman than the baseball writers ever realized."[26] An article in the Alexandra (LA) *News Leader* called Williams' remarks "unexpectedly beautiful."[27] When Wendell Smith asked Lou Boudreau, the great former shortstop who had managed both Paige and Williams in the Major Leagues, which players he felt were most deserving of being elected to the Hall of Fame, Boudreau said Paige "heads the list."[28]

Missing entirely from the media coverage was anyone directly asking officials from Major League Baseball or the Hall of Fame if they intended to follow Williams' suggestion and include Black players. Young's broadside at them was only in print. There is no record that he, or any other reporter, directly asked Frick, or Kerr, or anyone else associated with the Hall of Fame, what they thought of Williams' comment.

It's likely that everyone already knew the answer.

5. Change 79

* * *

As Williams noted in his speech, Ford Frick was no longer the commissioner of baseball when Williams made his remarks. In 1963, Frick announced that he would retire when his existing contract expired two years later. He spent those two years telling the owners what they had done wrong in limiting the commissioner's powers, not sharing television revenue, and not expanding the number of teams sooner. He also claimed that his proudest accomplishments during his tenure were "the integration of the races in baseball, the expansion of the game and my own baby, the Hall of Fame."[29]

At the end of the 1965 season, Ford Frick formally retired and accepted the position as chairman of the board of the Hall of Fame, where his portrait hung in the rotunda outside the plaque gallery. It is still there. The position gave Frick, and his determination to preserve his traditional views of baseball's past, the power to stand as one of the principal obstacles to the election of Negro Leagues players.

The leadership of the Hall of Fame during this time was made up of a mix of representatives of the Clark Foundation and former baseball writers. Former BBWAA member Frick was chairman of the board. The Hall of Fame's president was Paul S. Kerr, who had been vice president of the Clark Estate, as well as the director of one of the Clark family's other museums in Cooperstown, the Farmers Museum. He was elevated to president of the Hall of Fame upon the death of Hall founder Stephen Clark in 1961. The Hall's director was Ken Smith, former writer for the *New York Mirror* and author of a book about the Hall of Fame. Smith was a former secretary of the BBWAA.[30]

The campaign among many members of Frick and Smith's former writing brethren to elect Negro Leagues players to the Hall of Fame was continuing to grow. Dave Condon of the *Chicago Tribune* continued to raise the issue in his column. He used the twentieth anniversary of Josh Gibson's death as a reason to remind everyone of Williams' suggestion that Gibson be elected. "One is moved to consider the plea of one of baseball's all-time greats when he was admitted to the Cooperstown mecca last summer.... Ted deplored the fact that many deserving baseball players were not eligible for the hall.... Josh Gibson, and Satchel [Paige], belong in the hall."[31]

Stan Issacs used his column in *Newsday* to argue on Paige's behalf as well, citing the recent rule change that allowed Casey Stengel to be elected without waiting the required five years after retirement. "Paige is not even eligible because he didn't put in the minimum 10 seasons in the big leagues. That's an unfair rule because Paige was ready for organized baseball long before it was ready for him.... The BBWA waived the

80 Cooperstown's Back Door

rules to vote Casey Stengel into the Hall.... The same should be done for Paige."[32]

Steve Jacobson used the same platform to highlight the absurdity of the ten-year rule when it came to all Black players, noting that if Roy Campanella had been in the car accident that paralyzed him one year earlier, he wouldn't have completed the necessary ten years of Major League service to be eligible for the Hall of Fame. Despite having three Most Valuable Player awards to his credit, he couldn't be elected to Cooperstown. He also noted that Jackie Robinson barely played the necessary ten years, too. "[I]f it had taken Branch Rickey one more year to decide for baseball that Negroes were fit to compete with white men, then Jackie Robinson wouldn't have been eligible, either. He just made the required 10 years.... Satchel Paige, who was born ... into an era that said no Negro may play in the Major Leagues, may never be marked with one of those little brass plaques." Jacobson found all this preposterous, particularly in contrast to the Hall of Fame's ongoing efforts to collect memorabilia. He mocked the notion that the Hall of Fame could dedicate time and resources to collecting "the ball from Ed Head's no-hitter and the portrait of the general who didn't really invent the game," while ignoring more important issues like the eligibility of Black players who hadn't been allowed to play in the Major Leagues.[33]

The calls for the election of Paige reached the point that it was mentioned in routine news articles touting his appearances in cities where he continued to tour. "Satchel Paige, the ageless rubber-arm pitching star, is scheduled to appear on the mound for the Indianapolis Clowns when they meet the Baltimore Stars Wednesday night at 7:30 at Fairchild Park," proclaimed *The Daily Times-News* of Burlington, North Carolina. "The 'great one' is being expounded for a place in Baseball's Hall of Fame by many sports writers, not only for his major league career, but also for the additional 22 years of greatness in the Negro leagues.... Admission is $1.50 and 75 cents."[34] When Paige's tour took him to Chicago, there was Dave Condon, again using his column to make Paige's case for the Hall of Fame. "Among Negroes, Satchel always will be regarded as the greatest; too bad other fans do not have the same regard and demand that he be voted into the Hall of Fame."[35] Condon also posed the question to Lou Boudreau, Paige's former manager with the Indians. "Does Paige belong in the Hall of Fame? Well, not off what he did in the majors, but I do believe the Hall of Fame should have special categories for players such as Paige."[36]

Black journalists expanded on the subject, often not limiting themselves to making cases only for Paige or Gibson. A lengthy case was made in the *Pittsburgh Courier* for electing Rube Foster.[37] It ran next to a separate piece reminding readers of the "spans of domination" in Black baseball prior to Jackie Robinson's joining the Dodgers in 1947, and named twenty different Negro Leaguers who should be considered an "all-timer."[38] Doc Young lamented in the *Chicago Defender* that "no one seems to care" that no Hall of Fame was available to players like Paige, Gibson, Bullet Joe Rogan, Smokey Joe Williams, Oscar Charleston, and other "super-stars" of Black baseball.[39] Claude Harrison wondered in the *Philadelphia Tribune* is "maybe some day the Hall of Fame will realize that Gibson, Cool Poppa [*sic*] Bell, Slim Jones and others are just as much to do with the development of baseball as anyone else."[40] Sheep Jackson of the *Cleveland Call and Post* expressed optimism that the time was ripe for at least Paige to be elected because so many players and writers were advocating for him that the Hall of Fame couldn't ignore them.[41]

Absent from the debate was the loud, influential opinion of J.G. Taylor Spink, integration opponent and former editor of *The Sporting News*, who had died in December 1962. Taking his place was his son, C.C. Johnson Spink, described as "the antithesis of his hard-drinking, hard-driving father." The young Spink broadened the paper's coverage, both topically and editorially. It would no longer be only "The Bible of Baseball," but would cover all sports.[42] Rather than adopting the views of the editor alone, the paper reprinted articles from outside papers, and gave free reign to columnists like Leonard Koppett, who regularly criticized baseball's ongoing biases.[43] When Branch Rickey was inducted into the Hall of Fame in 1967, an editorial in *The Sporting News* lamented the Hall's decision not to break from tradition and allow Jackie Robinson to speak: "In the present turmoil of racial relations, his appearance on the platform could have been of dramatic value.... We have no idea what he would have said if he had been invited to speak at Cooperstown.... But, whatever the subject Robinson might have picked, the Hall of Fame's platform would have given him a chance to talk with conviction in a voice that would have been heard all over our troubled land."[44] It was a far cry from the days of Spink's father using the paper to write "No Good from Raising Race Issue," or advising Robinson to "stop, look and listen."

In the immediate aftermath of Williams' call for the inclusion of Negro Leagues players, one voice was conspicuously silent. Dick Young, the most popular columnist in the most popular paper in the largest city in the country, wrote almost nothing about it. He noted Williams' comment when he wrote a column about the induction ceremony, but he didn't endorse it or expand upon it.[45] A week later, he wrote a column in *The Sporting News* in which, at the very end, he noted that Frick,

82 Cooperstown's Back Door

Kerr, and other Hall of Fame officials should act on Williams' suggestion.[46] Otherwise, Young was silent on the subject. He wrote nothing else about it for the rest of 1966, and nothing at all in 1967.

This was entirely out of character for Young, whose tenacity in using his influential column to push agendas that resonated with him was legendary. He had just used that influence to benefit Casey Stengel. Two days after Stengel formally retired, Young wrote that the Hall of Fame's post-retirement five-year waiting period should be waived in Stengel's case. In fact, he mocked the fact that the Veterans Committee didn't meet every year, and that Stengel couldn't be voted upon until January 1967, even if the waiting period was waived.[47] Two months later, he wrote about Stengel's situation again, this time asking his readers to participate in a letter-writing campaign on Stengel's behalf to Paul Kerr at the Hall of Fame.[48] Two weeks later, he made Stengel's case again when answering reader mail.[49] A week later, he wrote that the BBWAA, at their annual winter meeting, had unanimously recommended that the Hall of Fame immediately elect Stengel.[50] Just before Christmas, Young again used a reader's letter to make Stengel's case, as well as to mock the reader's handwriting.[51]

The dawn of the new year didn't slow down Young's campaign. When writing about the going away party thrown for Ford Frick as he retired from the commissioner's office, Young reported that "somebody" asked Frick about Stengel's situation. Frick's reply was that he was working with Kerr, and they would "come up with something."[52] By the time it was finally announced on the last day of January 1966, that the five-year waiting period would be waived for Stengel, Young had mentioned Stengel's Hall of Fame situation seven times in five months. He had been so vocal that he had literally become part of the story, as the article in the *Daily News* noting the eventual change to the Hall of Fame's rule noted: "In explaining the sudden change, which was championed by sportswriter Dick Young ... Frick added that the five-year rule was waived in deference to any player or official older than 65."[53] A week later, Young reprinted his summary of Frick's comments at his retirement dinner, apparently to emphasize that the "something" Frick intended to "come up with" had now happened.[54]

Even with the Hall's rule now changed, Young didn't relent. He mentioned Stengel and the Hall of Fame again on back-to-back days in early March.[55, 56] Stengel was finally elected three days later as part of a special election by the Veterans Committee, and Young wrote the summary of that vote,[57] and then added his personal views on that decision in his column the same day.[58] Even then he couldn't stop writing about it, taking a figurative victory lap for his successful advocacy by mentioning Stengel's election three more times in the next six weeks.[59, 60, 61] The count of Young's drumbeats on this issue was up to 15 in the span of less than eight months, demonstrating conclusively that if sufficiently motivated by a subject, Young would use his enormous platform to keep it in the public eye, something he had not done to that point in support of electing Negro Leaguers to the Hall of Fame.

Then something changed.

On April 20, 1966, Dick Young used his column to write about an interview he conducted with Jackie Robinson two days earlier for the 20th anniversary of Robinson's first game in White baseball with the Montreal Royals.[62] The two men had an odd relationship. When Robinson first reached the Major Leagues, Young was the team's beat reporter for the *New York Daily News*. That paper was one of the few that paid for their reporters' expenses to travel with the team, rather than relying on the team to cover those costs. That gave *Daily News* reporters more freedom in covering the team, and Young used that freedom in an odd way. With Jackie Robinson the biggest baseball story in the country that year, Young used his place with the country's most widely read newspaper to barely report on Robinson at all. He didn't ignore him completely. Robinson's actions in each game were faithfully reported upon as needed. But he didn't comment upon the social impact of Robinson integrating baseball at all and deemphasized his importance to the team's success on the field.[63]

Over the years their relationship would evolve. Despite his frosty initial response to Robinson, Young demonstrated some sympathy toward the first Black players. He befriended Roy Campanella and co-wrote his autobiography in 1952. Robinson expressed some admiration for Young. "I had always respected Dick for being a newspaperman that went out and got stories and wrote them, regardless of whether or not they were going to hurt anybody as long as they were truthful."[64] Later, Young began to believe that Robinson's style in advocating for Black ballplayers and for civil rights in general was "too militant,"[65] while Robinson came to believe that Young was bigoted, commenting that Campanella was "lapping at the rears of prejudiced sportswriters."[66] In his final book, *I Never Had It Made*, Robinson wrote, "I used to think he was a nice guy personally, and I knew he was a good sportswriter. As time went by, Young became, in my book, a racial bigot."[67] Though defenders of Young disputed that charge, chalking his behavior up to nothing more than being opinionated and "ornery,"[68] Young did shows signs of intolerance. For instance, Young was in the habit of writing quotes from Roberto Clemente phonetically, emphasizing his thick accent, a practice Clemente detested.[69]

Still, Robinson respected him overall, and even though he felt that "Dick wrote the way he did because he didn't particularly like me,"[70] he agreed to the interview. In it, Robinson reminisced about that season in the International League, including the warm reception he and his wife received from Montreal fans, and the cruelty they experienced elsewhere. He talked about nearly suffering a nervous breakdown that year from the pressure on him and from remarks fans would make, and how he didn't think he'd be a Dodgers fan anymore once the players he played with were no longer on the team. Then the conversation shifted. Young didn't indicate how it shifted but, given his obsession over the past several months with Stengel, it's likely he raised the subject. Robinson was blunt in his views that Stengel was prejudiced against Black players, citing several players who were in a position to know.[71]

This, of course, was not a new allegation about Stengel. During the 1920s, when he was playing for the Giants, he was alleged to have yelled "Cuban n_____!" at pitcher Adolfo "Dolf" Luque during a game, resulting in Luque charging into the Giants' dugout and punching Stengel in the face.[72] While managing the Boston Braves in 1939, he was interviewed by Wendell Smith about the possibility of the Major Leagues being integrated. After admitting that he'd seen several Black players with the ability to play in the Major Leagues, he then repeated the anti–Black tropes about "unrest" and "troubles" in the Negro Leagues that might be brought to White baseball in the event of integration and "reflect on the game's name."[73] Stengel had been quoted as saying, supposedly as a joke, "When I finally get me a n____, I got one who can't run," upon the Yankees' signing of their first Black player, Elston Howard,[74] and had reportedly yelled racist insults at Robinson and Don Newcombe during a World Series game.[75] The possibility, or even likelihood, of his holding racist views was well known.

Despite certainly knowing about these events, Young remained a Stengel loyalist and pushed back on Robinson's allegation, noting that he'd seen no evidence of that during his years of close association with him. "It could be that they were guys who weren't playing regularly, and blamed it on prejudice," Robinson replied, "but I heard it long ago, too, when Stengel was with the Yankees. Porters on Pullman trains used to tell me things they heard, and I just couldn't root for Stengel, mainly because of that."[76]

If Young had a reply to that he didn't write about it, but it's notable that, after that column ran, Young stopped writing about Stengel almost entirely. There were write ups during the time of the actual induction ceremony in July,[77] but for the most part Young's obsession with Stengel appears to have been retired with the publishing of Robinson's comments about him. Whether that was coincidence or intentional isn't known.

What is known is that Young didn't immediately demonstrate the same zeal for Negro Leagues players' being elected to the Hall of Fame as he had shown for Stengel. He noted Williams' comments, and endorsed them a week later, but otherwise dropped the subject for a couple of years. When Satchel Paige signed a contract with the Atlanta Braves in 1968 in an attempt to reach the necessary Major League service to qualify for a pension, Young used the occasion to revive the idea that Paige deserved to be honored by the Hall of Fame despite not being eligible. That wasn't true, since Paige and any other former Negro Leagues player could have been inducted as a pioneer had the Hall's Veterans Committee chosen to do so, but Young argued for the Hall to add a "section at Cooperstown to include Satchel Paige and others who contributed richly to baseball history in the Negro leagues."[78] He then dropped the subject again for nearly another year.

These rare mentions of the issue make it clear that it was on Young's mind at least to some extent during this timeframe. He wasn't using his widely read column to adamantly tout the case of the Negro Leaguers, certainly not to the same extent he did for Casey Stengel, but he was on their side. Unknown then, at least publicly, was that Young was using his position within the Baseball Writers Association of America to advocate for the Negro Leaguers, and he was doing so at a time that coincided with new conditions in baseball and the country at large for Black players and people.

Dick Young was one of the most influential writers in the BBWAA, and finally used that influence to argue for the inclusion of players from the Negro Leagues in the Hall of Fame (courtesy of the Baseball Hall of Fame).

For Young, his decision to take this stand appears to have revolved around the first, and, at that point, only two Black men elected to the Hall of Fame. In July 1969, during an event for Hall of Fame members at All-Star Game festivities in Washington, D.C., Jackie Robinson and Bob Feller got into a spirited argument over the role of Major League Baseball in providing management or front office jobs to Black former players. During his remarks, Robinson commented that he wished more owners would offer managing jobs to Black players after they retired. Feller, during his comments, chose to challenge that notion, saying that "Players get what they deserve for what they perform, and nobody owes them anything," and added that everyone in baseball is "paid for your ability. Anybody who can do the job can get a job in baseball on ability alone." Robinson's response to that was to say that Feller "still has his head in the sand after 20 years."[79] Young attended the event and reported on the nasty exchange.

The BBWAA, of which Young was president at the time, was also meeting in Washington during the All-Star break. During their meetings, Larry Claflin of the *Boston Record-American* suggested that the BBWAA should take action to begin considering Negro Leagues players for the Hall of Fame. His motion called for experts on the Negro Leagues to be added to the Veterans Committee. The motion was approved by the full BBWAA.[80]

One week later, Roy Campanella was inducted into the Hall of Fame, just the second Black player elected. Young was in attendance in Cooperstown for the ceremony

Shortly after being the second Black player elected to Cooperstown, Roy Campanella (right) was tapped to serve on a committee that would recommend Negro Leagues players who were worthy of induction (Library of Congress).

5. *Change* 87

and to announce the BBWAA's decision to augment the Veterans Committee with Negro Leagues experts. He had a much closer relationship with Campanella than he had with Robinson, and wrote warmly about his friend's induction ceremony, while also noting his announcement that the BBWAA "is instituting machinery to vote into Cooperstown, worthy greats of the Negro leagues prior to the breakdown of the ignominious color line."[81] It had already been decided that Campanella would be one of those experts.

Regardless of Young's personal views of Robinson or his tactics, it's clear that he respected him He both respected and liked Campanella, and was moved by both Robinson's ongoing, fiery advocacy for equal right and Campanella's quieter way of making the same points. "When Roy Campanella speaks, you listen, because his voice sings. It is a melodic purr, soft and sensuous," Young wrote. He contrasted that style with Robinson's more strident approach of "screaming from the top of his lungs," though he admitted that was sometimes necessary. Mostly, he wanted to make it clear exactly how wrong he felt it was that someone like Campanella hadn't dared to dream of being able to play baseball at the highest level solely because of the color of his skin. "How does a boy dream of making the top of a game they would not permit him to play at the bottom?" Young wrote that he saw the need for both Robinson's aggressive methods and Campanella's more passive ones, and that their respective elections to the Hall of Fame proved they were both right. He also made it clear that they weren't the only Black players who were good enough to be included in Cooperstown. "Others belong, men like Satchel Paige and Josh Gibson, and maybe Pop Lloyd and Bill Wright and Slim Jones and Cyclone Williams, men whose exclusion from the Hall of Fame is based on being born black and in the wrong time."[82]

It's clear that, when first advocating for the Hall to admit players from the Negro Leagues, Young had been using the Campanella approach, writing about it infrequently, and without rancor. It's equally clear that in that summer of 1969, when the BBWAA, under his leadership, had voted to take the matter into their own hands, Young's approach had shifted. He was now intent on using the BBWAA's long-standing position in Hall of Fame voting to hit the leadership of the Hall right across the nose.

There was a tactical problem with the BBWAA's strategic action, however, and Young recognized it in his column the day after the announcement. "This has to be done through the cooperation of Bowie Kuhn, the new commissioner, and Paul Kerr, president of the Baseball Museum at Cooperstown."[83] As much influence as the BBWAA had over the Hall of Fame, they did not make the final decision regarding the makeup of the Veterans Committee or the eligibility of players from Negro Leagues to be considered. It was going to take the Hall of Fame to make that change, which meant it was going to take the agreement of a person who had spent decades doggedly defending and even romanticizing baseball's traditions, had been a major force in delaying integration in baseball, and viewed the Hall of Fame as his "baby."

It was going to take the agreement of the Hall of Fame's chairman, Ford Frick, and Ford Frick didn't want anyone from the Negro Leagues in the Hall of Fame.

The argument, according to Frick, had nothing to do with discrimination or the ability of the players from the Negro Leagues. It wasn't a question of whether they were great players who would have excelled in the White Major Leagues if given the opportunity. It was simply a question of the rules. Hall of Fame eligibility rules were quite clear, in Frick's view, and they required a player to have played ten or more years of Major League Baseball to be eligible for consideration. None of the players in question met that requirement, and therefore the hands of Frick, and everyone else at the Hall of Fame, were tied. The fact that the Hall of Fame set those rules and was free to alter them at any time was not an appropriate consideration, according to Frick, and Hall of Fame president Paul Kerr. To alter the rules to allow the Negro Leagues players to be eligible would be a lowering of the Hall of Fame's lofty standards, in their view, and their job was to protect those standards.

We know all of this because of the efforts of one person to broker a compromise between the Hall of Fame and advocates for the former Negro Leaguers. Bowie Kuhn, longtime attorney for the National League and newly installed Commissioner of Baseball, was not, under ordinary circumstances, someone who would be considered progressive. In the opening chapter of his autobiography, Kuhn made two different references to race that were entirely unnecessary, first referring to Rudy York as "the Cherokee first baseman," and then expressing confusion that St. Louis Cardinals owner Gussie Busch was "off the reservation" in calling for Kuhn's resignation.[84] In the opening sentence of the second chapter, he took issue with his acknowledged reputation of being an "Ivy League–Wall Street stuffed shirt," but then enumerated on the very next page how his mother's family had been in the United States since 1634, had "deep ancestral roots" in Washington, D.C., had a variety of notable people in her family tree ("five governors and two United States senators, in addition to various congressmen, judges and lawyers"), and was a distant relative to Jim Bowie.[85]

Kuhn notes that after completing his "honors degree in economics"

5. *Change* 89

at Princeton, he went to law school, then traveled through Europe after graduating at the age of 23 and joining the prestigious New York law firm of Wilkie, Owen, Farr, Gallagher and Walton. He'd chosen that firm from the variety of job offers he received because one of its founding partners, former Republican presidential nominee Wendell Wilkie, was one of his heroes, and he fondly recalled tallying convention results as a 13-year-old during the election of 1940.[86] His work at the firm included representing the National League and eventually becoming their counsel, from which position he routinely argued in favor of maintaining the reserve clause and arguing against free agency and the player's union in general. This is not the portrait of a progressive.

But, like the other complex figures involved in the issue, Kuhn was not quite as monolithic in his thinking as he seemed. Growing up, he'd held a job as a scoreboard operator at Griffith Stadium in Washington, D.C., where the Homestead Grays played half of their home games.[87] "Don't forget, I saw Josh Gibson and others play in Griffith Stadium where I was the scoreboard operator."[88] The argument in favor of inducting players from the Negro Leagues struck a sympathetic chord with him, particularly because he found the various arguments against admitting them to the Hall of Fame to be "unpersuasive and unimpressive." He felt those arguments were technical, and not based in fairness toward the players who, "through no fault of their own ... had been barred from the majors until 1947."[89] He was certain these were great players who would have proven their greatness if given the opportunity. "This was precisely the kind of situation that required the bending of rules."[90]

According to Kuhn, he decided to call a meeting between the involved groups at his office in an attempt to reach a resolution. It's not clear exactly when the meeting was held, Kuhn states only that it was "in early 1970." Depending on how early in the year it was held, Robert Peterson's book, *Only the Ball Was White*, published in April of that year, may have already been available. It had been reviewed and commented upon by several prominent writers, including Bob Broeg in the *St. Louis Post-Dispatch*[91] and Stan Isaacs in *Newsday*.[92] In the book, Peterson not only told the story of Black baseball, putting a relatively comprehensive history of it into the public's consciousness for the first in decades, but also added an impassioned call for players from the Negro Leagues to be elected to the Hall of Fame. He was explicit that this should be full membership, not limited to a mere display, or "some obscure corner of the museum.... I mean in the austere Hall of Fame where wide-eyed young fans now gape at the bronze likenesses of Honus Wagner and Ty Cobb and Babe Ruth and Walter Johnson and read summaries of their deeds."[93]

Peterson didn't stop there. He also provided specific rebuttals to the arguments against electing them. To those who argued that the Negro Leaguers didn't face top competition, he replied, "After a careful study of contemporary accounts I have the distinct impression that the top black clubs won somewhat more than half of their games against big-leaguers."[94] Addressing the idea that incomplete statistics prevented a clear picture of Negro Leaguers' greatness, he responded, "There is, however, plenty of testimony to the talents of the greatest black stars, not only from other Negro players but from white major-leaguers, some of them with niches in the Hall."[95]

To the notion that including the Negro Leaguers would lower the Hall of Fame's standard, Peterson countered that their inclusion would actually raise those standards. "Foster, Paige, Gibson, and Lloyd were among the most gifted baseball men of all time and of any color. To exclude them on the grounds that, except for Paige, they never competed in the big leagues is to raise not just an unreasonable standard but an impossible one. And so long as the Hall of Fame is without a few of the great stars of Negro baseball, the notion that it represents the best in baseball is nonsense."[96] He'd even done the math on the appropriate number of Negro Leagues players to elect. Noting that the Hall of Fame's membership included 68 players whose Major League careers took place during the period from 1900 to 1947, Peterson felt that it would be fair to add eight Black ballplayers from that time period. That would raise the total number of Hall of Famers from that era to 76, just over 10 percent of whom would be Black, a figure that would approximate the percentage of the American population that was Black during those years.[97]

It may be that the meeting Kuhn called preceded the publication of Peterson's book, but he mentioned it in his autobiography as having "focused greater attention on the accomplishments of Negro League players."[98] Regardless of the timing, it's clear it made an impact on Kuhn and many baseball writers and couldn't be ignored by the leadership of the Hall of Fame.

From the Hall of Fame, Frick and Kerr attended the meeting at Kuhn's office in New York City. From the BBWAA, president Young and secretary-treasurer Jack Lang of the *Long Island Press* attended. Kuhn presided, and three other officials from Kuhn's office, including Monte Irvin, the great outfielder from the Giants and, before that, the Newark Eagles of the Negro National League.[99] The positions of most of the participants were well-known, having been reported publicly over the years reported. Young, of course, had stated his views in his column and the position of the entire BBWAA had been reported when they voted to alter the makeup of the Veterans Committee the year before. Frick had defended the standards of the Hall of Fame and baseball generally for decades. Irvin, officially representing the commissioner's office but also informally representing the interests of the former Negro Leaguers since he'd played in those leagues himself, had publicly stated that he felt Frick and the league presidents didn't do enough to protect Black players against Jim Crow laws in the South, particularly during spring training each year. He said that Major League baseball could have applied significant economic pressure on cities and towns that enforced segregation, but instead elected to stand silent as teams purchased entire hotels to allow their players to stay together.[100]

That put Kuhn, who was sympathetic to the writers' position but also had a great deal of respect for Frick and the Hall of Fame, in the position of having to broker some form of compromise. Unfortunately, neither side seemed interested in that. During the meeting, Frick and Kerr maintained the view that Negro Leagues players were ineligible for good reasons, ranging from lack of statistics to accurately record their careers, to falling short of the ten-year Major League service rule, to lowering the standards of the Hall of Fame and angering existing Hall of Famer members. Young vehemently disagreed, apparently rather rudely. He was "passionate and unrelenting" in voicing his view that the Negro Leaguers should be admitted, and the meeting became "heated and unpleasant."[101] Despite agreeing with Young's position, Kuhn "was offended by his rudeness to Frick," and the two men had exchanged "heated words" in the middle of the meeting.[102] Not surprisingly, no compromise was reached.

That did not stop Kuhn. To his credit, he continued to have direct discussions with Kerr throughout most of 1970, attempting to convince him that the Hall of Fame needed to represent the Negro Leagues in some way. Peterson's book, and his recommendation that eight Negro Leagues players should be elected, was now widely available and reported upon. Separately, Roy Campanella gave a similar estimate of the number of Hall-worthy Negro Leaguers to Dick Young. When Young asked him how many players from the Negro Leagues had Hall of Fame credentials, Campanella replied, "Eight or nine," a number deliberately lower than the "twenty or thirty" he felt were deserving because he didn't want Young and others to dismiss it.[103] Young was less vocal on the issue than he had been, never writing about it in his widely read column during that entire year, a sign that negotiations were ongoing behind the scenes.

By July, progress had been made. Kuhn formed a committee, reporting directly to him, that would have the task of nominating Black players for the Hall of Fame. At that point, the committee was still unofficial, and it wasn't even clear who led it, or what would be done with their nominations. One report indicated that Young headed the committee.[104] Another indicated that Irvin was the chair.[105] Former sportswriter Joe Reichler, who had moved to working for Kuhn in the commissioner's office and was a non-voting member of the committee, claimed that he was the leader of the committee as Kuhn's personal representative.[106] What is clear is that the committee still hadn't met, wasn't funded, and still hadn't been approved by the Hall of Fame. "I've heard rumors," Kerr said, "but no one (not even the Commissioner) has talked to me about changing the rules. The board of governors of the Hall of Fame would have to vote on something like this."[107]

Still, it was clear that some kind of movement had taken place in the negotiations. As Frick had noted many times, he did not feel that it was baseball's function to "lead crusades," or "settle sociological problems." In an interview for one of Jackie Robinson's books, he had stated that the "breaking of the color line reflected changes taking place in the country at large. In other words, baseball was not a frontrunner in breaking the color line. Its tardiness in this respect was inherent in the attitude of American society."[108] True or not, this was Frick's view on the role baseball should play, and he likely brought that to his new position with the Hall of Fame. The Hall was intended to be a reflection of the game, which was a reflection of society at large. That society had now changed. The Civil Rights movement was in full swing. Martin Luther King, Medgar Evers, Malcolm X, and others had died fighting for the rights of Black people.

Prominent Black athletes, like Jackie Robinson, Jim Brown, Bill Russell, and Muhammad Ali, were using their positions to fight for change. Black baseball players were among the best in the game. Sportswriters, Frick's former brethren, were now adamantly in support of players from the Negro Leagues being admitted to the Hall of Fame. White Hall of Famers like Ted Williams, Bob Feller and Lou Boudreau were calling for their election as well. Peterson's book glorifying Black baseball was being read and quoted. The commissioner of baseball himself was in support of admitting the Negro Leaguers. The position of Frick, Kerr, and the rest of the Hall of Fame's leadership simply had to shift with the times.

In January 1971, it finally did. Kuhn's Special Committee on the Negro Leagues was convened after he finally convinced Kerr that admitting Negro Leagues players was the democratic thing to do and wouldn't diminish the Hall's standards.[109] In fact, the Hall's approval was only granted on the condition that the players wouldn't be full members of the Hall of Fame. They would instead have a separate "display" elsewhere in the Hall. There would be no plaques of Negro Leaguers in the Plaque Gallery.[110] When the committee's existence was announced formally on February 3, 1971, it explicitly said that the Negro Leagues players would be honored as "part of a new exhibit."[111]

The door to the Hall of Fame was not yet open for the greats of the Negro Leagues, but it had been unlocked.

Chapter 6

The Back Door

THE FULL CHARTER OF BOWIE KUHN'S new committee has been a point of debate ever since it was formed. The committee's members were known, for instance, but various people have been portrayed as the official or unofficial leader. The rules the committee was ordered to follow are well-documented, but whether they were given a limit on the total number of Negro Leagues players they could elect remains unclear. And perhaps the greatest mystery involving the committee's work is whether Kuhn pulled a fast one on the Hall of Fame's leadership, using public humiliation to achieve it.

Officially, Monte Irvin was the committee's chair, appointed by Kuhn. He was joined by several men who had been directly involved in the Negro Leagues. They included former players Roy Campanella, Judy Johnson and Bill Yancey, and former owners Ed Gottlieb and Alex Pompez. Sam Lacy and Wendell Smith, the Black sportswriters who had worked so tirelessly to see baseball finally integrated, were also on the committee. The final two voting members of the committee were Frank Forbes, a player for several Black teams before the Negro Leagues were formally founded who later became a scout for the New York Giants and a judge with the New York Boxing Commission, and Eppie Barnes, former first baseman for the Pittsburgh Pirates who went on to manage a semipro team in East Orange, New Jersey, which regularly played against Negro Leagues teams.[1]

Dick Young was on the committee as a non-voting member.[2] It's not clear why, since he had virtually no direct knowledge of the Negro Leagues and couldn't vote on the committee's selections anyway, but his forceful advocacy for the admission of Black players and his recent position as president of the BBWAA likely convinced Kuhn that he should be appeased. Kuhn's public relations director, Joe Reichler, was the final member. He also was not given a vote and claimed later to be the actual chairman of the committee, described by historian John Holway as "sort of an overseer to make sure the blacks on the plantation didn't get out of line."[3]

Just as notable as who was on the committee was who wasn't on it. Few would question the credentials of players Irvin, Campanella, or Johnson, or writers Lacy and Smith, or owners Gottleib and Pompez. But there were more knowledgeable people about the Negro Leagues who could have been included rather than Barnes or Forbes. Any number of former players, like Buck Leonard, Buck O'Neil, and Satchel Paige, had decades of direct knowledge of Black baseball that could have been tapped into. Historians like Holway and Robert Peterson had done years of invaluable research but were excluded. No one involved in selecting the committee's members has ever commented publicly on why these experts weren't included, other than Jackie Robinson, who reportedly wasn't asked to join because he only played one year in the Negro Leagues.[4]

The rules given to the committee regarding which Negro Leagues players they could consider were explicit. The players must have played in the Negro Leagues for at least ten years and must have played prior to the re-integration of the Major Leagues in 1947. Like their White counterparts, their selection must be agreed upon by 75 percent of the voting members of the committee, and would be based upon their "playing ability, integrity, sportsmanship, character, and their contribution to the teams they played on and to baseball in general." The committee was further limited to electing just one player per year, but this was later changed.[5]

Reports at the time, and in the years since, indicate that the committee was given a limit of eight or nine players they could elect. This was hinted at even before the committee officially existed. An article from July 1970, that included quotes from Young and named many of the eventual committee members six months before they were agreed upon, said that Young "heads a committee which expects to nominate approximately eight Negro Baseball stars for the Hall of Fame," and went on to suggest that figure came from Peterson's suggestion in *Only the Ball Was White*.[6] John Holway claims that there was a plan to list nine Black players on a single plaque.[7]

The committee was formally announced to the public on February 3, 1971. The release included the acknowledgment that any Black players elected would be honored in a separate exhibit, not in the existing Plaque Gallery.[8] The Associated Press story about the committee explicitly noted that any Negro Leaguers selected by the committee "will not actually be Hall of Famers," and added a quote from Kuhn noting that he "wouldn't call it a compromise. The rules for selection to the Hall of Fame are very strict and I think those standards are correct."[9]

Though the committee's initial task was to draw up a list of Negro

Leagues players who fit the election criteria, which would have included dozens of men,[10] by the time the news of the committee was released only 12 men were under serious consideration for election.[11] The AP story again made it clear that even that group was realistically down to two men, Josh Gibson and Satchel Paige, who would likely be the first elected.[12]

With just those two under serious consideration to be the first Negro Leaguer elected, Paige had a clear advantage over Gibson; He was still alive. Joe Reichler's status as a non-voting member of the committee begins to make more sense once the public relations aspects of the committee's work are taken into account. That was Reichler's specialty, and he later admitted in a letter to Effa Manley, former co-owner of the Newark Eagles, that "It is important, in my opinion, to honor the men who are still living so that they can make personal appearances, meet the press and public, and spread the Gospel of Negro Baseball. Except for Josh Gibson, a great player who passed away makes little impact upon the voters as well as upon the public and the press."[13] If the results of the committee's work are any indication, Reichler's view was the one they followed, as six of the nine players they ultimately elected were still living.

That included Paige, whose unanimous election by the committee was announced on February 9, 1971.[14] During the press conference at which the announcement was made, Kuhn was asked if Paige would be a Hall-of-Famer, and he acknowledged that he would not. "Technically, you'd have to say the answer to that question is 'No,'" Kuhn replied. "But I agree with those who say that the Hall of Fame is a state of mind, and the important thing is how sports fans view Satchel Paige. I know how I view him.'"[15] Kuhn was referencing something Young had written in his column the week before, already putting a spin on the decision not to give the Negro Leaguers full membership. Noting that any Negro League players elected by the committee would be displayed in a separate exhibit, Young felt they would still be referred to as Hall of Famers even if they technically weren't. "As far as I'm concerned, and I am sure as far as the fans believe, these men will be Hall of Famers and will be referred to, evermore, as Hall of Famers, for the Hall of Fame is not a pile of bricks in upstate New York; it is a state of mind, a list of great names, a wonderful dream."[16]

Young was not the only member of the committee who tried to put the best spin possible on the decision. Wendell Smith said, "None of us on the committee feels that any form of segregation is involved in setting up a separate section for the black leagues," noting that since the Negro Leagues didn't have sufficient statistics to document the players' achievements, "we just don't know for sure" if they'd have been stars in the Major Leagues. "I find no fault with the separate category."[17] Monte Irvin also backed the idea. In a 2005 interview, he said "If we had done it another way, it could have taken a longer time. It might have happened eventually, but we got it done right away."[18]

This was not the consensus view. A wide array of opposing voices spoke up, denouncing the decision as another form of Jim Crow. "If it's a special kind of thing, it's not worth a hill of beans," said Jackie Robinson. "It's the same damned thing all over again. If it were me under those conditions, I'd prefer not to be in it. They deserve the opportunity to be in it but not as black players in a special category."[19] Willie Mays was less direct, but also didn't approve of the decision: "The Hall of Fame is a big place. They could've had them all together instead of saying let's put those guys over here because they weren't in organized ball."[20] Paige's former boss, Bill Veeck, also disapproved: "A man like that doesn't need a side niche in the Hall of Fame. He shouldn't have to come in the back door."[21]

References to the Hall of Fame having front doors for some but only a back door for others became the general theme. An editorial in the *Detroit Free Press* noted, "It's a shame, in the literal sense of the word, that Satchel Paige had to use to back door to get into the baseball Hall of Fame."[22] Similar language was used by Hal Wood in the *Honolulu Advertiser*: "The greatest pitcher in the history of baseball finally made it into the Hall of Fame—even if it was by the back door."[23] Syndicated columnists Jim Murray blasted the decision.

In 1971, Leroy "Satchel" Paige became the first Negro Leagues player elected to the Hall of Fame. He was very nearly placed in a separate wing, prompting him to say, "I ain't going in the back door" (Library of Congress).

"They've segregated the Hall of Fame! ... They have taken Baseball's shrine, Cooperstown, and turned it into a 'Sorry, I can't serve you here—but if you'll step around the back' place.... Who in the world got the bright idea to dust off and put back a 'Colored Only' sign in this day and age? ... What is this—1840? Either let him in the front of the Hall—or move the damn thing to Mississippi."[24] Publicly, Paige was more willing to go along with the plan. "I'm proud to be in wherever they put me in the Hall of Fame."[25] But Paige's former teammate, Buck O'Neil, claimed later that Paige had told him "I want to be in the Hall of Fame, but I won't go in the back door."[26] A different version of Paige's thoughts about the separate display has been more widely reported. "I was just as good as the white boys. I ain't going in the back door of the Hall of Fame."[27]

Kuhn would have us believe that the public outcry was part of his plan all along. In his autobiography, he wrote that the complaints were something he had not only predicted but felt were necessary. "I knew that the furor would be heard by the board of directors and that the public outcry would be hard to resist. This is exactly what happened. By 1971, the board decided to give our committee the power to vote in members on a full and equal footing with everyone else." Only then does he note Paige's election, and how he was "spirited unto New York under the guise of receiving an award," going on to claim that Paige was "superb" at the press conference, showing no bitterness.[28] He omitted a comment made by Paige in *Sports Illustrated* a week later. "The only change is that baseball has turned Paige from a second-class citizen into a second-class immortal."[29]

Kuhn's version of events is difficult to believe, partly because his recounting of the timeline of Paige's election is wrong. By the time Paige was elected, the committee's existence had been widely reported for a week, with clearly leaked presumptions that either Paige or Josh Gibson was going to be first player elected. Dave Condon wrote in his column of February 5, 1971, that the leak came from Joe Reichler "a few weeks ago," when he told a group of reporters that not only would a Negro Leagues player be elected to the Hall of Fame a month later, but that it would be Paige.[30] It was even announced in advance that the committee's first election would take place the same week Paige was supposedly "spirited into New York" under false pretenses, so it's unlikely that Paige didn't know the true reason he was there. Additionally, Kuhn's implication that the Hall of Fame had already acquiesced to the criticism of having a separate display by the time Paige was elected was also inaccurate. The reality was far different. Kuhn, Paige, and others were all still being asked about the separate display at the press conference where Paige's election was announced.

6. The Back Door

The furor lasted for several months as the leadership of the Hall of Fame continued to resist admitting Paige as a full member. Everyone involved in the decisions came under fire. Kuhn said he was "placed under personal attack."[31] A substantial letter-writing campaign took place. People wrote directly to the Hall of Fame, complaining about their "policy of segregation."[32] Newspapers' Letters to the Editor sections ran complaints, including from prominent community leaders like Charles Grigsby, president of The New Urban League of Greater Boston, who wrote to the *Boston Globe* that the Hall's new segregated section was reflective of racism.[33] Robert Peterson, author of *Only the Ball Was White*, wrote an article for the *New York Times* that was syndicated in many newspapers, noting that Paige's entry into the Hall of Fame was "by the back door," and he could only be considered to be in the Hall of Fame "approximately."[34]

Prominent former players, including some members of the Hall of Fame, continued to speak out about the plan to segregate the Negro Leaguers. Retired pitcher Early Wynn, who had been a teammate of Paige's in Cleveland for one season, labeled Cooperstown the "Hall of Shame." Bitter over the fact that he hadn't been elected yet, Wynn felt the decision to segment the Hall of Fame into separate categories was wrong and hypocritical since the same decision hadn't been applied to other members of the Hall who had not played in the Major Leagues for ten years, like pioneers and executives.[35] Jackie Robinson continued to be vocal in his disapproval of the decision as well. He was quoted in the *Indianapolis Star* that April, saying that Paige was going into the "black man's Hall of Fame," and "deserves much better.... You'd never get me in that way."[36]

The campaign of complaints about the Hall of Fame's stance took long enough, in fact, that Dick Young changed his position on the issue. In June 1971, Young wrote that the committee only considered electing players who "would have made the Hall of Fame (not just the big leagues) if the opportunity had existed," and wouldn't be surprised if Paige's induction later that summer was as a full member of the Hall.[37]

Perhaps this change of heart was all part of Kuhn's plan, too, but that's doubtful. Writing fifteen years after the fact, from a position as a member of the Hall of Fame's board of directors, Kuhn would have us believe that part of his plan all along to have Negro Leaguers granted full membership was to publicly humiliate the Hall of Fame and damage his own reputation and the reputations of several members of the Special Committee on the Negro Leagues who supported the initial announcement of a separate display. It seems unlikely that Kuhn would have been allowed to remain on the Hall's board after an announcement

100   **Cooperstown's Back Door**

like that. Far more likely is that Kuhn, the Hall of Fame, and the committee didn't anticipate the level of outrage that would be expressed in the public and in the media, and Kuhn was trying to put the best spin possible on it when writing his memoirs.

Whether intentional or not, the pressure ultimately worked. The treasurer of the Hall of Fame, Howard Talbot, tracked all the letters received on the subject and reported to Kerr that the sentiment they expressed was overwhelmingly in favor of admitting Paige as a full member. This put Kerr and the rest of the Hall's board in the position of having to choose between all three principal constituencies: The public, the media, and the current members of the Hall of Fame.

Since the Hall's inception, it had needed all these groups to be successful. Catering to the public to ensure they would create an attraction that people would pay money to visit had been a key focus of the Hall's founders, but so had the knowledge that it would be difficult to sell the exclusivity of the Hall and collect the necessary artifacts to fill it if they players weren't happy with the result. Positive media attention provided the Hall of Fame with the publicity they so badly needed, which explains their deep attachment to the BBWAA as their primary voting body and the placing former sportswriters like Ford Frick and Ken Smith into prominent leadership positions at the Hall of Fame.

Kerr and the board were constantly under pressure from the existing members to keep the Hall of Fame's standards high. This is consistent with the behavior of the members of any exclusive club. Once they are admitted, they want to feel like it was an accomplishment, and want to keep the benefits of membership down to the fewest number of members possible. Plus, in this case, many of those members were complicit in the decisions that had kept baseball segregated for so long and were on record saying the quality of play in the Negro Leagues was not at a Major League level. That had been a standard excuse used to justify their bigotry, so agreeing to grant Negro Leaguers the game's highest honor as full members would fly in the face of their previous stance.

The current members were not unanimous in this view, though. Vocal support for Paige's full membership had come from Jackie Robinson and Roy Campanella, as would be expected, but also from baseball luminaries like Ted Williams, Bob Feller, and Lou Boudreau. Past statements from deceased members, like Lou Gehrig and Babe Ruth, were used as testaments to the skill of Paige and the other top players from the Negro Leagues. Even if the membership had been more unified, they were outnumbered, as the consensus of both the public and the media was on the side of admitting the Negro Leagues players as full members.

After Kerr and the Hall's board of directors weighed that against the pressure being applied by the media and the public, as well as by some of their more prominent current members, they backed down. On July 6, 1971, one day before his birthday, Paige was flown to New York on the pretext of getting an award and was told he would be inducted as a full member at his induction ceremony a month later.[38] Here we see the botched timeline Kuhn presented in his autobiography again, as he represented this event as taking place in February, close to the initial announcement of his election.

The announcement in the media the following day was particularly low-key when compared to the press conference called when Paige was elected. Short articles from wire services were all that appeared in most newspapers, buried deep in sports sections. There were no quotes from Paige, Kuhn or anyone representing the Hall of Fame. The UPI report that ran in the *Evansville Press* was typical. It noted only that Paige had been elected, that Kuhn and Kerr had made the announcement jointly, and that it was the new committee that had voted him in. The only note about the separate display was matter of fact: "However, it was stated that all players selected by this committee would be enshrined in a separate wing of their own in the museum. Paige will be inducted into the Hall of Fame along with seven others during the annual ceremonies in Cooperstown, N.Y., Aug. 9."[39]

However long it took, and no matter the clunky methods used, Satchel Paige took his rightful place in the Hall of Fame that August. As expected, his acceptance speech was funny and warm and filled with gratitude.[40] But later, after the formal ceremonies were over, Paige expressed some of the bitterness he felt, not just toward the Hall of Fame but toward baseball in general, for not allowing him and his Black peers to prove themselves in the White Major Leagues for so long.

A few years later, Paige was invited to an event for other players who had been elected and was asked to speak. He took the opportunity to express his view that too many Black players were being unfairly kept in the minor leagues instead of brought up to the majors where he felt they belonged. Joe Reichler, who was at the event in his public relations capacity for the commissioner's office, interrupted Paige and told him to sit down.

"I sat down," Paige later said. "They keep asking me to come back but I've never been back to Cooperstown."[41]

CHAPTER 7

The First Wave

THE SPECIAL COMMITTEE on the Negro Leagues elected a total of nine men over seven years. That was one more than the number recommended by Robert Peterson in *Only the Ball Was White*, but quite a bit had changed since then.

Peterson's recommendation was based on the proportion of Black people in the population during the years when baseball was segregated, roughly 10 percent, and the assumption that a similar percentage of the inducted players from that era should also be Black. When Peterson published his book, he noted that 68 players were in the Hall of Fame after playing careers that took place in the 1900 to 1947 period. That's why he recommended the addition of eight Black players from that era. Adding eight would bring the total number of Hall of Famers from that period to 76, and eight of them being Black would be 10.5 percent of the total, roughly in line with the percentage of Black people in the overall population of the United States.

During the years between Peterson's book being published and the Special Committee finishing their work, the Veterans Committee went through one of their most liberal periods of electing players. These were years when Frankie Frisch and Bill Terry were on the Veterans Committee and dominated the discussion of which players they would consider for election. They were backed by some of the BBWAA members on the committee with them, like Dan Daniel, Fred Lieb, and Roy Stockton, all of whom had covered Terry and Frisch's teams in New York or St. Louis.[1]

As a group, these men pushed through the elections of 19 players whose careers took place primarily during the time before baseball integrated. Most of them were former teammates of Frisch, Terry, or both. This means that the population of Hall of Famers from Peterson's window of 1900 to 1947 wasn't 68, it was 87. Adding eight players from the Negro Leagues wouldn't be enough to be proportional with the population. The Special Committee would have had to elect 10 Black players to be in keeping with Peterson's suggestion.

7. The First Wave

It should be noted that even adding 10 players from the Negro Leagues would have grossly underrepresented Black baseball in the Hall of Fame, because Peterson's original recommendation was a conservative one. He ignored the 19th century, when segregation in baseball began, and stopped at 1947 even though very few Black players reached the Major Leagues immediately upon Jackie Robinson breaking the color line. It wasn't until 1959 that every Major League team finally had allowed a Black player onto their rosters, and the 10 percent figure that Peterson uses as the proportion of Black people in the U.S. population wasn't reached in the Major Leagues until 1962.[2]

A more liberal period Peterson could have used would have been from the inception of the Major Leagues in 1872 (or 1876 depending on your views of the National Association) to 1962 when the Major Leagues finally had a percentage of Black players on its collective rosters that matched the Black population in the country. Using that span, the number of Hall of Famers whose careers mostly fell within it goes from 87 to 121. Only Jackie Robinson and Roy Campanella in that group were Black. To raise the level of representation to 10 percent, as proposed by Peterson, the Special Committee wouldn't have elected eight men, as he suggested, or the nine they did elect, or the ten they should have elected if we limit the period in question to the 1900 to 1947 timeframe. Under the broader timeframe of 1872 to 1962, the Special Committee should have elected 11 (9.8%) or 12 players (10.5%) depending on whether they wanted to round up the numbers. And that's still ignoring managers, executives, umpires, and pioneers, all of whom were excluded from Peterson's recommendation and from the committee's elections.

In addition to being armed with Peterson's reasoning, which clearly played a role in public opinion and Kuhn's campaign to change the Hall of Fame's position regarding the Negro Leagues, many of the committee members felt that more than nine Negro Leaguers belonged in the Hall of Fame. Roy Campanella was part of the committee, and he believed between 20 and 30 players from the Negro Leagues had credentials worthy of the Hall of Fame, a number he intentionally lowered to eight or nine when asked by Dick Young because he felt he wouldn't be believed.[3] The full committee had initially drawn up a list of 30 players they felt were qualified.[4] This matched with newspaper speculation as far back as the late 1930s, when writers like Jimmy Powers and papers like the *Chicago Defender* published lists of Hall-worthy Black players. Edwin Henderson, in his 1939 book *The Negro in Sports*, listed 20 Black players who he felt were qualified for the Hall of Fame. It's likely that committee members Wendell Smith and Sam Lacy, who had covered the Negro Leagues for decades and fought so long to integrate baseball,

104　　　　　　　　　Cooperstown's Back Door

felt that more than nine players deserved to be inducted. As the committee was doing their work in the early 1970s, contemporary accounts from former Negro Leaguers like Richard Powell[5] or longtime journalist A.S. "Doc" Young expressed the view that up to ten times as many players should have been inducted.[6]

And yet the committee still stopped after electing just nine. Why?

The explanation given by Monte Irvin was partly because "we'd done a good job," but also because "the powers that be at Cooperstown" had hinted that the committee should stop and disband. Rather than "embarrass anybody" or destroy the "spirit of cooperation," the committee decided to disband. "We took this from nothing to something. We got it started. We got a number of guys elected, and we felt it was time to back off a little bit."[7]

Irvin's assertion was disputed by the new chairman of the board at the Hall of Fame, Ed Stack, who insisted that no one at the Hall of Fame suggested the committee should disband,[8] and Bowie Kuhn publicly said he was not aware of any "quota" or limitation on the number of the committee's elections. However, Kuhn's spokesman, Joe Reichler, admitted that Kuhn was under pressure for the election of Negro Leaguers to stop.[9] Dick Young went even further. At a speech in Cooperstown years later, he admitted that a limit of nine players had been given to the committee from the outset, and that they disbanded as soon as that limit had been reached.[10]

Whether the committee had a true quota or were merely pressured by leadership at the Hall of Fame, it's inarguable that the committee chose to stop their work at the exact point they'd elected approximately the number of players suggested by Peterson in his book. Negro Leagues scholar John Holway insists that part of the original plan to have a separate Negro Leagues display was that it would be a single plaque listing a nine-man all-star team of Black players, and that's precisely what the committee did.[11] The nine players they elected fit each position:

Pitcher: Satchel Paige (1971)
Catcher: Josh Gibson (1972)
First Base: Buck Leonard (1972)
Second Base: Martín Dihigo (1977)
Third Base: Judy Johnson (1975)
Shortstop: John Henry "Pop" Lloyd (1977)
Outfield: Monte Irvin (1973)
Outfield: Cool Papa Bell (1974)
Outfield: Oscar Charleston (1976)

Dihigo, of course, was not a full-time second baseman. He pitched, played the outfield, and played at least 45 games at each infield position during this career. He had originally been chosen by the committee in 1975, but the Hall's board of directors had disapproved his election, noting that "the record is insufficient to establish a career of at least 10 years in the Negro Baseball Leagues in the United States prior to 1946."[12] An alternative explanation is that Dihigo was primarily viewed as a pitcher or utility player, neither of which would work toward an all-star team since Paige had already been elected to fill the pitching slot and no one had contemplated a place for a utility player. Two years later, with the seven men already elected by the committee and only a short-stop and a second baseman missing from their proposed all-star team, the board of directors reversed course and approved Dihigo's election, along with shortstop John Henry "Pop" Lloyd. Then the committee voted to disband.

Criticism was leveled at the committee for many reasons. The primary complaint was that, contrary to Irvin's view, they hadn't completed their work. Many more players from the Negro Leagues were at least as worthy of election as some of those the committee had selected. Additionally, since Reichler had made it known that he and the commissioner's office preferred living players, there have been accusations that this was unfair to better ballplayers who had already passed away.[13] Six of the nine men selected by the committee were still living. This included two members of the committee, Irvin and Johnson, another point of contention among critics of the committee's work. While no one disputed that they were excellent players, the fact that they were elected ahead of other players with better records and reputations left the committee open to the criticism that they had acted the same as White players on the Veterans Committee, who had developed a reputation for favoring their friends and teammates.[14]

A.S. "Doc" Young, longtime sportswriter in Black newspapers like the *Chicago Defender*, felt that the committee's work was an "embarrassing mistake," and the committee should be ended. "The pattern to this exercise is clear now," he wrote in 1975. "The committee is more concerned with honoring old-time Negro league players who are still alive than it is about historical accuracy, justice or right.... Committee members obviously don't give a cussword about the basic tenets under which a Hall of Famer should be elected."[15]

There were additional accusations that politics had been at play in the committee. Effa Manley wrote to Reichler that "a couple members of the committee picking them had a real hatred for [her husband and partner] Abe Manley and I am afraid his team The Eagles."[16] And, indeed, several great players who played for the Manleys with the

Newark Eagles had been passed over, including Ray Dandridge, Leon Day, Dick Lundy, Biz Mackey, Mule Suttles, and Willie Wells. Further criticism involved the passing over of Rube Foster, the founder of the first Negro National League, without whom the organized Negro Leagues may have never existed.[17] His omission was consistent with the committee's focus on more recent players from the Negro Leagues, and on players who primarily played in the eastern part of the country. Great players from earlier time periods or the more western teams, men like Foster, his brother Willie, Bullet Rogan, José Méndez, John Donaldson, Cristóbal Torriente, Willard Brown, Turkey Stearnes, and Hilton Smith, had been passed over.

The decision to include only one player at each position ended the election chances for every Negro Leagues pitcher as soon as it was announced that Paige had been the first player chosen. On the day it was announced that the committee had been formed, the *New York Daily News* ran a list of the 12 players most likely to be elected. It included all nine of the committee's eventual selections, which seems to indicate that the *Daily News*, the employer of committee member Dick Young, knew in advance which players would be elected.[18] Of the three who were not, two were deceased pitchers, Dick "Cannonball" Redding and Smokey Joe Williams. Since Paige was the only other pitcher on the list and was the only one still living of the three, Redding and Williams had no chance for election even before the committee voted. The same could be said for the third player on the list who was passed over, third baseman Ray Dandridge. He was still living, but played the same position as committee member Judy Johnson, and had played primarily for the Manleys in Newark; consequently he had no real hope of being chosen.

Because so many worthy players had been passed over, the committee was not unanimous in their decision to disband. Committee member Judy Johnson was vocal in his disagreement with the decision. "I didn't vote to disband it," Johnson said. "The disbanding of the committee is a bad thing. I'm feeling for the men who played with me and against me. They deserve the same thing I got."[19] Dick Young used his column to note that reform to the election process was needed, and though his focus was on the recent habit of the Veterans Committee to induct friends instead of more worthy players, he also noted that "there are some voices who believe more of the old time black players are worthy of consideration."[20]

Kuhn and the Hall's board of directors didn't immediately accept the committee's decision to disband. Instead, they tabled it, and formed a new committee that was tasked with reviewing the entire voting process for all players.[21] That even included the initial voting by the BBWAA for recently retired players, as that organization had threatened to withdraw from the voting process, and potentially "set up their own Hall of Fame," if the election process wasn't overhauled.[22]

There had never been a time when the BBWAA was pleased with the work of the Veterans Committee. Its existence was viewed collectively by the writers as an admission by the Hall of Fame that the writers were wrong sometimes, and the committee was needed to right those wrongs. For the most part, that wasn't a concept that the writers disagreed with as long as these corrections were limited in number, but once the committee's members began voting in dozens of their former teammates and friends in the early 1970s, the writers took issue. In 1973, the Hall of Fame agreed that the Veterans Committee could not consider a player unless he'd been retired for at least 25 years and reminded the committee members to "take into consideration the amount of votes received by a player from the voting membership of the BBWAA during the period of his eligibility."[23] In other words, stop electing the players who had been soundly rejected by the writers.

This agreement didn't last long because the Veterans Committee completely ignored the guidance they'd been given to consider a player's prior support from the BBWAA. In the next election after that agreement, the committee voted in Jim Bottomley, former teammate of late committee member Frankie Frisch, who had died by this point but not before teeing up Bottomley's election the year before.[24] Bottomley had never received more than 33 percent of the writers' votes, and if the modern standard was in place that requires a candidate to receive at least 5 percent of the votes to remain on the ballot the following year, Bottomley would have been dropped after his first year, when he appeared on less than 4 percent of the ballots.

In 1975, they did it again. They elected Billy Herman despite his never exceeding 20 percent on the BBWAA ballot, and Earl Averill, whose support topped out at less than 6 percent of the writers. In 1976, they rammed through the election of Freddie Lindstrom even though he only appeared on a BBWAA ballot five times and never got more than 4 percent of the votes cast. In February 1977, right around the time the Special Committee on the Negro Leagues was voting to disband, the Veterans Committee elected Amos Rusie and Joe Sewell. Neither of them had ever received more than 8 percent of the votes on any BBWAA ballot.

It was the cumulative effect of the Veterans Committee repeatedly ignoring the guidance they had received from the Hall of Fame that prompted the BBWAA to complain again and threaten to withdraw from the election process. C.C. Johnson Spink in *The Sporting News* described the relationship between the Veterans Committee and the BBWAA as a "feud," with the writers wanting to "kill off the committee."[25] He wasn't wrong. During the All-Star break in 1977, writers met and agreed that the Veterans Committee should be dissolved.[26] Three weeks later, Bowie Kuhn announced that he had been asked to form a committee that would investigate all three methods then in place to elect people to the Hall of Fame: the writers' vote, the Veterans Committee, and the Special Committee for the Negro Leagues.[27]

In October, the Hall of Fame announced what Kuhn's committee had recommended and the Hall's board of directors had approved. To achieve the primary goal of making peace between the Veterans Committee and the baseball writers, a compromise was struck. The Veterans Committee would not be abolished, as the BBWAA had suggested. It would, however, have its purview drastically curtailed. Beginning with the elections of 1978, the Veterans Committee would be limited to electing two people each year. They would continue to have full control over the selection of all managers, umpires, executives, and other pioneers. Among players, however, any that retired after World War II must have received at least 100 votes from the BBWAA in one or more of their annual elections to be eligible for Veterans Committee consideration. Anything less than that would make them ineligible.[28] This satisfied the writers' primary concern that the Veterans Committee had been showing up the writers by electing players they had soundly rejected.

In addition to this change, the Hall decided to accept the Special Committee on the Negro Leagues' decision to disband. All future elections of Negro Leagues figures would now fall under the Veterans Committee, subject to that committee's new limit on two annual selections. That made the Veterans Committee responsible for three distinct groups of possible inductees: players retired for at least 25 years (subject to the new restrictions just agreed upon), umpires, managers and other executives, and Negro Leaguers. A further limitation was that the committee could not elect multiple people from any one of those three categories in any given year. There would never again be an opportunity to elect multiple Negro Leagues representatives in the same year under the new rules.[29]

The size of the Veterans Committee was also changed. Instead of 12 members, it would now have 18. Since 75 percent of the committee had to agree on any candidates, it would no longer take nine "Yes" votes to elect someone, it would instead take 14. Among the new members of the Veterans Committee was former Negro Leagues player Roy Campanella[30] which would seem to be fair until it's recalled that he was part of the just-disbanded Special Committee that had declared their work done with no other worthy candidates identified. Campanella would be the only Black person on the Veterans Committee. The other 17 were all White.[31]

All these changes provided the appearance that Negro Leagues players were still eligible for election to the Hall of Fame, but the actual impact was to effectively shut down nearly all Negro Leagues elections for the next two decades.

The Special Committee on the Negro Leagues had put their all-star team in the Hall of Fame as directed, but then they essentially left the room, turned off the light, and closed the Hall of Fame's door behind them.

CHAPTER 8

Back to Obscurity

SIMPLE MATH TELLS US THAT the structure of the new Veterans Committee, with its two annual selections available and three groups to honor, should have resulted in the election of two Negro Leagues representatives into the Hall of Fame every three years. First implemented in 1978, by the end of the 1980 election cycle there should have been two new members of the Hall of Fame from each of the three groups: Two White players who retired at least 25 years earlier, two executives, umpires, or managers, and two Negro Leaguers. That would have been an equitable distribution.

In 1978, the Veterans Committee elected a White player, Addie Joss, and a White executive, Larry MacPhail, the same man who had authored the 1946 report about the danger integration posed to baseball's finances.

In 1979, the Veterans Committee elected a White player, Hack Wilson, and a White executive, Warren Giles, who was president and general manager of the Cincinnati Reds for several years after Jackie Robinson integrated the Major Leagues, but who never promoted a single Black player onto the Reds' Major League roster during that time. The Reds wouldn't have their first Black player until three years after Giles had departed to become the new president of the National League. It's worth noting that Giles had been a member of the Veterans Committee for 25 years. He left the committee for health reasons in 1978, died from cancer in February 1979, and was elected by his former peers on the committee a month later.

In 1980, the Veterans Committee elected a White player, Chuck Klein, and a White executive, Tom Yawkey, who owned the last Major League franchise to integrate its roster, the Boston Red Sox. Yawkey was also part of MacPhail's committee that recommended against the integration of the Major Leagues in 1946, one year after his team held a workout at Fenway Park for three Black players, including Jackie Robinson, only to ignore them later and remain segregated for another 14 years.

110

8. Back to Obscurity

Finally, in 1981, the committee managed to elect someone from the Negro Leagues, Andrew "Rube" Foster. Compared to most members of the Hall of Fame, and certainly compared to the three executives the committee had elected in the three years before him, Foster was wildly overqualified for election. He had been one of the greatest Black pitchers ever, as well as an exceptional manager of the Chicago American Giants, and founder and first president of the Negro National League.

Having elected exclusively White players and executives with their first selections, it would have been fair if the Veterans Committee had elected members of the Negro Leagues several years in a row to even out the distribution of their choices. They didn't do that, instead reverting to the pattern of electing one White player, Travis Jackson, and one White executive, Happy Chandler, in 1982. The did the same in 1983 when they elected George Kell and Walter Alston. By now the committee had elected 12 men in the first six years of their new structure. A fair distribution across the three groups they could select from would have seen them elect four Negro Leaguers in that time. Instead, they elected one.

Red Sox owner Tom Yawkey (shown with his first wife, Elise) was elected to the Hall of Fame in 1980. Years later, the Hall added a display that noted his troubling history of refusing to integrate his team (Library of Congress).

A change to their rules was implemented before the 1984 election. The limitation of having only one inductee from each group in any given year was removed. The committee was now free to elect two White players, or two Negro Leaguers, each year if they chose. Given that they'd already passed over the Negro Leagues far too often, this presented them an opportunity to play catch up and bring the representation of the Negro League among their selections back to where it should have been all along.

Instead, the Veterans Committee used this new rule to elect two White players in 1984, Pee Wee Reese and Rick Ferrell. Ferrell's former teammate Charlie Gehringer was one of the longest-serving members of the committee and had advocated strongly for his election. Let's pause here for a moment and compare the lifetime batting statistics of Ferrell and Biz Mackey, famed Negro Leagues catcher:

> Ferrell: .281 batting average, .378 on-base percentage, .363 slugging percentage.
> Mackey: .328 batting average, .390 on-base-percentage, .470 slugging percentage.

It's certainly true that the statistics for Mackey weren't as easily available or as comprehensively tabulated as they'd been for Ferrell or any other player from the White Major Leagues, but researchers like John Holway and writers like Robert Peterson and organizations like the Society for American Baseball Research, had been finding and publishing statistics from the Negro Leagues for some time by 1984. The committee had this information available to them, including Peterson's description of Mackey as "the finest catcher Negro baseball had produced."[1] And while Ferrell was likely elected mostly because of his defense, committee member Roy Campanella was on record as saying that Mackey had taught him everything he knew about playing defense as a catcher. Monte Irvin called him "an expert at blocking the ball," and lauded his intelligence and ability to set up hitters. "He was one of the great catchers," Irvin said. "He knew all the fine points."[2] Electing Rick Ferrell over Biz Mackey was one of the clearest indications possible that the Veterans Committee simply didn't take the players from the Negro Leagues seriously.

This was reinforced in 1985, when they elected two more White players, Arky Vaughn and Enos Slaughter. That was the same Enos Slaughter who participated in the Cardinals' proposed boycott of games against the Dodgers in 1947, and later spiked Jackie Robinson at first base.

In 1986, the committee elected two more White players, Bobby Doerr and Ernie Lombardi. It had been nine years since the Veterans Committee had been reorganized. In that time, they could have elected as many as 12 members of the Negro Leagues and should have elected at least six if they had distributed their selections evenly. Instead, they elected one.

One last glimmer of hope was given to advocates of the Negro

8. Back to Obscurity

Leagues in 1987, when the Veterans Committee elected Ray Dandridge. An exceptional third baseman, his credentials were better than those of Judy Johnson. Not only did Dandridge have better offensive numbers from Black baseball than Johnson had, but after baseball integrated, he had also played four seasons with the Minneapolis Millers, the Triple A affiliate of the New York Giants. He excelled there despite being in his late thirties, batting a combined .318 and serving as a mentor to Willie Mays when he joined the team in 1951. Though the Giants never promoted him to the Major League roster,[3] the statistics from his time in Minneapolis were readily available to the Special Committee on the Negro Leagues. He was one of the few Black players whose performance in White baseball was documented, yet he was passed over by the committee in favor of committee member Johnson.

This last bit of hope for Negro Leaguers was snuffed by the Veterans Committee the same year. With two slots they could fill, and no White candidates agreed upon, the second slot was available to elect another member of the Negro Leagues. Pitchers Joe Williams and Dick Redding had been the other two players named, along with Dandridge and the original nine Negro Leagues inductees, in a *New York Daily News* article as the twelve most likely to be elected back in 1971 when the Special Committee was first announced.[4] They were still available to be elected in 1987, but instead the Veterans Committee elected only Dandridge, passing over every other available Negro Leaguer.

The committee twisted the knife in 1988 when they elected no one. They had run out of White players, managers, umpires, and executives that they could agree upon, and dozens of exceptional Negro League players were available for them to elect, yet they decided to pass. In 1989 they agreed on two White people, Red Schoendienst, and umpire Al Barlick, but couldn't agree on any Black players.

In 1990, they elected no one again.

Bill Veeck was elected by the Veterans Committee in 1991, based in part upon his decision to integrate the American League in 1947 by signing Larry Doby. That signing, as well as his decision to sign Satchel Paige the next year, are both listed among his accomplishments on his Hall of Fame plaque. It certainly would have been fitting if the committee had elected to induct Doby with Veeck, but they didn't. In fact, they didn't elect any Black player to go into the Hall alongside noted racial pioneer Veeck. Instead, they elected Tony Lazzeri, who had been dead for 45 years and had a questionable case for induction.

Another umpire, Bill McGowan, was elected in 1992, along with pitcher Hal Newhouser, whose greatest seasons took place against a vastly reduced level of competition during World War II.

The committee again elected no one in 1993.

In 1994, the committee elected Leo Durocher and Phil Rizzuto. Durocher would have been Jackie Robinson's manager during his groundbreaking season in 1947 had he not been suspended for associating with gamblers and other underworld figures. As for Rizzuto, there is no serious case to be made that he was a better shortstop than Willie Wells, an elite player in the Negro Leagues for more than twenty years. The differences in their respective 162-game average seasons are startling:

Rizzuto: 155 hits, 86 runs, 4 home runs, 55 RBI, 15 steals, .273 average, .706 OPS.

Wells: 201 hits, 145 runs, 22 home runs, 136 RBI, 25 steals, .330 average, .943 OPS.

In the 17 elections after the Special Committee on the Negro Leagues disbanded and responsibility for electing players from the Negro Leagues was given to the Veterans Committee, a total of 34 individuals could have been elected; 28 of them could have been from the Negro Leagues after the change before the 1984 election that allowed the Veterans Committee to have both of their annual selections come from the same group. An equal distribution between the three groups for which the Veterans Committee was responsible would have seen 11 or 12 selections from each. Instead, the distribution was as follows:

- White Players—16
- White Executives, Managers, Umpires—9
- No Selection, left vacant—7
- Negro Leaguers—2

It should come as no surprise that former members of the Negro Leagues and advocates for their place in baseball history were not pleased with the Hall of Fame during this time.

Buck Leonard publicly advocated for Willie Wells' election,[5] as did Cool Papa Bell, who added that Turkey Stearnes was also deserving, so much so that "if they don't put him in, they shouldn't put anybody in."[6] Joe Black, a veteran of both the Negro Leagues and the National League, criticized the Hall of Fame for not properly honoring Black players. Of the original Special Committee he said, "You are not going to make up for 100 years by picking just one player a year," but he was equally critical of the Veterans Committee, claiming that they were unfairly "closing out" players from the Negro Leagues. "I think they have got to do more if they really want people who visit the Hall of Fame to say that Negro ball played a part."[7]

8. Back to Obscurity 115

Former Kansas City Monarchs infielder Othello "Chico" Renfro agreed. He described the Hall of Fame's display as being "one table set aside for Negro baseball."[8] Outfielder Ted Page labeled any assertion that there were no more players from the Negro League who were worthy of the Hall of Fame "totally untrue." He acknowledged that the original Special Committee had a difficult task but was critical of the results. Page was part of a group of ten Negro Leagues veterans who petitioned the Hall of Fame to either racially balance the Veterans Committee or reinstate the Special Committee on the Negro Leagues but with different members who would more closely examine earlier Negro Leagues teams and give greater weight to the results of barnstorming games against White teams. "How can you tell me a Webster McDonald, who was 14–3 against white major leaguers, or a Smokey Joe Williams, who was 20–5–1, or a Willie Wells (a .410 hitter against whites) don't deserve it? How can you keep them out?"[9]

Members of the Veterans Committee heard the complaints but fell back on the claim that the lack of consistent statistics from the Negro Leagues made the task of evaluating those players difficult. "It's elusive, it's frustrating," said Bob Broeg, columnist for the *St. Louis Post-Dispatch* and a member of the Veterans Committee. "I know you can get over-statisticized in baseball, but it's still important."[10] Some, like Joe Cronin, barely saw any Negro Leagues games, and claimed to rely on the opinion of fellow committee member Roy Campanella. Unfortunately, Campanella's personality wasn't consistent with being a strong advocate for his Negro Leagues peers. He was amiable, and uncomfortable raising difficult issues. "Grin and bear it, don't whine," was the description applied by his biographer, Neil Lanctot, regarding issues of racial equality.[11] Even if Campanella had a more forceful style, relying solely on his experience in the Negro Leagues would have left committee members with only a narrow glimpse of the players in those leagues. Campanella played in the Negro Leagues only from 1937 to 1945, and never saw Joe Williams or Bullet Rogan or Cristóbal Torriente or a host of other Negro League greats.

To address the possible inequities in the voting process, in 1978 the Veterans Committee had voted to request a change in the number of people they could elect in one year from two to three. This would have allowed them to elect someone from each of the three groups that fell under their purview every year, but the request wasn't approved by the Hall of Fame's board of directors.[12] Rather than address the inequity themselves by rotating their annual selections among the three groups, the Veterans Committee instead used the board's disapproval as an excuse to continue bypassing almost all candidates from the

Negro Leagues. Their line of thinking and inflexibility in considering other candidates allowed Negro Leagues scholar John Holway in 1978 to predict the next three players the committee would elect. "Unless the board of directors agrees to a rules change, [Hack] Wilson presumably will garner the players' slot next year, forcing [Joe] Williams and the other blacks to wait still another year. And the year after that, Chuck Klein would be expected to shut them out. Thereafter it would be Johnny Mize, and so on."[13] This was precisely what happened, though the election of Rube Foster as an executive broke the all–White pattern in the year Mize was elected.

In June 1982, a group of 40 living veterans of the Negro Leagues voted to select an all-time All-Star team from those leagues. In the process, they identified many players they felt were the best at their positions and therefore at least as deserving of induction into the Hall of Fame as those that had been elected by the Special Committee on the Negro Leagues. They agreed with the committee on some members, including Satchel Paige, Josh Gibson, Buck Leonard, Judy Johnson, Monte Irvin, Oscar Charleston, and Cool Papa Bell. Rube Foster was selected as the manager. But the group also voted Newt Allen of the Kansas City Monarchs as the best second baseman in Negro Leagues history, and Willie Wells as the best shortstop. They voted equally for Johnson and Ray Dandridge at third base, and for Willie Foster and Luis Tiant, Sr., as the best left-handed pitchers.[14] Their views of these players were material to Hall of Fame selections, considering the often-expressed complaint that reliable statistics from the Negro Leagues weren't available to the members of Special Committee on the Negro Leagues or their successors on the Veterans Committee, and yet it appears they weren't being taken into account.

The solution, according to Ed Stack, chairman of the Hall of Fame's board of directors, was to educate the members of the Veterans Committee about eligible Black ballplayers. But, as Holway noted in 1978, the Hall itself wasn't providing much of that education. "Less than one wall [in the Hall of Fame] is devoted to the black half of baseball history," Holway wrote. "The new, expanded Hall, due to open in 1979, will contain 12 rooms—48 walls. Again, only one of the 48 walls will be devoted to black history. By contrast, an entire room will be devoted to the history of baseball in ancient Egypt and other pre–American antecedents."[15]

Having someone like Holway on the committee would have been an excellent place to start. Vacancies on the committee were somewhat common, as its members were older and often passed away or resigned for health reasons. Three new members were added to the committee

8. Back to Obscurity

in 1978, just one year into the new structure. All three—Joe L. Brown, Allen Lewis, and Birdie Tebbets—were White, and had no firsthand experience with the Negro Leagues, and that would be typical for most of the time the Veterans Committee operated.

The Hall of Fame deviated from that standard in 1981, to the benefit of everyone associated with the Negro Leagues. The committee had a vacancy that year after the death of writer Fred Lieb. That would be the same Fred Lieb who believed in the myth that Abner Doubleday invented baseball[16] and later equated the death threats Hank Aaron received during his chase for the home run record with the racist nicknames some of Babe Ruth's teammate had for him. The Hall of Fame filled that vacancy by naming John J. "Buck" O'Neil to the committee.

Buck O'Neil had been associated with professional baseball for nearly fifty years at that point, first having signed to play for the Tampa Black Smokers in 1933.[17] He played first base, reaching the Negro American League in 1937 with the Memphis Red Sox but then joining the Kansas City Monarchs for the rest of his career. He took over as player/manager of the Monarchs in 1948 and continued managing the team until 1955. He resigned after that year when the team was sold and became a scout for the Chicago Cubs, helping to find and sign players like Lou Brock and Billy Williams. In 1962 he joined the Cubs as a coach, becoming the first Black coach in Major League history. In later years, he would also scout for the Kansas City Royals.

O'Neil had definite ideas about the representation of the Negro Leagues in the Hall of Fame, beginning with the fact that he disagreed with Satchel Paige as the first person chosen. Though he and Paige were close friends, O'Neil felt that the Negro Leagues wouldn't have existed without the "genius and ambition" of Rube Foster[18] and it was Foster, not Paige, who should have been the first person from the Negro Leagues elected by the Special Committee.[19] It is not coincidental that in O'Neil's first year on the Veterans Committee they elected a Negro Leagues representative for the first time, or that the man they elected was Rube Foster.

Buck O'Neil's advocacy for the Negro Leagues was constant, but the structure of the committee and the near-complete lack of knowledge of the Negro Leagues on the part of the White members of the committee made it nearly impossible to collect the minimum 14 votes needed to elect any of them. O'Neil felt that part of the problem was that the Negro Leagues players hadn't been publicly voted on in the past. Unlike their White counterparts, there was no discussion of Negro Leaguers accomplishments each year when a new ballot was announced, nothing to bring them into the consciousness of most White players or fans.

Cooperstown's Back Door

This placed them at a disadvantage, in O'Neil's view, with the members of the Veterans Committee.[20]

Regardless of the reasons for the committee's failure to elect a representative number of people from the Negro Leagues, the situation was frustrating for the surviving veterans of those leagues. After years of that frustration building up, they decided to do something about it.

In 1979, a reunion of Negro Leagues veterans was held in tiny Ashland, Kentucky. Nestled along the Ohio River, Ashland is a small city of about 20,000 people, tucked into a corner of Kentucky that borders both West Virginia and Ohio. The closest city of any size in Huntington, West Virginia, home of Marshall University, about fifteen miles to the east. The closest city with a Major League team is Cincinnati, more than two hours away by car. The photos of the city produced by a Google search mostly show a small, quaint downtown area, a few parks, the new medical center that is the area's largest employer, and a lot of views of the river and the bridge that spans it to the Ohio side.

For a small city, Ashland is the hometown of a surprising number of notable people, including singers Naomi and Wynonna Judd, game show hosts Chuck Woolery, and serial killer and cult leader Charles Manson. It has several ties to the Major Leagues as well, being the birthplace of umpire Charlie Reliford, pitcher Don Robinson, and 2006 National League Cy Young Award winner Brandon Webb. The even smaller village of Greenup, Kentucky, about fifteen miles down the river, was the home of former Negro Leagues star Clint Thomas, and that accident of birth was the reason why the reunion was held in Ashland instead of anyplace more prominently associated with Black baseball.

At the time, the editor of one of the newspapers in the region, *The Greenup County Sentinel*, was a man named Tom Stultz, and he was a big baseball fan. More specifically, he was a big fan of the Negro Leagues, and was outraged that so many great stars of those leagues were being passed over for the Hall of Fame each year. "The tragedy of it," Stultz said, "is that all were great baseball players, really great, in the old Negro Baseball League. And they belong in the Hall of Fame. Twenty-five were nominated at one time [in 1971], but only nine ever were selected.... They are still eligible, but I'm afraid they'll be dead if nobody does nothing to get them the recognition they deserve. They are, after all, some of the greatest names in baseball."[21]

So dedicated was Stultz to this cause that he decided to be the person to do something about it. He burned up the phone lines ("I hate to look at my telephone bill next month.") and organized a reunion that was intended to be far more ambitious than just a friendly gathering of former competitors and teammates. "Our purpose is fivefold," Stultz

8. Back to Obscurity

said. "One, to honor Clint Thomas; two, to honor all the greats of the Negro League; three, to help preserve a part of sports history; four, to rally national support for a benefit game annually to help these stars financially; and five, to encourage greater Hall of Fame recognition for the black players."[22]

Stultz's efforts were surprisingly effective. He contacted Bowie Kuhn's office and spoke with Monte Irvin, which opened the door to contacts with other Negro Leagues stars and Major League teams. His efforts resulted in commitments from over a dozen Black stars, including Thomas, Judy Johnson, Buck Leonard, Turkey Stearnes and Ray Dandridge. Former baseball commissioner, and one-time governor of Kentucky, Happy Chandler, also attended, as did former Major League stars Bob Feller and Ernie Banks. To no one's surprise, Satchel Paige committed to attending but then didn't show up. "He just might be fishing at some pond he saw on the way over here," Leonard said.[23]

From those who attended, the reunion received glowing reviews. "I think it's a great idea," said Irvin, "especially in this quaint setting. It kind of reminds me of Cooperstown."[24] Thomas, the locally born guest of honor, said, "This reunion is one of the greatest things that's ever happened. Why, I haven't seen some of these players in 25 or 30 years."[25] Jake Stephens, who had played shortstop on the Hilldale Club in the 1920s, had only recently been released from the hospital but attended the reunion anyway. "This has been just like medicine to me," he said.[26] The first three of Stultz's five purposes for the event had been met. Thomas and the other players had been honored, and they had done their part in preserving part of sports history.

The reunion's final two purposes weren't achieved. There was no mention of an annual exhibition game to raise funds to help any Negro Leaguers who were struggling financially, and there was no movement at all in garnering more recognition for Negro Leagues veterans from the Hall of Fame. In the next Veterans Committee election after the reunion, Negro Leagues veterans were again bypassed, this time in favor of Chuck Klein and Tom Yawkey, a man with such a troubling history regarding race that the new ownership group of the Red Sox successfully lobbied the city of Boston to remove his name from the street outside of Fenway Park.[27] According to one account, no Negro Leagues players were even listed along with the "others under consideration" in the March 1980 Veterans Committee election, though relatively obscure players like former Pirate and Dodger shortstop Glenn Wright were finalists despite never receiving more than 7 percent of the votes cast in any election conducted by the BBWAA.[28]

Despite the limited impact of the first reunion and the departure of the event's organizer, Tom Stultz, to Chicago after selling his small local paper, a new organizing committee arranged for a second reunion back in Ashland the following year. In June of 1980 an even larger group of former players convened, including most of the same players as the year before but also Willie Wells, Buck O'Neil, Don Newcombe, Jimmie Crutchfield, Dick Seay, Chet Brewer, and others. The guest of honor was Effa Manley, former co-owner of the Newark Eagles.[29] The effect on the newcomers was much the same as it had been the year before. Crutchfield said that the reunion made him feel better than he had in years,[30] while Monte Irvin, who attended not only as a former player but also representing baseball commissioner Bowie Kuhn, announced that plans for the next year's reunion were already in the works. Financial sponsors, including a beer company and Colgate Palmolive, had already pledged money to make the next event "bigger and better."[31]

While the camaraderie and reminiscing were the same, one of the priorities of the reunion changed dramatically. No longer content with Stultz's vision to simply "encourage greater Hall of Fame recognition for the black players," the players announced that they intended to open their own Negro Baseball Hall of Fame in Ashland. Former player Othello "Chico" Renfro, who had changed careers and was then a sportscaster in Atlanta, served as the group's spokesperson. "If you could take a trip to Cooperstown and see the one table set aside for Negro baseball," Renfro said, "you would know the place for the Negro Baseball Hall of Fame is here in Ashland, Kentucky."[32] The sentiment was backed by former pitcher Joe Black, who noted that the Baseball Hall of Fame hadn't done enough to honor Black players and urged the continuation of the event and the formation of a separate Hall of Fame. "Each of these gentlemen deserve a place in the sun."[33]

Fairly quickly, the idea of a separate Negro Baseball Hall of Fame was slightly modified. Rather than call it a Hall of Fame, the organizers changed the name of the proposed site to the Negro Baseball Hall of History. Essentially a museum of Black baseball history, it was intended as "a forerunner of a full scale Negro Baseball Hall of Fame,"[34] and had the backing of Bowie Kuhn. At a press conference announcing the new plan, Irvin read a statement from Kuhn that said "It will be good for the country and good for baseball. I fully endorse the proposal to preserve this era.... These players deserve this memorial, particularly as they continue to be an inspiration for today's black and white Americans."[35]

The intention was to open the museum in early 1982.[36] It was expected to cost approximately $3 million, of which just $30,000 had been publicly pledged at the time the project was announced. Governor John Y. Brown of Kentucky said that the state intended to donate

8. Back to Obscurity

121

a building to house the museum's exhibits and memorabilia. At a projected cost of $750,000, it would be nearly 11,000 square feet when finished and would be managed by the same local Tri-State Fair and Regatta organization that had taken over the planning for the annual reunions.[37]

For a time, it appeared the Hall of History might become a going concern. With the backing of Kuhn and a couple of sponsors, plus the attention of the veterans of the Negro Leagues, they were able to attract even bigger names to reunion. In 1981, more than sixty former players attended the reunion, including Willie Mays. The guests of honor were Judy Johnson and Satchel Paige, who attended the event for the first time and took the opportunity to again express his displeasure with the Baseball Hall of Fame. "When I told 'em at Cooperstown that players from the black leagues shouldn't have to play at all in the minor leagues, they told me to sit down. They didn't want to hear about that. I ain't been back to Cooperstown. I ain't going back. Don't get the idea they ran me out. They didn't. I just ain't going back. I'll come here though. I'll come here every year if I can."[38] Mays added his enthusiasm and support for the reunion and planned Hall of History, saying that he would have a word with other Black stars like Henry Aaron and Ernie Banks to attend the reunions in the future. He felt it was owed to the Negro Leagues veterans who made his entry in the Major Leagues possible. "I look around this room and I see faces of men who couldn't do what I did because they didn't have the chance, but they dreamed the dreams I did when they were 15, too." He pledged to donate "a roomful of trophies" to the planned museum and suggested hosting a golf tournament as a fundraiser.[39]

That money was needed, because the grandiose plans for a separate building and a permanent staff ran into problems almost from the beginning. The building intended to be used to house the museum was turned into a childcare center when it became clear that operating funds for the museum weren't going to materialize. One financial study was conducted which indicated over $1 million would need to be raised to allow the museum to begin operating, and nearly $200,000 more would be needed annually to operate it. The initial donation drive, which included a letter from Bowie Kuhn, raised only $40,000. Instead of having almost 11,000 square feet of dedicated space when the museum finally opened in June 1982, it was instead housed in just one room of the Jean Thomas Museum, the former home of a prominent White woman from the area.[40]

The final reunion was held in Ashland in November 1983, with Bowie Kuhn in attendance for the first time. "I wasn't about to miss this one, since this would be the last time I would be in office."[41] Though Kuhn promised to do his part to keep the reunion going, even the event he attended nearly didn't happen. "It was kind of shaky this year," said Buck Leonard, after the usual sponsor, Schlitz Brewing Company, pulled out.[42] No sponsors were found the next year, and a tentative sixth annual edition of the reunion in 1984 had to be cancelled. There were no reports of planning for any reunions in Ashland after that. Without the reunion to draw visitors, and with the Jean Thomas Museum in too remote an area to draw baseball fans on its own, in June 1985, The Greater Ashland Foundation agreed the collection should be relocated to Cooperstown. "This is a part of baseball history that should be recognized," said museum director Mary Lou Putnam. "I'm convinced it will have a happier home in Cooperstown."[43]

Representatives of the Hall of Fame expressed their excitement acquiring the collection. "We installed a Negro League exhibit in 1980 with some memorabilia, but what we had until now is about the size of this picture," said Hall of Fame director Howard Talbot as he indicated one of the photos from the collection. Referencing the Hall's current exhibit, the same one that Chico Renfro once referred to as "one table set aside for Negro baseball," Talbot acknowledged that the Negro Leagues artifacts collected by the Ashland museum in less than five years was more impressive than the one the Hall of Fame had gathered in nearly fifty years. "I came because I wanted to look at it firsthand. I had heard about the exhibit, but I didn't realize it was such a wonderful collection," Talbot said. "With this material, we'll be able to more than double the size of the exhibit."[44]

In Bowie Kuhn's view, the consolidation of the artifacts with the Hall of Fame's collection was a good thing. He had personally backed the Ashland museum effort but felt that incorporating the collection with the Hall of Fame's was a better option. "This display will in time be seen as a real treasure, since the day is coming when we will have no one left to attend those reunions and tell the wonderful tales of the Negro Leagues."[45]

Not everyone agreed with Kuhn's view. In April 1984, before the last tentative Ashland reunion was cancelled, there was speculation that the memorabilia collection stored in the Jean Thomas Museum might be moved to Kansas City as part of plans to redevelop the YMCA Building where the Negro National League was founded in 1920.[46] That move never happened, but plans continued in Kansas City to redevelop the area near 18th and Vine Streets where the YMCA Building was located. An annual Heritage Celebration was held in the area each year, drawing attention to the rich Black history in the neighborhood, which had

8. *Back to Obscurity* 123

been the home of several jazz clubs and thriving Black-owned businesses.[47] That included the offices of the Kansas City Monarchs on 18th Street. The building was gone by the mid–1980s, but a plaque had been installed marking the location.[48] The Black Economic Union in Kansas City made the area a focal point of their efforts, and included the prior location of Municipal Stadium, former of the Monarchs, in their planning.[49] The city applied for and received a federal grant to assist in their efforts.[50]

The history of jazz and baseball were intertwined in Kansas City. The great musicians who lived or visited Kansas City all stayed in the same area hotels as players from the Monarchs or their opponents. The players went to the area's jazz and blues clubs in the evening and socialized with the performers. They became friends, and sometimes more than friends. Ted Strong, who played shortstop and the outfield for the Monarchs, married blues singer Julia Lee.[51]

In the middle of all this activity in the 1930s and 1940s was a man who was still around in the highest circles of baseball in the 1980s to tell the stories about it. He still lived in Kansas City, having adopted it as his hometown, and fondly recalled the days of seeing Count Basie, Cab Calloway, Billie Holiday, and Bill "Bojangles" Robinson in the dining room of Kansas City's Streets Hotel.[52] He still scouted for the Kansas City Royals, and attended the Ashland reunions, and also worked closely with the Hall of Fame. In fact, he was a member of the Veterans Committee, and experienced firsthand the difficulties in getting anyone from the Negro Leagues elected.

The man was, of course, Buck O'Neil. With the Ashland reunions ended, and the dreams of a separate Negro Leagues Hall of History in tatters, and with the Hall of Fame dragging its feet in electing Negro Leaguers, O'Neal had an idea to do something about the situation.

And he knew just the place to do it.

CHAPTER 9

The Second Wave

THROUGHOUT ITS HISTORY, the Baseball Hall of Fame has tried to mirror society as closely as possible. When it was founded, this strategy was the surest means of building public support and attendance.

That strategy continued through the years of segregation in baseball, and World War II, and the postwar years through the 1950s, which included the disintegration of the Negro Leagues once the top Black talent in baseball was finally allowed to play in the White Major Leagues. Few people, including Black people, were paying attention to the Negro Leagues during these years, and it was convenient for the Hall of Fame to do the same.

Something changed beginning in the 1960s. American society fought over civil rights, and Black Americans, as well as some baseball historians of all races, began calling attention to the remarkable talent level and quality of play in the Negro Leagues. Bob Feller called for Satchel Paige to be elected to the Hall of Fame based mostly on his career in the Negro Leagues, but he did that in 1962 before the Hall of Fame's leadership was ready to listen. Ted Williams forced them to when he said the same thing about Paige and Josh Gibson on the steps of the Hall of Fame in 1966.

In his 1970 book, *Only the Ball Was White*, Robert Peterson told the history of the Negro Leagues and called for the induction into the Hall of Fame of as many as eight players from the Negro Leagues from the 1900 to 1947 period. The book caught the attention of the American public generally and prominent sportswriters who began writing more about the Negro Leagues. Among those paying attention was Bowie Kuhn, the new Commissioner of Baseball, who began advocating for the election of Negro Leagues players to the Hall. Suddenly the Hall of Fame was in the position of having to do something about their lack of recognition of the Negro Leagues if they wanted to continue reflecting American society. To the credit of the Hall of Fame's leadership, they shifted. True, they did it through what Ted Williams later called "a half-assed

9. *The Second Wave* 125

program," but they shifted, nonetheless.[1] Nine men from the Negro Leagues were elected to the Hall over the next few years, and provisions were made for future elections through the Veterans Committee.

But the Hall's leadership still didn't want controversial spotlights shining on the institution, so they ended the high-profile elections of Negro Leaguers as soon as they could. For nearly twenty years, almost no one else from the Negro Leagues was elected, and that would have remained the case if further catalysts hadn't arisen that forced the Hall of Fame to shift again.

In the early 1990s, several of those catalysts emerged again, and Buck O'Neil was involved in all of them.

* * *

In June 1985, the National Baseball Hall of Fame and Museum took over the memorabilia collection that had been housed at the Negro Leagues Hall of History in Ashland, Kentucky, when that organization stopped operating. Despite more than doubling the Hall of Fame's collection, little was done to enhance the presentation of the Negro Leagues in the museum. The existing display was updated and augmented with the added pieces from Ashland, but the press release sent out about it in May 1986, received almost no attention.[2] This did not sit well with veterans of the Negro Leagues. It seemed to O'Neil and his peers that "a lot of people want to forget those days as if they never happened."[3]

O'Neil had lived in Kansas City since his playing days with the Monarchs and stayed there throughout his 32 years scouting and coaching for the Cubs. He and his wife, Ora, had adopted the city as their hometown, though neither of them was from there. Ora taught in the local school system, while Buck eventually began scouting for the Royals.[4] They were deeply involved in the city and understood the once-thriving jazz district at the intersection of 18th and Vine Streets, where Buck and other members of the Monarchs and their opponents had socialized, had fallen into disrepair.

Plans to redevelop the area were discussed throughout the 1980s. An annual Heritage Celebration was started in 1983, bringing prominent musicians to the city to celebrate the city's lengthy history of jazz excellence as well as to encourage economic investment. As early as 1984, redevelopment discussions included adding a Negro Leagues component. The YMCA Building where the Negro National League was founded in 1920 is just two blocks from 18th and Vine, and the Monarchs offices were in the neighborhood as well, so including Negro Leagues history in the planning was a natural fit. The idea was put forward to have the Negro Baseball Hall of History collection moved from Ashland to Kansas City.[5] It never materialized before the collection was moved to Cooperstown the following year, but the idea of a prominent Negro Leagues memorial of some sort in Kansas City never left O'Neil's mind.

Others in the city felt the same. Two of the more prominent researchers into the history and records of the Negro Leagues happened to live in Kansas City. After meeting at a convention for collectors in the 1970s, Phil Dixon and Larry Lester began collaborating on an effort to interview Negro Leagues veterans, find box scores of Negro Leagues games, and collect photos and memorabilia. They had pennants from the New York Black Yankees and Homestead Grays, and over seven thousand photographs. Their goal was to preserve the history of those leagues because they found that existing documentation about the Negro Leagues was misrepresentative or incomplete, where it existed at all. "We believe that to be a true baseball historian and fan, you can't ignore this very important part of it," Lester said. "As a black child growing up in Kansas City and a fan of baseball, I became a fan of the old leagues. There's a strong history there. We're trying to preserve that."[6]

Also present in Kansas City were the Motley brothers, Bob and Don. Bob Motley had been a Negro Leagues umpire, and Don was a local Ban Johnson League coach and bird dog for the Kansas City Royals who helped find local player like Frank White for the team's inventive new Royals Academy. Both were deeply interested in preserving the history of baseball in Kansas City as well.

It was a perfect confluence of opportunity. The city was the founding location of the Negro National League. The location of the building where that happened was in a historic district that the city wanted to redevelop. Perhaps the most prominent Negro Leagues veteran lived in Kansas City and was a member of the Hall of Fame's Veterans Committee. And the first attempt to develop a museum for the Negro Leagues had failed. When editor Tom Stultz of little Greenup, Kentucky, had first devised the idea of a reunion of Black players from the Negro Leagues, he expressed his wish that "some big city mayor … would have been behind this instead of a poor, country weekly editor."[7] Over a decade later, he was going to get his wish.

In November 1990, the formal organization of the Negro Leagues Baseball Museum in Kansas City was announced. Frank White and his old coach, Don Motley, were named as vice presidents. Larry Lester was the secretary and research director. Phil Dixon was the museum's spokesperson. Cubs legend Ernie Banks was one of the museum's ten

9. *The Second Wave*   127

board members. A former senior research associate of the Baseball Hall of Fame, W. Lloyd Johnson, was named the director of the museum. And Buck O'Neil was elected the museum's first president.

The Negro Leagues Baseball Museum, or NLBM, struggled at first, just like the one in Ashland. Most of those struggles were the same: funding and facilities. The city was committed more to the creation of a Jazz Museum and was finding it difficult to spread the money around to all the various parts of the 18th and Vine redevelopment effort. Disagreements between the proponents of those disparate efforts complicated the development further. A countrywide recession made it even more difficult to raise funds, though the NLBM conducted seminars and traveling exhibits to raise awareness. Still, the NLBM persisted, and had advantages that the Ashland effort did not. The first, of course, was O'Neil, as he was a remarkably engaging spokesperson for the Negro Leagues in general and the NLBM in particular. The museum also had the buy-in of most local leaders who viewed the effort as critical to the city's redevelopment efforts.

Even more powerful for the NLBM was the fortunate timing of another project in which Buck O'Neil was closely involved. In September 1994, while the NLBM was still housed in a single temporary room in Kansas City, struggling to get attention and funding, filmmaker Ken Burns' latest documentary series, *Baseball*, was broadcast on PBS. The entire country was introduced to the Negro Leagues and Buck O'Neil, who, with his ready smile and upbeat stories, became the face and voice of Negro League baseball.

* * *

There was no more popular creator of documentary films in the United States in the early 1990s than Ken Burns. He had already been nominated for two Academy Awards for best documentary feature and had won two Emmy Awards for his landmark PBS series *The Civil War* in 1990. That series had set new standards for viewership on PBS, averaging more than 14 million nightly viewers of the five-night, nine-episode, ten-hour series. Nearly 40 million people who watched at least one episode. It was the most-watched program in the history of public television, with people drawn to the series' unique method of using period photographs and actors voicing historical figures, interspersed with interviews of historians and public figures. Little known writer and novelist Shelby Foote became a star after appearing in many of the interview segments of the series.

Four years later, Burns released *Baseball*, also on PBS. While it was not as viewed by as many people as *The Civil War*, it still drew millions of viewers each night; the average audience share of 7 percent compared to 13 percent for *The Civil War*. Both series had nine original episodes,[8] though the run time of *Baseball* was considerably longer, over eighteen hours. Like *The Civil War*, the series won the Emmy Award for Outstanding Information Series and produced a breakout star from the group of interview subjects.

That star was Buck O'Neil.

His place as the voice of the series was very much planned in advance. Before the first episode even aired, television critics in newspapers across the country praised his presence in the series. "Shelby [Foote] was great," said Geoffrey C. Ward, Burns' co-writer of both *Baseball* and *The Civil War*, "but this came from the Church of St. Buck." Before the premiere, Burns traveled across the country with O'Neil during the baseball season, visiting ballparks to promote the series. "He's like family now," Burns said of O'Neil. "I love him."[9] At a luncheon with PBS executives, Burns was politely told to be quiet so they could hear more of what O'Neil had to say, then gave him a rousing ovation when he was done. He was described as a raconteur without rancor, and Burns was explicit in describing him as the star of the series. "People kept saying to me, 'Who's the Shelby Foote? Who's the Shelby Foote?' I have had the great good fortune of interviewing hundreds of people, but I have never met a man like Buck O'Neil. He is the heart and soul of this film. Shelby Foote would be lucky to be compared to Buck O'Neil."[10]

Once the series was finally broadcast, the reviews of both it and O'Neil were mostly glowing. One reviewer declared that O'Neil's "elegance and wisdom make him everybody's role model."[11] Another described his "gentle warmth" and "overpowering sense of dignity."[12] In his home state of Florida, he was called simply "the voice of baseball" in a front-page story in the *Tampa Tribune*.[13] Even in the few reviews that were critical of the series, O'Neil was immune from criticism. One labeled the entire series "Burns' boner," but still conceded that O'Neil "sparkled throughout."[14] The ESPN anchor Keith Olbermann was unsparing in his criticism of the series, saying it lacked credibility and that Burns demonstrated "bad editorial judgment and historical fudging," prompting Burns to label Olbermann "a pettyminded nitpicker." And yet, amidst that nasty exchange, Olbermann conceded that he "loved Buck O'Neil's reminiscing on the old Negro Leagues."[15]

Olbermann and other critics of Burns who argued that the series focused too much on myths and not enough on facts were not wrong. Some egregious fact-checking errors were made. For instance, despite having the president of the Negro Leagues Baseball Museum at their

9. The Second Wave   129

disposal, Burns and his partners claimed in the series that "in riot-torn Chicago, Andrew 'Rube' Foster created one of the most successful Black enterprises, the Negro National League."[16] Foster and his cohorts founded the league in Kansas City, of course, a widely reported fact they could have easily found on their own even if they didn't have O'Neil available to tell them. But regular viewers didn't seem to care. They felt the series was long at times, and somewhat dry, but loved O'Neil. He was called "far and away, the star of the series."[17] One viewer said the series had "too much George Will and Doris Kearns Goodwin and not enough Buck O'Neil. Not nearly enough!"[18]

Inevitably, O'Neil's new stardom led to great visibility for the Negro Leagues Baseball Museum as well. In interview after interview, O'Neil's role in the museum was mentioned. He was described as "a legend" in Kansas City, and "our only choice to lead the project" of starting the museum.[19] While the series was still airing, readers of the *Arizona Republic* were told to plan a visit to Kansas City just to see the museum.[20] According to the museum's director, Don Motley, they received "hundreds and hundreds of calls a day" after the airing of the series, which provided more exposure than the museum could have dreamed of achieving with its tiny advertising budget. "It's all over the country now," Motley added.[21]

Burns went even further than simply mentioning the museum and decided to provide it with a direct financial benefit. When he played in a celebrity hitting contest at the 1994 All-Star game to raise money for charities, Burns, who also sat on the museum's board of directors, designated the NLBM as his recipient.[22] He decided to license *Baseball* products, something he avoided doing with *The Civil War* only to see others sell unlicensed products based on the series. Rather than allow that to happen again, he licensed 25 different products, ranging from key rings to leather jackets, with the proceeds going in part to the NLBM. Within weeks of the series premiere, Burns anticipated writing an initial $25,000 check to the museum, something he wanted to personally hand to O'Neil. "I can't wait to see his face," Burns said.[23]

Beyond just O'Neil or the museum, the popularity of the series turned the public's attention to the Negro Leagues as well. Charles Strouse interviewed several Negro Leagues veterans, and his write-up appeared in dozens of newspapers in the Knight-Ridder syndicate.[24] Alan Robinson wrote a syndicated column for the Associated Press about the Pittsburg Crawfords that appeared in dozens more.[25] ESPN's sports documentary series *Outside the Lines* had an episode about the Negro Leagues a month after *Baseball* aired. The show's producer, Bud Morgan, made the analogy that as a painting on a canvas ages,

130 Cooperstown's Back Door

sometimes an original image that had been painted over begins to come through. "Now the Negro Leagues are coming through in American culture and American consciousness."[26]

Because of the new place the Negro Leagues occupied in the country's consciousness, thanks to the efforts of O'Neil, Burns, and others, the leaders at the Hall of Fame decided another reassessment of their position was in order. As Hall of Fame board chairman Ed Stack said later, "It was becoming clear that Negro Leaguers were not going to be elected using the existing process."[27]

At the meeting of the Hall of Fame's board of directors in January 1995, the parameters for elections by the Veterans Committee were changed. For a period of five years only, as many as four people could be elected by the committee each year instead of the previous limit of two.[28] Two slots, as usual, would continue to go to one player and one executive, manager, or umpire. The two new slots, however, were reserved for players from two specific categories, one each for a player from the Negro Leagues and a person from 19th-century baseball, with those two new slots required to be filled for each of those five years. As in previous years, there was no restriction on the Veterans Committee using either of their first two slots on a player or executive from the Negro Leagues as well, but since they'd only done so twice in 17 years, the reality was that this new rule was going to see just one Negro Leagues player elected each year.

The reason given for this change was the age of the people who could reasonably recall the Negro Leagues or anyone from 19th-century baseball. It was felt that those with memories of those eras were dwindling in number, and even fewer of them eligible to serve on the Veterans Committee, so the time to recognize them was now.[29] This was, of course, preposterous in regard to 19th-century players, all of whom had been dead for quite some time by 1995, but it was a valid point regarding players from the Negro Leagues, whose accomplishment weren't as well documented with statistics and newspaper accounts and required memory and word of mouth to evaluate. A far more likely reason for the Hall of Fame's change of heart was the publicity *Baseball* drew to the Negro Leagues, including the performance and elevated national profile of O'Neil, who was still a member of the Veterans Committee and had been fighting, mostly in vain, for the committee to properly honor the Negro Leagues greats who had been overlooked.[30]

The Hall was explicit that this new arrangement would expire in five years. There were even hints that after this five-year window, both Negro Leaguers and anyone from 19th-century baseball would no longer be eligible for the Hall of Fame.[31] Buck O'Neil found the limit too

9. The Second Wave 131

extreme. "The Hall only gave us five years to rectify this unfair situation, which isn't enough time, because we've got more than [five] players who should be in the Hall of Fame. Just off the top of my head I could rattle off a dozen."[32] John Holway named nearly a dozen men as well, projecting that the "next wave" of Negro Leaguers to be elected would include Mule Suttles, Bullet Joe Rogan, Willie Wells, Jud Wilson, Willard Brown, Turkey Stearnes, Cristobal Torriente, Biz Mackey, John Beckwith, Willie Foster, and J.L. Wilkinson.[33]

The new rules made that technically possible, but highly unrealistic since it would require the committee to use multiple slots for Negro Leaguers each year, something they had proven unwilling to do. O'Neil's comment about a dozen worthy candidates, written in 1996, proves that he knew the annual limit was really one, because the Hall of Fame's rules for the Veterans Committee wouldn't have prevented a dozen Negro Leaguers from being elected in that five-year span. In fact, they could have elected 20, four each year. Nothing precluded the committee in 1995 from electing J.L. Wilkinson as an executive, Bud Fowler as a 19th-century player, Bullet Rogan as the Negro Leagues representative, and Turkey Stearnes as a second 20th-century player. But, as O'Neil well knew, the unspoken limit was one Negro Leagues representative each election, and no more.

In 1995, that representative was Leon Day, an excellent multi-position player who pitched as well as played outfield and second base. He was not, in John Holway's estimation, the right choice. Though Day had a great career, he was far from the best available candidate from the Negro Leagues, in the view of Holway and other experts, who felt that Rogan, Stearnes, Willie Foster or Willie Wells were far more deserving.[34] The Hall had established an advisory group led by Bill Guilfoyle, vice president of the Hall of Fame, and that group had produced a list of eight players from the Negro Leagues they felt were worthy of induction.[35] Why only eight men were listed as candidates is unclear, particularly since the group was heavily influenced by O'Neil, who had at least a dozen players in mind. The shortened list was likely another signal from the Hall of Fame that their appetite to admit more representatives of the Negro Leagues was limited. Heavily influenced by O'Neil, the final list was made up entirely of players O'Neil had listed "off the top of [his] head." Objectively, Day was less qualified than other pitchers on the list, and was clearly less accomplished than Rogan, who, like Day, had also been an excellent hitter when he wasn't pitching. He was also less qualified than Cannonball Dick Redding, one of the first men listed as a likely inductee back in 1971 when the Hall first started admitting Negro Leaguers.[36]

132   Cooperstown's Back Door

But Day had two factors in his favor, at least in terms of being elected that year. The first is that he had been a teammate of Monte Irvin with the Newark Eagles, just as Ray Dandridge, the last inductee from the Negro Leagues, had been. Irvin sat on the Veterans Committee for years doing the same thing White members of the committee had traditionally done, advocating for his former teammates and friends. Day's association with Irvin is likely the reason why he made the eight-person list of finalists over Redding and others.

The second advantage Day had, if it can be called one, was that he was gravely ill and not expected to live much longer. O'Neil later acknowledged that he had pushed for Day's election due to his failing physical condition. "The reason I wanted Leon in was that he was still alive, living down in Baltimore in ill health."[37] The Hall of Fame had a long tradition of electing players who were either on their deathbed or had just passed away, choosing to provide the player or their loved ones some measure of comfort rather than electing more deserving candidates. They'd done so in 1948, when Phillies general manager Herb Pennock died suddenly of a cerebral hemorrhage while walking into the New York hotel where National League owners and executives were holding their winter meetings. Pennock, the same man who had called Branch Rickey the year before and told him he couldn't bring Jackie Robinson to play in Philadelphia, was voted into the Hall of Fame two days later, despite having been passed over in seven prior years of voting without receiving more than 53 percent of the votes cast.[38]

The Hall did it again in 1952, electing Harry Heilman a few months after he passed away, and again in 1954 just two weeks after Rabbit Maranville died. It had become somewhat of a standard in Hall of Fame voting and, in 1995, it was Leon Day's turns to receive the Hall's sympathy. His election was such a foregone conclusion that it was noted in newspapers at the time the rule change was announced, almost three weeks before the votes were cast, that "Leon Day will almost certainly be the choice from the Negro League category." Day died a week after being told of his election.[39]

In the remaining four years of the window established by the Hall, some of the best players in the history of the Negro Leagues were elected. Bill "Willie" Foster was chosen in 1996, Willie Wells in 1997, Charles "Bullet Joe" Rogan in 1998, and "Smokey" Joe Williams in 1999. Three of the four were included in the group of players Holway had identified as being members of the likely next wave of Negro Leaguers to be inducted, and all four were from the list the advisory group had produced in 1995. As a bonus, Larry Doby was also elected by the Veterans Committee in 1998, the only year in the five-year window in which the

9. The Second Wave
133

committee used a second slot for a Black player. Doby was elected primarily for his accomplishments in the Major Leagues, not for his brief time playing with the Newark Eagles, but it didn't hurt that his former teammate, Monte Irvin, continued to have significant influence on the committee.

During these annual elections of Negro Leaguers, the Hall of Fame finally opened a larger, more complete display dedicated to the history of the Negro Leagues. In June 1997, just after the 50th anniversary of Jackie Robinson's breaking the color barrier, the Hall opened "Pride and Passion: The African-American Baseball Experience," dedicated to the history of Black baseball. It was noted to have an interactive component, the first exhibit in the Hall of Fame to include one. "It's as significant as anything we've ever done, to have an exhibit that tells a story that's as old as professional baseball," said curator Ted Spencer. "We want people to come out of the exhibit shaking their heads, 'Wow! We didn't realize.'"[40] Rachel Robinson, Jackie's widow, was the keynote speaker at the exhibit's opening, and Buck O'Neil and Larry Doby helped her cut the ceremonial ribbon.[41]

Though the Hall of Fame was explicit in 1995 that the Veterans Committee's new annual maximum of four players would only last for five years, in practice it continued for two additional election cycles after it should have expired in 1999. This allowed for the elections of two more Negro Leaguers from the list of finalists Bill Guilfoyle's advisory group had developed, Turkey Stearnes in 2000 and Hilton Smith in 2001. Smith's election was viewed in some circles as favoritism on the part of Buck O'Neil, since Smith had been his teammate with the Kansas City Monarchs for many years.[42] It might have been true that favoritism was involved in O'Neil's input into the original list of candidates selected by the advisory board, because four of the eight finalists the group produced were former teammates of O'Neil.

In terms of the order of election, though, it's difficult to see favoritism from O'Neil at play. The first three men elected under the new guidelines, Day, Foster, and Wells, were not teammates of O'Neil. Bullet Rogan, elected fourth in 1998, was the first of O'Neil's teammates to be elected by the committee. The election of Joe Williams in 1999 meant that all four of the players who had not been O'Neil's teammates had been inducted into Cooperstown by the committee. The only three finalists who were not elected in that original five year window were teammates of O'Neil and had the Hall of Fame's original five-year window been unchanged, they would have been passed over. Once they decided to extend the Veterans Committee's new mandate, only former O'Neil teammates remained from the list of finalists Guilfoyle's group had produced.

All the activity involving O'Neil and the forced election of Negro Leaguers stirred resentment among some members of the Veterans Committee. Jerome Holtzman, who joined the committee in 1998, later said that members of the committee were under the impression that all worthy Negro Leaguers had already been elected or would be by the time the five-year window closed and were not pleased when O'Neil told them that he "forgot a few" and the elections should continue. They felt that it wasn't a transparent process since there was no way for them to research who they were voting on. "O'Neil was doing all the spade work, and whoever he said should get in got in."[43]

It's certainly true that research into the Negro Leagues was more difficult in the late 1990s than it is now, and that records and accounts of Negro Leagues players and games were scarce compared to the White Major Leagues, but Holtzman strains credulity to claim the members of the Veterans Committee did not know "who we were voting on." Robert Peterson's *Only the Ball Was White* had been available nearly thirty years by that point. The only finalist not mentioned in that book was Hilton Smith, but his career had been covered extensively elsewhere, including John Holway's book *Blackball Stars*, in which it was noted that "many blackballers insisted [he] was as good as Satchel."[44] An article in *Newsday* in 1993 noted that Smith had been featured in a traveling exhibit of photographs from the Negro Leagues that was on display at that year's All-Star Game in Baltimore, with Don Motley of the Negro Leagues Baseball Museum also describing him as being "as good as Satchel Paige."[45] Similar documentation was available for each of these players, as books and articles about the Negro Leagues and their individual players had been growing in number and popularity for many years, particularly after Burns' *Baseball* aired. The complaints of Holtzman and others on the committee seemingly had more to do with not wanting to take the time to read about these players rather than a lack of resources about them.

Regardless of whether the resentment toward O'Neil was fair, it was real. He had become the face of the Negro Leagues and of the movement to remember them and have them recognized. He'd written a book, and been a guest on David Letterman's show, and the subject of countless articles. He was a guest speaker all over the country, gaining notoriety that eluded others who fought for the same cause.

That resentment was about to cost him dearly.

CHAPTER 10

The Second Special Committee

THE HALL OF FAME DECIDED after the 2001 Veterans Committee election that yet another change was needed. Their reasons for that were simultaneously discouraging and encouraging for Negro Leaguers and those who supported them.

The discouraging part was the overall sense from existing members of the Hall of Fame and from the baseball writers that it had become too easy to be elected via the Veterans Committee. The ongoing induction of Negro Leaguers each year troubled some writers, including Jerome Holtzman, who was a member of the Veterans Committee as well as baseball's official historian despite not having any training in the field of history. His view was that "some on the Veterans Committee" were displeased with the continued annual inclusion of a Negro Leagues representative in the committee's elections and felt that Negro Leaguers had become overrepresented in the Hall of Fame. But those concerned members only spoke about the issue privately, "because nobody wanted to stand up publicly and say we got enough black players in there, as it could be interpreted as being anti-black."[1]

Holtzman was right, such sentiment could be interpreted that way, because it was clearly "anti–Black." It was also factually wrong regarding Hall of Fame representation. Through the 2001 elections, more than 84 percent of the 277 members of the Hall of Fame were White. Fewer than 7 percent had been inducted for their time in the Negro Leagues. Only one Black player whose career took place largely before the Negro Leagues were founded, John Henry Lloyd, had been elected. No managers or umpires from the Negro Leagues had been elected, then or now, and only one executive, Rube Foster. A look at individual years when one or more of the Negro Leagues was in direct competition with the White Major Leagues shows vast disparities in both the number and percentage of players from each league who eventually reached Cooperstown. (See chart.)

135

	Total AL/NL Players	Elected to HOF by thru 2001	Percentage Elected	Total Negro League Players	Elected to HOF by 2001	Percentage Elected
1920	495	30	6.1%	178	2	1.1%
1921	492	33	6.7%	176	3	1.7%
1922	497	38	7.6%	157	3	1.9%
1923	513	40	7.8%	287	9	3.1%
1924	529	47	8.9%	338	10	3.0%
1925	526	51	9.7%	322	9	2.8%
1926	502	52	10.4%	336	9	2.7%
1927	512	52	10.2%	309	10	3.2%
1928	505	53	10.5%	278	7	2.5%
1929	510	53	10.4%	276	11	4.0%
1930	493	53	10.8%	195	7	3.6%
1931	492	48	9.8%	145	4	2.8%
1932	491	52	10.6%	351	6	1.7%
1933	460	51	11.1%	166	9	5.4%
1934	487	47	9.7%	165	10	6.1%
1935	484	44	9.1%	176	11	6.3%
1936	481	41	8.5%	152	12	7.9%
1937	498	41	8.2%	326	10	3.1%
1938	502	37	7.4%	328	9	2.7%
1939	533	37	6.9%	282	7	2.5%
1940	514	34	6.6%	319	6	1.9%
1941	546	38	7.0%	270	5	1.9%
1942	512	32	6.3%	299	8	2.7%
1943	519	22	4.2%	310	6	1.9%
1944	548	16	2.9%	301	5	1.7%
1945	547	16	2.9%	322	7	2.2%
1946	633	28	4.4%	321	7	2.2%
1947	544	35	6.4%	309	4	1.3%
1948	542	31	5.7%	292	3	1.0%
Average	514	39.7	7.7%	265	7.2	2.7%

You're reading that chart correctly. As of 2001, when Holtzman made his complaint that the Negro Leagues were overrepresented in the Hall of Fame, nearly 8 percent of all the players who suited up in the American and National Leagues in any given year between 1920 and 1948 were eventually elected to the Hall of Fame, compared to less than 3 percent of the players in the Negro Leagues. In any given year of the

10. The Second Special Committee 137

Negro Leagues' existence, about one-third of all Major League players were playing in the Negro Leagues, but they made up just 15 percent of the players from these years who were elected to the Hall of Fame. At the time Holtzman claimed that members of the Veterans Committee felt the Negro Leagues were overrepresented, there wasn't a single year of the Negro Leagues' existence in which the percentage of Hall of Famers from those leagues met or exceeded the percentage of Hall of Famers from the White Major Leagues. Even today, looking back, only three years—1936, 1944, and 1945—saw the Negro Leagues have a percentage of Hall of Famers as high or higher than the percentage that were elected from the White Major Leagues.

Furthering the notion that the sentiment expressed by Holtzman was more related to race than to qualifications was the fact that it came at a time when the Veterans Committee was facing renewed criticism for lowering their standards to elect a White player. For decades, the committee was seen as being dominated by personalities who were more interested in getting their friends and teammates elected than with correcting mistakes made by the BBWAA in prior elections. For every sound selection of someone like Arky Vaughan or Johnny Mize, outstanding players who were simply overlooked by the writers, there were many more cases of players like George "Highpockets" Kelly, or Chick Hafey, or Freddie Lindstrom, or Rick Ferrell, or Nellie Fox. Even as Holtzman and the other members of the Veterans Committee he claimed to speak for were complaining that Hilton Smith was unfairly rammed through the committee by Buck O'Neal in 2001, they were ramming through the election of Bill Mazeroski in the same year.

As usual, Mazeroski had a strong advocate with a personal connection to him on the Veterans Committee: Joe L. Brown had been the general manager of the Pirates for Mazeroski's entire Major League career, and he now chaired the Veterans Committee. He could have selected anyone to announce the results of their election but kept that duty himself so he could have the privilege of telling the world that Mazeroski had been elected. "In my opinion, he should have been elected the first time he was eligible," Brown gushed. "He's the best second baseman of all time. I don't think anybody came close." Despite being a member of the committee since 1979, nearly the entire time it had been considering Negro Leagues players, Brown still knew so little about the Negro Leagues that he botched Hilton Smith's name during the same press conference, calling him "Milton Smith" instead.[2]

Notwithstanding Brown's glowing opinion of Mazeroski, his election proved to be the breaking point for many members of the BBWAA and the leadership of the Hall of Fame. Though he was an excellent

138   Cooperstown's Back Door

defensive player and hit one of the famous home runs in baseball history to win the 1960 World Series, Mazeroski's career was well below the standard for the Hall of Fame that had been established through decades of elections. Based on traditional statistics, Mazeroski's offensive numbers are among the worst in the Hall of Fame. His .260 batting average is fourth lowest among position players. He scored 769 career runs, higher only than Negro Leaguers for whom we have incomplete data and four catchers who each played before World War II. He stole just 27 bases, a figure lower than everyone in the Hall of Fame other than noted slow-footed sluggers like Harmon Killebrew, Willie McCovey, and David Ortiz.

Modern statistics portray much the same picture as the traditional ones. Mazeroski's career OPS, or On-base percentage Plus Slugging percentage, was just .667, lower than only six non-pitchers in the Hall of Fame. The OPS measure can be adjusted to account for a player's run-scoring era and home ballpark, with the result being called OPS+. It's put on a scale for which 100 indicates a League-average result. Anything lower than that is below-average, and Mazeroski's career OPS+ mark of 84 is the fourth lowest in the Hall of Fame, ahead of only Luis Aparicio (82), Rabbit Maranville (82) and Ray Schalk (83). Additional modern statistics like WAR (Wins Above Replacement), which accounts for both his poor bat and excellent glove, don't help him. Not counting Negro Leagues players, Mazeroski's career WAR total of 36.6 is in the bottom-ten among position players in the Hall of Fame. Everyone lower than him, like Kelly, Lindstrom, Ferrell, and Schalk, is considered a mistake by the Veterans Committee, someone elected simply because they had friends or admirers on the committee, just as Mazeroski did in the person of Joe Brown. Jay Jaffe's JAWS (Jaffe WAR Score) system for scoring a player's worthiness for the Hall of Fame places Mazeroski 50th among second basemen, with all his scores well below the averages for other second basemen in the Hall of Fame.

The argument for electing Mazeroski was his excellent defense, augmented by his famous Series-winning homer. His defense was excellent, earning him eight Gold Gloves. His career marks for double plays, range factor per nine innings, and Total Zone Runs as a second baseman are still the most in baseball history, and he's widely considered the best defensive second baseman ever, as Joe Brown noted during the announcement. The problem with this argument is that Mazeroski is not the only person for whom it can be made. Mazeroski's career is nearly identical to Frank White's, the great defensive second baseman of the Kansas City Royals. Each won eight Gold Glove Awards, and each had dramatic postseason homers. Mazeroski's defensive numbers are

10. The Second Special Committee

a bit better than White's, but White's offensive numbers are a bit better than Mazeroski's. There's very little to distinguish between them. Using Bill James' Similarity Scores methodology to compare players, White and Mazeroski are each other's most similarly comparable player, yet White was never seriously considered for induction into the Hall of Fame, either by the BBWAA or the Veterans Committee, while Mazeroski found himself elected by the committee a decade after being passed over by the writers 15 times, never having reached even 45 percent of the votes cast.

The response to Mazeroski's election was mixed at best. Many writers and fans praised his selection as refreshing, happy to see defense emphasized for a change. Others felt his election was a sign that the Veterans Committee needed to be changed or even eliminated. Jon Heyman wrote that the committee "didn't distinguish itself" by electing Mazeroski, openly comparing him to White and others who had been emphatically passed over by the writers and advising the Hall of Fame to have the committee "stick to managers, executives, umpires and Negro League players."[3] One writer suggested, "Isn't it time for baseball to do away with its Hall of Fame Veterans Committee?" He went on to say the committee "seems to hand out seats in Cooperstown the way Bill Clinton hands out pardons."[4] Another pointed out that the committee was "supposed to rectify mistakes not create new ones,"[5] while fans wrote in with their views that the committee was "in left field,"[6] or to ask the usual questions about how Mazeroski could be have been elected ahead of someone they preferred more, like Gil Hodges.[7]

More important to the leadership of the Hall of Fame was the collective opinion of its members, and those members were not happy about Mazeroski's election. Health issues had forced Ted Williams to be absent from the Veterans Committee's meeting when the vote that elected Mazeroski was held and he was reportedly unhappy about the result. He had opposed his election in the past, which contributed to Mazeroski falling short by one vote in the prior year's election.[8] At the annual dinner for Hall of Famers held during induction weekend, other members expressed their disapproval. Joe Morgan, the great second baseman who was also vice chairman of the Hall's board of directors, reported that members felt "It's becoming too easy to get into the Hall of Fame."[9]

Jane Forbes Clark, who had become chairman of the Hall's board of directors the year before, and Dale Petroskey, who had become the Hall's president in 1999, were sympathetic to the opinions of their members. When combined with the ongoing disapproval of the annual election of Negro Leagues veterans by many members of the Hall of Fame,

140 Cooperstown's Back Door

the disagreement over Mazeroski's election caused the Hall of Fame's new leadership to act. Two days after Mazeroski's tearful speech at his induction ceremony, the Hall announced that the existing format for the Veterans Committee was completely changed. Instead of having just 15 members chosen from executives, players and media members, the committee would now be comprised of all living Hall of Famers, plus all living recipients of the Ford C. Frick Award and the J.G. Taylor Spink Award. Existing committee members whose terms had not yet expired could continue, but all other existing members of the committee were removed, including Joe L. Brown. In total, there would be 90 members of the committee, subject to change only by the deaths of its members or the election of new Hall of Famers. As with the BBWAA voting, a person must receive 75 percent of the votes cast to be elected by the committee.[10]

Mazeroski had only been eligible for the Veterans Committee to consider because of an exception to the eligibility rules that were revamped in 1992. Tired of individual members of the committee forcing through the election of old teammates who had received almost no support from the BBWAA, a new rule was established that required a player to have received at least 60 percent of the BBWAA vote for the committee to consider them. Two exceptions were made. The first was to allow all players who played before 1945 to remain eligible. The second was to allow any player who received at least 100 votes in any BBWAA election between 1945 and 1991 to also remain eligible.[11] This exception kept Mazeroski eligible because he received between 100 and 143 votes in every BBWAA election, 1986 to 1991. The new format eliminated distinctions of this sort. The committee could now consider any player who had played ten or more years in the Major Leagues. As part of the new process, the committee would not any longer vote annually. Votes would take place every two years for players, and every four years for managers, executive, and umpires.[12]

If the intention was for it to be more difficult for the Veterans Committee to elect anyone to the Hall of Fame, the new system worked perfectly. In 2002 there was no election, per the new rules.

> In 2003 no one was elected by the Veterans Committee.
> In 2004 there was no election.
> In 2005 no one was elected by the Veterans Committee.
> In 2006 there was no election.
> In 2007 no one was elected by the Veterans Committee.

Four managers and executives were elected in 2008, and finally another player was elected in 2009, Joe Gordon, but the effect of these

10. The Second Special Committee

changes was to slam shut the Veterans Committee as a potential source of new members of the Hall of Fame. The Committee, and its replacement incarnation as the Era Committees, elected just three players between 2002 and 2017—Gordon in 2009, Ron Santo in 2012, and Deacon White in 2013.

This could have been devastating for the former members of the Negro Leagues and their advocates who were still hoping to see more of them elected. Fortunately, Clark and Petroskey were sympathetic to their cause, and were also committed to having a proper place in the Hall for the Negro Leagues and those who played in them. In July 2000, the same month that Clark replaced Edward Stack as chairman of the Hall's board of directors, the Hall of Fame sought and received a $250,000 grant from Major League Baseball to be used in conducting a thorough study of Black baseball from 1860 to 1960. "The documentary record of the African American contribution to our national pastime is incomplete and this endeavor will go a long way toward filling those gaps," said Petroskey when the grant was announced.[13]

Early the next year, about a month before Hilton Smith became the last Negro Leagues player ever elected by the Veterans Committee, the Hall's leadership announced that they had reviewed proposals from groups that sought to conduct the study and selected the group that would do so. It was headed by Larry Hogan, a Negro Leagues researcher and history professor, as well as the co-chairs of the Negro Leagues Committee of the Society for American Baseball Research, Dick Clark, and Larry Lester.[14] That was the same Larry Lester who had been, along with Buck O'Neil, one of the initial officers of the Negro Leagues Baseball Museum in Kansas City.

It was the first time the Hall of Fame had sponsored an academic study, and it had an ambitious set of goals. They included the completion of a "properly documented historical narrative on the history of African-American baseball between the years 1860 and 1960" that would be comprehensive and objective, as well as the development of a database of statistics from the relevant Black leagues and players. Biographical essays of relevant members of the Black community would be included, along with a comprehensive bibliography resource guide. The study would also be charged with identifying "artifacts which may be available for exhibition or display by the museum," and with creating an oral history and curriculum materials on the subject of Black baseball that could be used in schools.[15]

Originally planned to be completed in 2003, the timeline was extended once the scope of the work became clear.[16] Over the next four years, Hogan, Clark, and Lester coordinated the work of 50 or

142   Cooperstown's Back Door

more historians and researchers as part of the study. The group pulled together data from existing databases as well as a review of box scores from 128 newspapers. The result was a database of 3,000 daily records as well as league and all-time leaders. It included, by their estimation, all league-sanctioned games from the 1920s, more than 90 percent from the 1930s, and between 40 and 50 percent of the league games from the 1940s and 1950s.[17] The group submitted their final study to the Hall of Fame in 2005. Called "Out of the Shadows," it included the database, an 800-page manuscript, and complete bibliography.[18]

While the study was a remarkable achievement by itself, more important from the perspective of those who wished to see the Negro Leagues not just studied but honored was the decision by the Hall of Fame in July 2005 to hold a special election dedicated solely to candidates from the Negro Leagues. It would be held in February 2006, and the Hall of Fame did not limit the number of candidates that could be elected.[19]

The first step was to identify possible candidates. This task was assigned to a five-person screening panel consisting of the three leaders of the recently-completed study—Hogan, Clark, and Lester—as well as Adrian Burgos, who specialized in Latin American baseball, and Jim Overmyer, whose focus was on 19th-century baseball and eastern teams from Black baseball. No sportswriters or veteran players were included, though input was sought from a variety of sources, including Monte Irvin and Buck O'Neil, in developing an initial list of 94 candidates.[20] The screening panel met in November 2005 to narrow that list and produced a ballot of 39 candidates.[21] It included[22] the following:

Newt Allen	John Beckwith	William Bell	Chet Brewer
Ray Brown	Willard Brown	Bill Byrd	Andy Cooper
Rap Dixon	John Donaldson	Frank Grant	Pete Hill
Sammy T. Hughes	Fats Jenkins	Home Run Johnson	Dick Lundy
Biz Mackey	Effa Manley	Oliver Marcelle	José Mendez
Minnie Miñoso	Dobie Moore	Buck O'Neil	Alejandro Oms
Red Parnell	Spottswood Poles	Alejandro Pompez	Cumberland Posey
Dick Redding	Louis Santop	George Scales	Mule Suttles
Ben Taylor	C.I. Taylor	Candy Jim Taylor	Cristobal Torriente
Sol White	J.L. Wilkerson	Jud Wilson	

Some of the finalists were quite familiar at this point. Speculation about Cannonball Dick Redding being a likely inductee dated back 35 years to the initial vote on Negro Leagues players in 1971,[23] and he had been touted as a great pitcher by Babe Ruth as far back as 1933.[24] Willard

10. The Second Special Committee 143

Brown had been the only candidate not elected from the eight-person list that were selected one at a time between 1995 and 2001. Minnie Miñoso had a notable career in the integrated Major Leagues and had been the subject of publicity stunts as recently as 2003 that kept him in the public eye. These and others were considered as near locks for election, given that there was no limit on the number of candidates the committee could elect.

Then, of course, there was Buck O'Neil.

Before the committee had even been announced, a campaign had begun to get O'Neil elected to the Hall of Fame. The profile he'd developed in the years since Burns' *Baseball* documentary aired made him the face of the Negro Leagues to many, and as the story of his life and career became known, pleas for him to be elected mounted for several years. Sometimes the appeals were direct and specific. He was touted as a worthy candidate in 2002 by two Hall of Famers he had scouted, Lou Brock and Ernie Banks. "Buck deserves to be in the Hall as a scout," said Banks. "Scouts are so important, but they've been forgotten by Cooperstown."[25] Sometimes the messaging was more subtle. When the Hall of Fame arranged to have forty-seven of the living sixty-two members of the Hall visit the White House in March 2001 to commemorate the start of the new baseball season, they invited O'Neil to attend as a special guest, including him in the group despite not being a member.[26]

Two months after that event, in May 2001, Joe Posnanski dedicated one of his columns in the *Kansas City Star* to making the case for O'Neil's election, and started a petition drive so readers could lend their support to the cause. He made it clear that "Buck O'Neil would not want us doing this. Buck's too modest, too involved, too intent on helping other people. But it's time for us to do this whether he wants it or not." He went on to say "everybody knows he belongs in the Hall of Fame. There's no real argument against him"; then he noted his playing career was good, and he won five pennants as a manager, and was the first Black coach in Major League history, and was a remarkable scout who discovered Banks, Brock, Joe Carter, and Lee Smith, in addition to being an outstanding spokesperson for the history of the Negro Leagues and great influence on the game. Posnanski cited O'Neil as the person who "got the Negro Leagues Baseball Museum built," and that the museum was the best location to go sign the petition supporting O'Neil's election. Yes, there would be technicalities to work out, Posnanski continued, as O'Neil's position on the Veterans Committee in 2001 complicated the question of whether he could be voted upon. He also noted "there are all sorts of politics involved."[27]

That petition drive wasn't successful, of course, but the issue of

144   **Cooperstown's Back Door**

O'Neil's candidacy was taken up again in 2005 when the new special election for Negro League members was announced. Bob Kendrick, at the time a spokesperson for the NLBM but now its president, said in July 2005, "You have to look at what he's done for the game overall. You have to look at what he's done in his entirety." The NLBM's executive director, Don Motley, said "Buck wouldn't get off the Veterans Committee because he felt like there were better players at the time who should be in," thereby sacrificing his own eligibility to advocate for others. "But Buck has done so much for baseball," Motley continued. "He should be in the Hall. He's the greatest ambassador baseball has ever had."[28]

Though four years had passed since Posnanski's petition drive, and the complication of O'Neil's place on the Veterans Committee was no longer a factor, Posnanski proved to be correct when he noted "there are all sorts of politics involved."

Larry Lester, one of the leaders of the group that conducted the Hall's years-long study, and a member of the select committee that narrowed down the ballot to 39 finalists, was named as one of the dozen members of the broader special election committee that would conduct the final vote. He had a long history studying the Negro Leagues and had been one of the founding officers of the Negro Leagues Baseball Museum before departing in 1995 after a falling out with Don Motley, the museum's executive director. Lester explained the issue as being "a different view on quality of life," noting that the working environment at the NLBM under Motley's leadership was one in which "people use profanity, where people talk down to each other." Officials at the NLBM gave a different point of view. Motley asserted that Lester's departure stemmed from his disagreement with a new accounting structure Motely had implemented. "He controlled the checkbook, he controlled buying, he controlled the museum," Motley said of Lester. "I began to make him accountable for everything."[29]

Complicating the situation was a nasty legal fight over tape recordings of interviews with Negro Leagues stars that John Holway had loaned to the museum in 1993. When Holway had asked for the tapes to be returned in 1998, the museum told him they couldn't be located.[30] In 2004, Holway sued the museum, seeking $750,000 in damages to compensate him for the loss of earnings he claimed he could have received from licensing the tapes.[31] After several fits and starts, including having the suit thrown out in Virginia for being the wrong venue, Holway switching attorneys several times,[32] and the new judge limiting Holway's potential damages to one dollar, the trial went forward on February 6, 2006, in Kansas City. Lester, who had been the conduit for bringing the tapes from Holway to the museum in 1993, testified that he had delivered them. Motley said he didn't remember receiving the tapes, and the museum sued Lester.[33] O'Neil made an appearance to testify about the museum's security measures. The trial lasted just two days, and the jury found for the museum on the grounds that Holway hadn't filed suit within the five year statute of limitations. Holway vowed to appeal.[34]

The verdict was reached two weeks before the committee voted on Buck O'Neil's candidacy for the Hall of Fame.

Only 11 members of the committee were in the room to vote. Robert Peterson, groundbreaking author of *Only the Ball Was White* and a member of the committee, had passed away on February 11, but not before submitting his ballot. The committee chose to accept his ballot rather than replace him on the committee, so his votes were cast before the group's discussion of each candidate two weeks later.[35] Former baseball commissioner Fay Vincent chaired the meeting but did not have a vote. Several of the Hall of Fame's leaders, including Petroskey and Clark, were also present. Clark reminded the group that there was no limit of the number of candidates they could elect but reiterated that the Hall of Fame's high standards should be upheld.[36]

Each candidate was discussed in the room, starting with the group that had received unanimous support from the five-person screening committee in October. After each group had been completed, voting was done by paper ballot and tabulated outside the room, with no votes publicly cast. Then the next group of candidates would be discussed, and the process repeated until all 39 had been reviewed and initial votes taken.[37] After this initial round of voting, two candidates were resubmitted to the group for further discussion, most likely because they had come close to the nine votes needed for election. One of these candidates was Louis Santop, and after further discussion and a follow-up vote, he was elected.

The other candidate returned for discussion was O'Neil. Before the committee's meetings had even begun, Lester had made a comment to Ray Doswell, another member of the committee as well as the NLBM's curator, that O'Neil's election was in doubt. He noted that mock elections held by the Society for American Baseball Research had largely failed to elect O'Neil, making his case "a hard sell."[38] Though he was listed as a manager, his case was more muddled, since he had also made contributions to baseball as a player, coach, scout, and overall ambassador of the game. O'Neil's entire body of work was to be considered, something Fay Vincent stressed to the committee when he urged them to reconsider their initial votes.[39]

If any of them did, it didn't change the result; 17 candidates had

Cooperstown's Back Door

been elected, nearly doubling the number of representatives of the Negro Leagues in the Hall of Fame. Among those elected was Willard Brown, the last of the eight candidates considered by the Veterans Committee during their annual election of Negro Leagues players from 1995 to 2001. Effa Manley, co-owner of the Newark Eagles, became the first and, so far, only woman in the Hall of Fame. Players who had been overqualified for election for decades only to be passed over as lesser White players were elected finally got the honor they deserved. The great catcher Biz Mackey, passed over in favor of Rick Ferrell by the Veterans Committee, was elected. So was Mule Suttles, a Triple Crown winner whose supporters had been forced to watch hitters of much lower caliber, like Chuck Klein and Hack Wilson, be elected over him.

The committee stopped at 17 though, leaving out many candidates who had been highly touted for years. Cannonball Dick Redding was passed over again, as was John Donaldson, two of the greatest pitchers in baseball history, victims of the committee's focus on the 1920 to 1948 period for which the recently completed study had developed better documentation and statistics. Also omitted from those elected was Minnie Miñoso, a victim of the fact that most of his career was played in the Major Leagues instead of the Negro Leagues, which many on the committee felt disqualified him from consideration.

Also left out was Buck O'Neil. When called with the news that he hadn't been elected, O'Neil said, "That's the way the cookie crumbles," then he rejoiced that 17 had been elected and volunteered to speak at the induction ceremony.[40]

O'Neil may have handled the disappointment well, but most others did not. Columns and editorials in newspapers across the country mocked the results. Hall of Famers like Lou Brock, Ernie Banks, and Bob Feller expressed disbelief. Both a senator and a congressman from O'Neil's home state of Missouri made statements calling for the Hall of Fame to act. Upon hearing the results, baseball commissioner Bud Selig repeatedly asked, "How can this be?"[41]

Motley openly accused Lester of organizing a faction of the committee to vote against O'Neil's election due to his ongoing feud with Motley and the NLBM.[42] Doswell expressed befuddlement that O'Neil had been passed over after no negative comments were made about his candidacy during the committee's discussions. "With all of the candidates, we made a point to talk about the positives and the negatives," he said. If anyone had any negatives, they didn't speak up. "Unlike all the other discussions, his was different in that way." He added that he felt Lester was at the center of the movement against O'Neil's election. "I don't have any proof to say this, but I think ultimately it centered on

10. The Second Special Committee

Larry Lester. They [Lester and his supporters] think Larry should have been head of the museum, they're friends of Larry, he has helped them in their research, vice versa, and ultimately he is coloring the vision of the museum."[43]

Lester defended the committee's decision, noting that they had all voted their consciences. "There are reasons the committee did not think he was in the top one percent. Buck knows how I voted. Buck knows me." When directly asked how he voted, Lester replied, "Ask Buck." According to O'Neil, he had no idea how Lester voted. "Larry knew me more than anybody else on that panel. I don't know how he voted."[44]

Buck O'Neil never got to speak on his own behalf, but he selflessly spoke for the 17 members of the Negro Leagues who were elected in 2006. He passed away less than three months later (courtesy of the Baseball Hall of Fame).

Though the Hall of Fame retained the paper ballots, they have elected not to release them. The committee members had agreed before the vote not to reveal how they had voted, so we may never know what kept O'Neil from being elected or how close he came.[45, 46] What we do know is that the 17 elected representatives of the Negro Leagues were given only 37 total minutes during the induction ceremony on July 30, 2006, barely two minutes per person.[47] O'Neil spoke on their behalf, rejoicing in their election, thanking God, and leading the crowd in singing "The greatest thing in all my life is loving you."

Ten weeks later, he was dead.

It would be 16 years before the Hall of Fame elected another member of the Negro Leagues.

CHAPTER 11

Over It

AFTER THE 2006 ELECTIONS, the HOF made it clear that they considered the Negro Leagues issue to be a closed topic. Brad Horn was a spokesman for the Hall of Fame at the time and said the Committee was "intended to review those candidacies on a one-time consideration. It doesn't mean there's not another opportunity in the future, if and when more research emerges. But this was a project to evaluate those individuals who really stood out. It's not intended to be a yearly event."[1] This stance held for almost two decades, even though the Veterans Committee continued to elect White people from the Negro Leagues era, further skewing an already uneven distribution of inductees.

In 2008, the committee elected Billy Southworth, whose managerial career and principal success took place while the Negro Leagues were still organized and functioning. They also elected Walter O'Malley that year. Though O'Malley's ownership of the Dodgers didn't begin until the Negro Leagues were winding down, he did play a role in killing them off, as he was co-owner of the Dodgers along with Branch Rickey when the team signed Jackie Robinson and set the precedent of not compensating the Negro Leagues teams for the players who made the jump to the Major Leagues. The next year Joe Gordon was elected by the committee, and virtually his entire career was played while baseball was still segregated.

The Veterans Committee was eliminated after the 2010 elections, replaced by what has become known as the Eras Committees. Initially, these consisted of three separate committees, each of which was dedicated to a separate period and would hold an election every three years. Two of those committees precluded consideration of the Negro Leagues entirely, because they covered periods from 1947 onward. Only the Pre-Integration Committee covered the era in which the Negro Leagues were still organized and thriving.[2] The name of that committee drew the ire of Joe Posnanski, who mocked the choice in an article for *NBCSports.com*, asking if the Hall of Fame had considered more accurate names like the Segregation Era or the Jim Crow Era. He also wondered why the Hall seemed committed to finding White people to honor from that era while refusing to elect more dark-skinned players that hadn't been permitted to play in the Major Leagues.[3]

That committee held an election for the first time in 2013, and no Black players, managers or executives were elected. They did elect James "Deacon" White, a barehanded catcher from the 19th century who had been dead for nearly 75 years. In the 12 months preceding the election, White's name appeared just once in any newspaper in the country, an article in *Newsday* about the players who had committed the most errors in history.[4] No one was clamoring for his inclusion in the Hall of Fame. Meanwhile, during that same period, Minnie Miñoso's name appeared in newspapers more than 600 times, and Buck O'Neil's 229 times. O'Neil would have celebrated his 100th birthday in late 2011, and the Negro Leagues Baseball Museum celebrated the event by raising funds to develop the Buck O'Neil Education and Research Center in Kansas City. There was a tribute event hosted by comedian Anthony Anderson, and a gospel concert in his honor, and a charity run.[5] Unlike Deacon White, O'Neil and Miñoso remained very much in the public consciousness but remained outside the Hall of Fame.

The committee met again in 2016, and no Black candidates were even nominated.[6] When asked about the last decade in which no Negro Leagues players had been elected, Hall of Fame spokesperson Brad Horn acknowledged that candidates from the Negro Leagues were not even eligible. "In 2006, the Hall of Fame said [the special committee] served as the final consideration for the Negro Leaguers," Horn said. "But, we kept the door open for new research to be considered. [The current policy] doesn't mean that it won't happen at some point."[7] New Hall of Fame president Jeff Idelson, who had taken over the position from Dale Petroskey in 2008, confirmed the Negro Leagues candidates weren't eligible, and that the Hall of Fame had no intention of including them again "unless new research came out that would warrant another look."[8]

That does not mean that the Hall of Fame and their new leadership did nothing to honor the Negro Leagues during this time. The outcry from failing to elect Buck O'Neil in the 2006 special election prompted the Hall to dedicate a statue to O'Neil in 2008. It is located on the museum's first floor, one of the first things visitors see after passing through the ticket counters. At the same time, they also established the Buck O'Neil Lifetime Achievement Award. It is given "not more than once every three years to honor an individual whose extraordinary efforts enhanced baseball's positive impact on society, broadened the game's appeal, and whose character, integrity and dignity are comparable to the qualities exhibited by O'Neil."[9] O'Neil was the award's first recipient in addition to being its namesake. Joe Garagiola, the man once accused of having hurled racist insults at Jackie Robinson during a game in 1947, received the award in 2014, his longtime career as a broadcaster and work as a philanthropist having surpassed the long-ago incident that always caused him anguish and regret. "That it's the Buck O'Neil award is really special to me," Garagiola said. "We were close friends and he was always someone looking out for the other guy."[10]

When he wasn't elected to the Hall of Fame in 2006, the Hall dedicated a statue to Buck O'Neil on the Hall's first floor, once of the first things visitors see after entering (courtesy of the Baseball Hall of Fame).

Also in 2008, the Hall of Fame agreed to a request from Jackie Robinson's family to alter his plaque to note his breaking of the color barrier. The original plaque said nothing about it, listing only his accomplishments on the field. That had been Robinson's preference at the time, having requested that only his play on the field be considered when the baseball writers considered voting for him. Idelson noted that an update to the plaque's wording had been discussed for several years, but nothing was done until Rachel Robinson contacted the Hall of Fame and agreed to the change. "I think he would understand now," she said of her late husband, "that we need to go beyond that and we need to think in terms of social change in America. He would want a part in that. I don't think he would object."[11] The new plaque adds his nickname, Jackie, as well as a new final sentence: "Displayed tremendous courage and poise in 1947 when he integrated the modern major leagues in the face of intense adversity."[12]

A year after creating the Buck O'Neil Award, the Hall of Fame partnered with the American Library Association to create a touring exhibit that was named for the Hall's permanent exhibit about Black baseball, "Pride and Passion: The African American Baseball Experience." The exhibit toured the country for four years, stopping everywhere from the Natrona County Public Library in Casper, Wyoming,[13] to the Harlem Branch of the New York Public Library.[14] Along the way, some familiar names participated in the exhibit. Ray Doswell, the curator of the Negro Leagues Baseball Museum and a member of the 2006 special committee that had passed over Buck O'Neil, was the keynote speaker when the exhibit opened in St. Joseph, Missouri.[15] Committee member Larry Lester, whose conflicts with the NLBM had been the speculative reason behind O'Neil's omission, spoke when the exhibit reached the Harper Woods Library near Detroit. So did Phil Dixon, the NLBM's first spokesperson when it opened in 1990.[16]

In 2014, the NLBM developed an exhibit of artwork entitled "Shades of Greatness: Art Inspired by Negro Leagues Baseball." Doswell coordinated a tour of the exhibit around the country that included a stop at the Hall of Fame.[17] The Hall of Fame's cooperation with the NLBM came at a critical time, as the museum had been struggling financially during a contentious leadership change following O'Neil's death,[18] and faced competition from other cities that hoped to capitalize on the increased popularity of the Negro Leagues by opening their own museums.[19]

While these were good steps, none of them altered the fact that former Negro Leagues players, managers, umpires, and executives remained ineligible for future elections by the Eras Committees. While they were ineligible, those committee continue to elect people, further skewing the already unequal distribution of Hall of Famers away from proper representation for the Negro Leagues. In addition to Southworth and O'Malley being elected in 2008, the Veterans Committee elected manager Dick Williams. They also elected former commissioner Bowie Kuhn and former Pirates owner Barney Dreyfuss, each of whom was involved in either keeping the Major Leagues segregated or in limiting the number of Negro Leaguers elected to the Hall of Fame.

The 2009 election saw Joe Gordon elected by the Veterans Committee. In 2010 it was manager Whitey Herzog and umpire Doug Harvey. In 2011, the first year of the new Eras Committees, executive Pat

152   Cooperstown's Back Door

Gillick was elected, followed by Ron Santo in 2012. Deacon White wasn't alone in the 2013 election. He was joined by former Yankees owner Jacob Ruppert and umpire Hank O'Day. In 2014, they elected managers Bobby Cox, Tony LaRussa, and Joe Torre. In total, the Veterans Committee and its replacement Eras Committees elected 16 people in the decade following the special election for the Negro Leagues in 2006. All 16 of their new inductees were White.

There had been opportunities during these years to elect Black and Latino players, even though members of the Negro Leagues were ineligible.

- The 2007 Veterans Committee ballot included future Hall of Famers Tony Oliva and Minnie Miñoso, but they weren't elected. They had been joined on the ballot by several minority candidates, like Maury Wills, Don Newcombe, Vada Pinson, Luis Tiant, Curt Flood, Al Oliver, Dick Allen, and Bobby Bonds. All were passed over.[20]
- In 2008, while the Veterans Committee was electing five new members, no minority candidates were on the final ballots.[21]
- In 2009, Oliva, Wills, Tiant, Pinson, Oliver, and Allen were all on the final ballot but were passed over again.[22]
- The 2010 election, like 2008, was dedicated to managers, umpires, and executives, and again no minority candidates were on the ballots.[23]
- The 2011 ballot for the Expansion Era Committee included Dave Concepcion, Vida Blue, and Al Oliver. Concepcion came the closest to being elected, receiving eight of the 16 votes cast. Both Blue and Oliver received fewer than eight, their exact total not being released by the Hall of Fame.[24]
- Four minority candidates were on the ten-person ballot for the Golden Era Committee in 2012. Miñoso came the closest to election, receiving nine votes, followed by Oliva with eight. Neither Allie Reynolds not Tiant received at least eight votes.[25]
- Since 2013 was one of the years the Pre-Integration Committee met, there were obviously no minority candidates on the ballot.[26]
- It was the Expansion Era Committee's turn again in 2014, and only two minority candidates were on the ballot: Concepcion again, and Dave Parker. Neither received enough votes to have their totals released by the Hall of Fame.[27]
- The Golden Era Committee met again in 2015, and had several holdovers from their 2012 election, including Oliva, Miñoso, and

Tiant. They were joined by Dick Allen and Maury Wills again, so minority candidates comprised half of the ten-person ballot. None were elected. Both Allen and Oliva received 11 votes, one vote shy of election. Wills received nine, Oliva eight. Tiant got fewer than three.[28]

- The 2016 election brought back the much-maligned Pre-Integration Committee, which continued to exclude minority candidates. They failed to elect anyone, prompting Jay Jaffe to call for yet another overhaul to the process of electing those who fall outside the authority of the BBWAA to elect.[29]

During this decade when the Veterans and Eras Committees were ignoring minority candidates, the voters from the Baseball Writers Association of America were doing the opposite. Of the 18 inductees they elected during these years, half were Black or Latino. The work of the BBWAA was all that was keeping the membership of the Hall of Fame from being even more drastically skewed than it was.

And it was skewed, particularly for the years the Negro Leagues existed. Even after the Negro Leagues special election in 2006, players, managers, and umpires from those leagues were underrepresented in the Hall of Fame compared to their peers from the White Major Leagues. During the period from 1920, when the Negro National League was founded, through 1948, the final year in which the Negro Leagues were recognized as Major Leagues, the average proportion of players in the White Major Leagues compared to the Negro Leagues was a little more than two-to-one. Some years, when only one Negro League was operating, the percentage of Negro Leagues players in the top tier of baseball was as low as 23 percent, but in other years when two Negro Leagues were operating that percentage was as high as 40 percent. The average was 265 Negro Leagues players per season, compared to 514 in the White Major Leagues, which means the Negro Leagues, on average, represented 34 percent of the players in these years.

The Hall of Famer players from this period are not distributed in the same way.

Hall of Famers from 1920–1948, through the 2016 elections.

	Players	Managers	Umpires	Executives	TOTAL
AL/NL	65	6	3	8	82
Negro Leagues	23	0	0	5	28
TOTALS	88	6	3	13	110

Players from the Negro Leagues accounted for 26 percent of the Hall of Famers whose careers primarily took place during these years, rather than the 34 percent that would represent a fair proportion. Instead of 65 Hall of Fame players from the White Major leagues and 23 from the Negro Leagues, the distribution would have been 58 from the White Major Leagues and 30 from the Negro Leagues if Hall of Fame selections mirrored the proportion of rostered players in those respective leagues. Likewise, assuming the same percentages should apply to managers, umpires, and executives, we would expect two Negro Leagues managers instead of none, and one Negro Leagues umpire instead of none. Only among executives was the distribution fair to the Negro Leagues, with five of the 13 Hall of Fame executives being from the Negro Leagues, about one more executive than equity would have dictated.

And this is just the period that included the organized Negro Leagues. Black baseball existed long before Rube Foster organized the Negro National League in 1920. Through the 2016 elections, 83 people whose careers took place primarily before 1920 were elected to the Hall of Fame. Only seven of them were from Black baseball: players Pete Hill, John Henry Lloyd, José Méndez, Louis Santop, and Ben Taylor, and pioneers/executives Frank Grant and Sol White. Many of the best Black players and managers in history came from this period, but the absence of organized leagues served as a convenient reason to overlook most of them.

Hall of Famers from before 1920, through the 2016 elections.

	Players	Managers	Umpires	Pioneers/ Executives	TOTAL
White leagues	59	4	3	10	76
Negro Leagues	5	0	0	2	7
TOTALS	64	4	3	12	83

Writers like Jay Jaffe began to take notice of the discrepancy, and pointedly asked Hall of Fame leaders about the continued exclusion of Negro Leaguers from consideration by the Eras Committees. In Jaffe's case, he took the further step of labeling the answers he received "troublesome," noting that "it's unseemly to prevent [Negro Leaguers] from consideration in this context alongside their historical contemporaries, most of whom have already had numerous chances."[30] He wasn't alone. Joe Posnanski, one of the most widely read baseball writers in the country, wrote about the embarrassing name of the Pre-Integration Committee.[31] In a February 2016 interview he noted that the Hall of Fame's handling of the Negro Leagues had been "tone deaf." While he believed that the best Negro Leagues players had already been elected to the Hall of Fame by that point, he noted that some had been omitted, and that it made the Hall of Fame look terrible in focusing on the continued election of obscure White players from that period when Black players remained ineligible. Posnanski wrote that White players and other contributors from that period were already overrepresented in the Hall of Fame. "I have absolutely no idea why they would have a biennial committee especially designed to elect more Major Leaguers from that time.... I think the Hall of Fame made a mistake by simply closing the book on the Negro Leagues. That said, if they were going to do that, it would look a lot better if they also would close the book entirely on pre–1947 baseball."[32]

Not many people associated with the Negro Leagues were still alive by 2016, but their surviving family members continued to advocate for their place in the Hall of Fame. Julian Duncan's grandfather, Frank Duncan, Jr., was a very good catcher for the Kansas City Monarchs and became their manager later in his career. He was the first professional manager Jackie Robinson had, and his teams compiled a .570 winning percentage while winning two pennants and a World Series. There are several managers enshrined in the Hall of Fame with lesser résumés than Duncan, and that's before considering his playing career or the fact that he and his son, Frank Duncan III, are believed to be the first father-son combination to play together in a Major League game. He was one of the initial 94 people considered by the screening panel for the Negro Leagues special election in 2006. The fact that he could never again come any closer to being considered for the Hall of Fame bothered Julian Duncan a great deal, not only for his grandfather but for all worthy Negro Leaguers who had been shut out. He was particularly unhappy that Buck O'Neil was no longer eligible. "I called Buck O'Neil 'Uncle Buck,'" he said. "That's how close our families were, and we were close for our whole lives."[33]

After a decade of excluding individuals from the Negro Leagues from further consideration for the Hall of Fame, the Hall announced a series of sweeping changes two days before the 2016 induction ceremony was held. Ozzie Smith, the great shortstop for the Padres and Cardinals, was named as a member of the Hall of Fame's board of directors. He was just the third Black member of the 16-person board, joining fellow Hall of Fame players Joe Morgan and Frank Robinson. Some changes to the election process for the Ford C. Frick Award were also included in the announcement.

But the main news was that the Era Committees were to undergo a complete overhaul. No longer would they be broken into three committees, each voting once every three years. Instead, there would be four committees, with three having much narrower time periods for which they were responsible. The Pre-Integration Committee was eliminated, and the new structure deemphasized 1947 as the break point between eras. Moving forward, candidates from more recent time periods would be given closer and more frequent examination. The Golden Days Era Committee would meet once every five years and would be focused on the years from 1950 until 1969. The Modern Baseball Era and Today's Game Era Committees would cover the periods from 1970 to 1987 and 1988 to 2016, respectively, and would each meet twice in every five years. The final committee, covering all baseball played before 1950, was named the Early Baseball Era Committee.

The good news for supporters of the Negro Leagues was that they would be eligible again, and included in the Early Baseball Era Committee. All committees could consider players, managers, umpires, and executives, so there were no excluded groups within the new structure.

The bad news was that the Early Baseball Era Committee would meet far less frequently than the others three, just once every ten years. Further bad news was that the initial schedule that was released slated the committee would be the last to meet, in 2021, and wouldn't meet again until 2030. "There are twice as many players in the Hall of Fame who debuted before 1950 as compared to afterward," said board chairman Janes Forbes Clark, "and yet there are nearly double the eligible candidates after 1950 than prior. Those who served the game long ago and have been evaluated many times on past ballots will now be reviewed less frequently."[34]

Logically, that decision made a great deal of sense. The packing of the Hall of Fame with players from earlier eras had been a problem for some time, one noted by historians and researchers for many years. The BBWAA had complained about this for decades, going so far as to threaten to dissociate the organization from the Hall if something wasn't done to curb the number of passed-over players who were being elected by the Veterans Committee. The many alterations to that committee that followed had done little to stem the flow, so the 2016 restructuring was a step in the right direction.

Unfortunately, by solving that problem the Hall of Fame created another. The Negro Leagues existed entirely in the window of time that would now be considered the least. They were no longer completely shut out of the Hall, which was a positive step, but they were grouped into the same category as the overrepresented Early Baseball Era when they were, if anything, underrepresented. The new structure promised little hope of ever correcting that.

Little did anyone know at the time that monumental changes to baseball and society would lead to yet another restructuring just four years later.

Chapter 12

Another Effort, More Hope

SINCE ITS FOUNDING, THE LEADERS of the Hall of Fame have tried to align the Hall's positions with public opinion, and with the positions of the Major Leagues. During the 1930s and most of the 1940s that meant segregation, a position that didn't change until Black players, who had finally broken the color barrier, became eligible through the normal processes for Hall of Fame elections. The Negro Leagues and its players were ignored, excluded from the record books and from the Hall of Fame as if they never existed.

Only dramatic changes in society triggered responses from baseball leaders and their partners at the Hall of Fame. The upheaval of the Civil Rights Movement in American society during the 1960s compelled people as disparate as Ted Williams and Dick Young to ask why the Hall of Fame continued to close its doors to the Negro Leagues, and those inquiries finally resulted in change. The same thing happened in the early 1990s, when the popularity of Ken Burns' *Baseball* documentary and its star, Buck O'Neil, propelled the image of the Negro Leagues to new heights in American popular culture. The Negro Leagues Baseball Museum opened, furthering that image even more, and new leaders at the Hall of Fame and in baseball reacted again.

In between these changes were lengthy down periods when the Negro Leagues and its greatest players were largely ignored again. Society was more interested in Reaganomics and action movies in the 1980s than they were with old Black ballplayers, so the attempts to raise awareness through annual reunions failed, and the Hall of Fame followed the trend by largely overlooking Negro Leagues players during their Veterans Committee elections. After the 2006 mass election of 17 individuals from the Negro Leagues, the Hall of Fame simply stopped making them eligible for the next 15 years, and society didn't really pay attention. Buck O'Neil was dead, the Negro Leagues' most recognizable voice silenced, and the few voices that emerged in the aftermath went mostly unheard.

12. Another Effort, More Hope

As the balloting for the first election for the Hall's new Early Baseball Era Committee approached in 2020, it would require some further catalyst in society to raise the awareness of the Negro Leagues again and force change at the Hall of Fame. That had always been their history, to reflect society instead of asking society to reflect, and there were few signs that the Hall of Fame intended to alter that course.

Sadly, for American society, but fortunately for those supporters of the Negro Leagues who continue to hope they will be fairly recognized in the Hall of Fame, sweeping societal changes were exactly what arrived in 2020.

In March of that year, the Covid-19 pandemic crashed full-force into the United States. Everyday life was immediately and drastically altered, as tens of thousands of people died, and quarantine conditions were imposed. People stayed home. Sports leagues stopped in place. Shortages of goods and food prevailed. Fights erupted over health issues, like wearing masks, social distancing, and the accelerated development of vaccines. Lines were drawn and sides were taken. The stock market crashed. Jobs were lost, or entirely reinvented as millions figured out ways to work from home. It was a full reassessment of American life.

The pandemic had a disproportionate impact on lower-income communities and populations.[1] People in those communities had less access to quality healthcare, and fewer options to earn money as the economy largely shut down or reinvented itself. These populations have longstanding systemic distrust of governmental agencies, which made it harder for healthcare workers to convince them to take a government-backed vaccine once it was available. These lower-income communities are disproportionately comprised of people of color, so America's Black and Hispanic population were among those hit the hardest. Hispanic and Black people were five and three times more likely to die of Covid-19 than White people during the pandemic's first year.

In the swirl of closures and deaths, the death of Breonna Taylor, shot by police in her home in Louisville, Kentucky, went largely unnoticed when it occurred on March 13, 2020.[2] It was the latest in a series of shootings of unarmed Black people by law enforcement. Two months later, George Floyd was murdered by officers of the Minneapolis Police Department who kneeled on him as he lay face down on the street during an arrest for supposedly using a counterfeit twenty dollar bill. One officer kneeled on Floyd's neck for eight minutes, despite Floyd's pleas for help and statements that he couldn't breathe. Eventually he lost consciousness, but the officer remained on his neck. Floyd died of cardiac arrest.[3] The entire event was recorded on video, which was livestreamed on Facebook even as the events were happening. Other recordings were available for the public on the internet within hours.[4]

Beginning the next day, protests were organized in several cities. In Minneapolis, the focus was on the death of George Floyd. In Louisville, the protests were centered on the death of Breonna Taylor, as the results of the investigation into her death had been reported to the Attorney General of Kentucky just days before Floyd's murder in Minneapolis. Elsewhere, the names of other unarmed Black victims of police violence were recalled. Though organized as peaceful protests, some violence and vandalism occurred, and police responded by using tear gas and rubber bullets against some protestors. The confrontations escalated over the next several days. By June 6, nearly 14,000 arrests had been made nationwide.[5]

During the first week of protests, statements were issued by the leadership of the National Football League,[6] National Basketball Association,[7] and National Hockey League.[8] Each expressed solidarity with the cause of the protestors in fighting against racial injustice, and recognized and shared in the "pain, anger, and frustration," behind the protests. Major corporations in most industries made similar statements, publicly denouncing racism and discrimination and pledging to support efforts to fight them. Major League Baseball, however, was relatively slow to take a stance. It wasn't until June 3, nine days after Floyd's death and several days after his peer commissioners in other leagues had already issued statements, that MLB commissioner Rob Manfred finally followed suit.[9]

The delay did not sit well with many Black players. Pitcher Marcus Stroman shared the MLB statement on Twitter, adding the comment, "Took long enough.... BLACK LIVES MATTER!" Many teams had issued statements prior to MLB acting. Miami Marlins co-owner and CEO Derek Jeter said that protestors should not be demonized, and that he had hope that his children could be free of living in a society where they were judged by the color of their skin. "I hope that their White friends grow up to recognize that it is not only enough to verbalize their non-racist views," he continued, "but also to participate at an active level to eradicate racism." Some White players, like Adam Wainwright of the Cardinals and James Paxton of the Yankees, used their platforms to support the demonstrations of their Black teammates.[10]

The unrest came at a time when the percentage of Black players in baseball was at one of the lowest points in history. After peaking near 19 percent of all Major League players during the 1970s and 1980s, the percentage of Black players in Major League Baseball steadily dropped for

12. Another Effort, More Hope 161

thirty-plus years.[11] By 2020, only 8 percent of the players on big league rosters were Black,[12] and the perception was that baseball had become a White person's sport. Adam Jones of the Baltimore Orioles had said just that. In 2016, after quarterback Colin Kaepernick of the San Francisco 49ers protested police brutality against Black people by taking a knee during the national anthem before an exhibition game, prompting other athletes to follow suit, no baseball players joined in the protests. When asked why, Jones said, "We already have two strikes against us already, so you might as well not kick yourself out of the game. In football, you can't kick them out. You need those players. In baseball, they don't need us. Baseball is a white man's sport."[13] The delay from Major League Baseball in condemning the racism that was being protested across the country didn't help this image.

In August, Jacob Blake was shot in the back by police officers in Kenosha, Wisconsin, setting off another round of protests and confrontations between police and demonstrators. Three days after the shooting of Blake, players for the Milwaukee Bucks protested his killing by walking off the floor during preparations for their first-round playoff game against the Orlando Magic and refusing to play the game. The Magic joined the protest by refusing to accept a forfeit.[14] The NBA quickly announced that all playoff games were postponed for the next few days. Players in other sports joined the protests. In Major League Baseball, where the season has just begun three weeks earlier after lengthy delays due to the Covid-19 pandemic, players on the Milwaukee Brewers and Cincinnati Reds struck, forcing the postponement of their game on August 26.[15] Two other games were postponed by players strikes later that day, and seven were postponed the following day. August 28, designated as the delayed date to celebrate Jackie Robinson Day across Major League Baseball, saw players from the Houston Astros and Oakland Athletics walk off the field in protest, forcing the game's postponement.[16]

These events took place just days after the Hall of Fame announced that the Early Days Era Committee, the only Era Committee that could consider the candidacies of individuals from the Negro Leagues, would no longer be meeting in 2020 as planned. Both that committee and the Golden Days Era Committee had been scheduled to vote on candidates that winter, but the Hall of Fame decided that would not be advisable due to the ongoing Covid-19 pandemic, which continued to have surges of new variants. Those committees traditionally meet in person, and the Hall of Fame had been strict in enforcing that rule. In fact, Bill Mazeroski's election in 2001 was likely due to the absence of Veterans Committee member Ted Williams. He was a vocal opponent of Mazeroski's election, but with recent open-heart surgery, he missed that year's committee meeting. Williams was not permitted to vote remotely, so only 14 votes were cast. That lowered the number of votes needed for election from 12 to 11, just enough for Mazeroski to squeeze into the Hall.[17]

That election was the driving force behind a large-scale restructuring of the Veterans Committee, but one thing the Hall of Fame did not change was the need to have the committee meet in person. Though most businesses in the United States had adapted to remote working conditions by that point in the pandemic, going so far as to issue cameras to their employees to hold meetings by video, the Hall of Fame elected not to change their in-person standard for the Eras Committees. "The Era Committee process," said Hall chairman Jane Forbes Clark, "which has been so effective in evaluating Hall of Fame candidates, requires an open, yet confidential conversation and an in-person dialogue involving the members of the 16-person voting committee."[18]

The pandemic, social unrest, and the missteps of Major League Baseball and the Hall of Fame all occurred during what should have been a year-long celebration of the Negro Leagues. February 2020 marked the 100th anniversary of Rube Foster's founding the Negro National League at the Paseo YMCA building in Kansas City. The Negro League Baseball Museum had planned a series of events to recognize the anniversary, and the initial celebrations were held in February. A reception was held at the museum on the night of February 13, featuring an exhibit of original art.[19] Major League Baseball and the Major League Baseball Players Association announced a joint donation of one million dollars to the museum, and plans for ongoing celebrations by Major League Baseball throughout the 2020 season.[20] The NLBM planned to wrap up the celebration with a Centennial Gala held in November to coincide with Buck O'Neil's birthday.[21] Almost all of that was derailed by the Covid-19 pandemic, which not only made large gatherings impossible, but also cancelled most of the MLB season.

The social unrest that followed served to amplify a key point that was often made by the NLBM's president, Bob Kendrick. "This story is so much more than just a baseball story. This is a story of social injustice. It is story of the civil rights movement. And it's a story of overcoming all of that adversity stacked against them. The social justice upheaval we're experiencing, it magnifies and quantifies the value of our museum to a greater extent."[22] Though most of the planned celebrations of the 100th anniversary of the founding of the Negro National League had to be postponed, the NLBM pushed ahead with a "Tip Your Cap" campaign in June. Prominent figures in baseball and American society were encouraged to tip their cap to the Negro Leagues and record a message as they did so. It was an enormous success, as well-known Americans from Magic Johnson to Paul Rudd sent their messages, often wearing replica Negro Leagues jerseys or hats. The baseball community participated as well, with several members of the Hall of Fame recording messages, including Henry Aaron, George Brett, Reggie Jackson, Derek Jeter, and Ozzie Smith, as well as active players like All-Stars Mike Trout and Corey Seager. Four former presidents of the United States—George W. Bush, Jimmy Carter, Bill Clinton, and Barack Obama—all sent messages as well, each wearing the cap of their favorite team.[23]

Though the response by Major League Baseball, the Hall of Fame, and the baseball community at large was slow in reacting to the sweeping movement for social justice, they did not ignore it entirely. They began to act shortly after the challenging, truncated season ended. In October, the Baseball Writers Association of America announced that its members had voted to remove Kenesaw Mountain Landis' name from the Most Valuable Player Awards. Several former recipients of the award, both Black and White, had expressed concern about his name being associated with the award earlier that year. "I was always aware of his name and what that meant to slowing the color line in Major League Baseball," said Hall of Fame shortstop Barry Larkin. "Of the racial injustice and inequality that Black players had to go through." Fellow Hall of Famer Mike Schmidt said, "If you're looking to expose individuals in baseball's history who promoted racism by continuing to close doors to men of color, Kenesaw Landis would be a candidate." He added, "Removing his name from the MVP trophy would expose the injustice of that era. I'd gladly replace the engraving on my trophies."[24]

In August, 28 members of the Democratic Caucus in the U.S. House of Representatives wrote to baseball commissioner Rob Manfred and to the BBWAA asking for Landis' name to be removed from the award. "Given that Commissioner Landis perpetuated baseball's 'Gentlemen's Agreement,' to keep Black players out of the major leagues, we agree it is time to remove his name from the award, and move toward a more inclusive award designation," they said in the letter. In a response to the letter, Manfred signaled his agreement while simultaneously pointing the finger at the BBWAA as the administrators of the MVP award. "I am pleased by the BBWAA's decision to take up this matter as soon as possible and I assure you I will monitor it very closely."[25] Two months later, the BBWAA voted to remove Landis' name. "Landis, baseball's first commissioner, served from 1920 to 1944 and notably failed to integrate the game during his tenure," said BBWAA president Paul Sullivan in the organization's announcement. "A motion was made in July by longtime member Ken Rosenthal, and after an online discussion of

164   **Cooperstown's Back Door**

the issue the BBWAA membership voted this week to remove the name, beginning in 2020."[26]

Four months later, the BBWAA also voted to remove J.G. Taylor Spink's name from the annual award given to recognize a distinguished, longtime baseball writer. Within days of the former MVPs calling for Landis' name to be removed from the Most Valuable Player award, some writers began calling for Spink's name to be removed as well. Bob Nightengale, writing in *USA Today*, noted "We are tearing down statues and monuments for what they represent. We are changing state flags for what they symbolize. Finally, we are demanding change in this country. It's time for the Baseball Writers' Association of America to step up, too. It's time for the BBWAA to remove the name—J.G. Taylor Spink—associated with the greatest honor given annually to a baseball writer." He went on to enumerate the various racist stances taken by Spink during his time as owner and editor of *The Sporting News*, and quoted former recipients of the award, like Paul Hagen and Peter Gammons, as they agreed it was time to remove Spink's name.[27] In the announcement in which it was noted that the award would be known as the BBWAA Career Excellence Award moving forward, the president of the BBWAA, C. Trent Rosecrans, noted that the change was not taken lightly and was only done after "substantial research and conversation with and among members" of the BBWAA was done before the matter was put to a vote. The research indicated that "Spink's *Sporting News* contained 'racist language, ugly stereotypes, and derogatory portraits of Negro League players and other black Americans during Spink's time as publisher, especially in the era before Jackie Robinson made his MLB debut in 1947."[28]

The long, difficult year for baseball was capped in December with the announcement from Major League Baseball that seven Negro Leagues would be given formal recognition as Major Leagues, effective immediately. It was the first time in more than fifty years that baseball had conveyed Major League status on leagues other than the American League and National League. The last time it had been done, in 1969, a committee of five White men representing the commissioner's office, the American League, the National League, the Baseball Hall of Fame, and the BBWAA, had recognized four defunct all–White leagues and passed over every Negro League as being worthy of Major League status.[29] That action was later described by Bob Kendrick as "Racism in its purest form."[30]

MLB's new stance on the Negro Leagues was noted as "long overdue" by commissioner Rob Manfred. "All of us who love baseball," Manfred said in a statement, "have long known that the Negro Leagues

12. Another Effort, More Hope

165

produced many of our game's best players, innovations, and triumphs against a backdrop of injustice. We are now grateful to count the players of the Negro Leagues where they belong: as Major Leaguers within the official historical record." Seven leagues were included in the recognition: the Negro National League (I) (1920–31), the Eastern Colored League (1923–28), the American Negro League (1929), the East-West League (1932), the Negro Southern League (1932), the Negro National League (II) (1933–48) and the Negro American League (1937–48). The statistics for these leagues would become part of the official Major League record book after a review of available data by the Elias Sports Bureau, the official statistician of Major League Baseball.[31]

Unfortunately, as with most things related to baseball in 2020, the announcement was not without controversy. The first sentence of the announcement rankled some Negro Leagues advocates. "Commissioner of Baseball Robert D. Manfred, Jr. announced today that Major League Baseball is correcting a longtime oversight in the game's history by officially elevating the Negro Leagues to 'Major League' status."[32] The word "elevating" struck many the wrong way, as it conveyed the notion that the Negro Leagues had been a lesser set of leagues that were now being lifted in some way by MLB's leadership decades later. Jerry Hairston, Jr., who played in the Major Leagues for 16 years and was the grandson of former Negro League All-Star Sam Hairston, said, "'Elevate' is not the word. It's to recognize the Negro Leagues. They were already elevated."[33] The NLBM president Bob Kendrick said that his first reaction upon hearing the news was "I don't need you to validate me."[34] "We were somebody then. We've always been somebody," said Rose Hunter, stepdaughter of Hall of Fame first baseman Buck Leonard. "We don't need somebody else to tell us we were great. They're acknowledging it because we already knew it. We always knew it." Negro Leagues researcher Gary Ashwill noted of the announcement, "It doesn't make them major leaguers because they were already major leaguers."[35] The lack of an apology in the announcement also wasn't well-received. "In 2020," wrote Clinton Yates, "joining the globe in recognizing that Black folks are real people without whom you could never survive is not a reason to say, 'you're welcome.' It's a reason to say sorry."[36]

The good news that Negro Leagues records would be incorporated into the official Major League record book was further diminished by the delay in doing so. The MLB announcement noted the "decades-long research" of the community of baseball researchers who had focused their energy on the Negro Leagues. It gave particular commendation to Ashwill and his partners in building the Seamheads Negro Leagues Database, and online archive of the most complete set of statistics of

Negro Leagues players, teams, and leagues.[37] It isn't a complete history of those leagues, as official league records are scarce and many of the games played in those leagues were not reported upon in media sources. The database also doesn't include statistics from the non-league barnstorming games that Negro Leagues teams routinely played to earn money and grow the fanbase.[38] Even so, it is an invaluable record of the achievements from those leagues and was diligently compiled over decades of work by volunteer researchers.

At the time of MLB's announcement, the database included statistics from 73 percent of the known Negro League games played from 1920 to 1948. Ongoing research continues to find more data and refine the quality.[39] That was sufficient for the team that runs the Baseball-Reference.com website, the leading online source for baseball statistics. In June 2021, the site announced that it had licensed the data from Seamheads and began to make it available to its users, the culmination of a nearly year-long effort that had begun months before Major League Baseball announced that the Negro Leagues were being recognized as Major Leagues.[40] In February 2023, another popular online source for baseball statistics, Fangraphs.com, announced that they had also licensed the Seamheads data and made it available online.[41]

Major League Baseball did not follow suit. Initial negotiations with Seamheads for the use of their database broke down, reportedly over issues related to who would control the data and how it would be used.[42] In the spring of 2023, MLB decided instead to launch their own effort. They partnered with Retrosheet, which controls a separate database of game-level Major League baseball statistics and had not previously been involved in compiling data from the Negro Leagues. The effort to compile that data from scratch was estimated to take at least five years, meaning Negro Leagues accomplishment likely wouldn't be incorporated into official MLB records until sometime in 2028, nearly eight years after MLB announced the change in the official status of the Negro Leagues. That delay didn't sit well with descendants of great Negro Leagues players. "I'm shocked," said Sean Gibson, great-grandson of Josh Gibson. "It's sad. I feel like Major League Baseball jumped the gun. They should have had all that worked out before they made the announcement."[43]

In November 2023, MLB announced that they had finally reached an agreement with Seamheads to use their database. The Retrosheet effort would continue to help augment that data, but the Seamheads data would serve as the statistical base.[44] Unfortunately, there is still no timetable for having that data appear in official Major League records. "History is process, not product," said official MLB historian

12. Another Effort, More Hope

John Thorn in explaining why no timetable existed for completing the work. A Negro Leagues Statistical Review Committee will work with Elias Sports Bureau to audit the accuracy of the data, then "create baselines that do not leave us with absurd results," said Thorn, "with the single-season ERA leader having 30 innings pitched or guys who played 18 games and had fewer than 100 at-bats being listed among to .400 hitters."

Whatever that work ultimately produces, some advocates of the Negro Leagues feel it will still be an incomplete representation of the Negro Leagues. "They should have included every game—against major leagues teams, barnstorming, local teams—against all teams," said Kendrick. "There's a possibility of marginalizing players who are almost mythical." He also felt that the story of Negro League baseball could never be reduced to just statistics. "No stats give you the greatness of Satchel Paige, the power of Josh Gibson, the speed of Cool Papa Bell. I don't ever want to lose the story. I don't want the legend and the lore to go away. That's what makes the Negro Leagues special."[45]

That, the legend and lore of the Negro Leagues, has always been something the Hall of Fame struggled to represent. As MLB finally recognized the Negro Leagues, and researchers built databases of their statistics, and the NLBM continued to battle through the pandemic and social upheaval to celebrate the Negro Leagues centennial, the Hall of Fame had to assess their own telling of that history, and how they should adapt to the new landscape in baseball and society at large.

This assessment would take place under new leadership. Longtime president of the Hall of Fame Jeff Idelson had announced his retirement from the position in April 2019 after 11 years in the role. He was replaced by Tim Mead, who assumed the role in July 2019 after a forty-year career as an executive with the Los Angeles Angels. He had most recently served as the team's Vice President of Communications, a role he had just vacated when Angels pitcher Tyler Skaggs died of a drug overdose on July 1, 2019. A team employee, Eric Kay, who worked for Mead in the team's communications department, had sold Skaggs the drugs he used to overdose. Kay was charged criminally in Texas and was eventually convicted and sentenced to a 22-year prison term.

The investigation into Skaggs' death and the role Angels employees played in it was taking place during Mead's first few months at the Hall of Fame, as was the Covid-19 pandemic and the social unrest and demonstrations following the murder of George Floyd. Less than two years after assuming the role, Mead announced in April 2021 that he was stepping down the following month, citing concerns related to his family. "I made the recent leap with every intention of following in the footsteps of my predecessors, in continuing their efforts in maintaining the Hall of Fame as a critical component of the game," Mead said in a statement released by the Hall of Fame. "Try as I might, even with the unwavering support of my family, these last 22 months have been challenging in maintaining my responsibilities to them."[46]

His resignation apparently wasn't expected, as no replacement had been found by the time it went into effect. Idelson returned on an interim basis as the Hall of Fame searched for its next president. On June 28, they announced that Josh Rawitch, then serving as the Senior Vice President of Content and Communications for the Arizona Diamondbacks, would take over the role.[47] The next day, Mead was named as a defendant in a pair of lawsuits by the family of Tyler Skaggs, alleging that Mead was aware that Eric Kay was a drug addict and that he was selling drugs to Angels players, including Skaggs, but allowed him to remain employed anyway.[48] Mead has denied the charges.[49]

Rawitch assumed the Hall's presidency during a clearly turbulent time. It showed few signs of abating. The Covid-19 pandemic had not yet ended, and civil unrest over issues regarding race continued in society, exacerbated by deep political divisions over the results of the 2020 presidential election and ensuing attempt to seize the Capitol and stop the certification of the results. Baseball found itself deeply involved in much of the unrest. Just two months before Rawitch was named to lead the Hall of Fame, Major League Baseball announced that the All-Star Game and MLB Draft that were scheduled to be held in Atlanta that summer would be moved to a different venue over concerns about a new law in Georgia that was viewed by civil rights advocates as an attempt to suppress the voting rights of minorities.[50] In MLB's official statement announcing the move, Rob Manfred said that the game and the draft were being moved as a demonstration of the sport's values, pledging the organization's support of voting rights and opposition to unfair obstacles to voting. "Fair access to voting continues to have our game's unwavering support."[51] The game and draft were ultimately held in Denver.

The Hall of Fame was reconsidering how they chose to tell the story of Black baseball even before Rawitch was hired. Their small two-room display for the entire history of Black baseball, which had been renamed "Ideals and Injustices," was more than twenty years old by the spring of 2021. Other than a statue of Buck O'Neil on the museum's first floor, and the plaques of actual members, there was almost no mention of Black baseball or the Negro Leagues anywhere in the museum's three floors of displays outside of those two rooms. They realized it was time to reconsider that. Tom Shieber, senior curator at the museum, noted

12. *Another Effort, More Hope* 169

that the Hall was seeking outside help in updating their presentation of Black baseball. "It's time to re-examine it and start afresh, and that's a great challenge," Shieber said. "With new research, new understanding, new attitudes and new technologies, there are new possibilities for what we can do."[52]

The re-evaluation came at a time when no one from the Negro Leagues had been elected to the Hall of Fame in 15 years, the longest gap between Negro Leagues inductees since Satchel Paige became the first Negro Leagues member of the Hall in 1971. This did not sit well with advocates of the Negro Leagues, including Larry Lester, a member of the Special Committee on the Negro Leagues that had elected the last Negro Leagues representatives to the Hall in 2006. "Statistically speaking, from 1920 to 1948, two point five percent of all white major leaguers are in the Hall of Fame," Lester said. "For the same period, less than one percent of Black players are in the Hall of Fame. That tells me there are more names that need to be recognized." He went on to note that while any other worthy Negro Leagues candidates were no longer living, it was still important to honor them and, more importantly, tell their stories. "It's time for their place on the pantheon, time for their place in history," Lester said. "They must be included in your narrative, your history of baseball."[53]

Part of that narrative, and the re-examination of how the Hall of Fame presented issues related to the rampant racism in the game's history, involved re-writing the wording on some displays, both in the museum and online. While the Hall of Fame did not, for instance, alter the plaque of Tom Yawkey, as suggested by *Boston Globe* columnist Dan Shaughnessy,[54] they did add wording to Yawkey's page on the Hall of Fame website. It now concludes by noting that Yawkey had a complicated legacy that included his organization's being the last Major League franchise to field a Black player. "As the sole owner of the Red Sox, Yawkey ultimately bears the responsibility for the inaction of his franchise."[55] The Hall also added a sign at the entrance to the plaque gallery that noted the complicated legacies some of its members had. It reads:

> "Enshrinement into the National Baseball Hall of Fame reflects the perspective of voters at the time of election. The plaques on these walls recognize Members for their accomplishments in the game.
> Our Museum exhibits, Library archives, and educational resources address the totality of their careers, as both part of a society and a game that always strive to improve.
> The National Baseball Hall of Fame and Museum's mission is to Preserve History, which is what we seek to do throughout the Museum."[56]

170 Cooperstown's Back Door

Hall chairman Jane Forbes Clark was aware of the calls to remove the plaques or even rescind the memberships of some of its members, like Yawkey, whose name was removed from the street outside Fenway Park in 2018 over his views and actions related to integrating baseball. Clark didn't agree with steps that drastic but understood why they were called for. "I don't feel in any context that one should expunge history, that one should erase history," Clark said. "Part of our mission is not only to honor excellence and connect generations, but it's to preserve the history of the game, and that's what we're doing: We're reacting to the evolution of society and society wanting a deeper understanding of underlying racism—its causes, its history, and how it continues to affect the game."[57]

Part of that additional context included the addition of placards on some of the Hall's existing displays, outlining the controversial views and actions of some of the game's key figures. A display with Kenesaw Mountain Landis now includes the wording, "As the most powerful person in baseball, Landis had the greatest ability to effect change, but his lack of overt action in promoting integration gave tacit approval to maintaining the status quo of a segregated system." Another for Cap Anson noted that he "used his stature to drive minorities from the game."[58]

Rawitch took over the Hall's presidency in September 2021, and brought a lifetime of baseball experience to the role. Despite being just 44 years old when he was named to the post, he had been working in baseball for over twenty-five years, starting as a teenager with the Dodgers, then as a reporter with Major League Baseball Advanced Media, and ultimately with the Diamondbacks. He speaks Spanish and has extensive international experience working with baseball organizations in Asia and Latin America, including work with the World Baseball Classic. In the month leading up to taking over the role, he traveled cross country with his family, stopping at a variety of baseball and museum venues. "Museums borrow good ideas from other museums," he said. "I'm learning as much as I can as fast as I can."[59] He has expressed an interest in modernizing the museum's displays beyond the ongoing contextual updates. That includes not only the displays in the museum, but how the Hall is presented to the public outside of the physical building in Cooperstown.

Rawitch recognized that people consume information differently, even at museums, and he wanted the Hall of Fame to adapt to those changes by including simple steps such as the addition of QR codes to their exhibits that patrons could scan with their phones for additional information. He used his experience with his son to inform him about the sorts of exhibits that would attract younger fans, and what

12. Another Effort, More Hope 171

a critical role social media would play in the museum remaining relevant. "Sometimes there's the bad side of it when you see what happens on Twitter and that's not ideal, but ultimately what we have to remember is that there are millions of young kids that are consuming most of their life's news through social media outlets. We're going to start a Tik-Tok account and we're doing all sorts of things that will hopefully keep us relevant to that generation."[60]

Though Rawitch had an eye on the future of the Hall, he also continued its focus on telling the story of baseball's past, while taking particular care to establish more multicultural ties between the Hall of Fame and Black, Latin, and Asian communities. His tour of baseball venues included a stop at the Negro Leagues Baseball Museum in Kansas City.[61] When the Jackie Robinson Museum opened its doors in New York City in July 2022, Rawitch was in attendance.[62] For the election of David Ortiz to the Hall of Fame in January 2022, Rawitch made the announcement in both English and Spanish.[63] He was present in Los Angeles for the retirement of Jaime Jarrín, longtime Spanish-language announcer for the Dodgers, and requested Jarrín's headset to put on display in Cooperstown,[64] and attended the Mariners' ceremony to induct Ichiro Suzuki into their Hall of Fame.[65]

The Hall took another important step toward the proper recognition of the Negro Leagues when the Eras Committees announced in December 2021 that Bud Fowler, Minnie Miñoso and Buck O'Neil had all been elected. In Kansas City, O'Neil's adopted hometown, watch parties were held in anticipation of hearing O'Neil's name finally announced, even though it was possible he would be passed over again. Bob Kendrick, who hosted a gathering at the NLBM, felt it was an important moment to share. "Because this is history," he said. "Whether it's good or bad remains to be seen. But it is still history, and it's still a moment in time in this organization's history. We need to capture that.... We'll be part of it together." When asked about the possibility that O'Neil again wouldn't be elected, he joked, "I'll either have a whole bunch of people to hug or a whole bunch of shoulders to cry on."[66]

In a suburb of Kansas City, a different watch party was hosted by Phil Dixon, the NLBM's first spokesperson when it was founded and a member of the Special Early Baseball Overview Committee that helped determine which candidates would be on the Early Baseball Era Committee ballot. Noting the 2006 election in which O'Neil had been passed over, Dixon said "They had the wrong people voting." It was an ironic statement given that his party was attended by Larry Lester, one of the voting members of the 2006 committee and the subject of speculation that he'd worked to block O'Neil's election.[67]

Bud Fowler (center of the back row), the local Cooperstown kid, was finally given his rightful place in the Hall of Fame in his hometown (courtesy of the Baseball Hall of Fame).

The chances of that happening again were much lower this time. The Hall of Fame had stressed to the committee members that each candidate's full baseball career should be considered, not just their record in the category in which they'd been nominated. That allowed the committees to consider, for instance, Gil Hodges' playing career and his managing career when considering his candidacy. That helped him finally get elected after falling short for several decades. The decision to recognize the Major League status of the Negro Leagues helped as well, as the full records for Miñoso could now be considered, a fact that likely pushed his long-delayed candidacy over the top. Both of those changes helped O'Neil's case, given that his long career crossed between the Negro Leagues and Major Leagues, and encompassed a variety of roles, all of which were noted by Rawitch during the official announcement. He took the added step of repeating the announcements of the elections of Miñoso and Tony Oliva in Spanish for audiences watching in Latin America.[68]

Rawitch was asked if the elections of Fowler and O'Neil, in particular, were an effort by the Hall of Fame to make amends for "past sins."

12. Another Effort, More Hope 173

Rawitch said they weren't, noting, "I would say it's really just to make sure that everybody's given a fair shake. In some cases, it may just be that the lens of time has changed the perspective of baseball."[69] That hesitation to admit any past wrongdoing on the part of the Hall of Fame continues to be a drag on some areas where progress could be made. There have been calls to remove Ford Frick's name from the annual award given for broadcasting excellence. Some of those calls have been based on the fact that Frick was barely a broadcaster himself, and therefore shouldn't have a broadcasting award named for him.[70] Others feel some consideration should be given to Frick's poor overall record on the subject of integrating baseball and integrating the Hall of Fame. Popular baseball writer Joe Posnanski cited that troubling track record while also noting that the BBWAA had voted to remove the names of Kenesaw Mountain Landis and J.G. Taylor Spink from two of their awards. He argued that precedent should be followed by the Hall of Fame, particularly when Frick's lack of a real broadcasting career was considered.[71]

They made one change to the Frick Award in 2022 that allowed for a more multi-cultural view of future recipients. Moving forward, voting for the award would be based on a ten-person ballot developed by the Hall each year, with at least one candidate being a foreign-language broadcaster.[72] Jacques Doucet, the French-speaking broadcaster for both the Expos and Blue Jays, was the first such candidate. He was the only foreign-language announcer on both the 2023 and 2024 ballots for the award. It would still, however, be named for Frick. When asked about the possibility of renaming the award for Vin Scully after he passed away in August 2022, Rawitch expressed sympathy for the notion of recognizing Scully, but would not commit to changing the name of the Frick Award.[73] To do so, even as a means of honoring Scully, could be viewed as an admission that one of the Hall of Fame's founding fathers, a person whose portrait hangs in the rotunda outside the plaque gallery, was deserving of the same fate suffered by Landis and Spink. That was a step the Hall of Fame wasn't ready to take.[74]

There were steps the Hall was ready to take in 2022. Some of them were small but significant, like the closer cooperation between the Hall of Fame and the NLBM in Kansas City. Immediately after the induction ceremony, Buck O'Neil's Hall of Fame plaque was brought to Kansas City and displayed at both the Negro Leagues Baseball Museum and at the Royals' annual Salute to the Negro Leagues game at Kauffman Stadium.[75] It was part of a more visible effort by the Hall of Fame to loan culturally significant objects to other baseball organizations across the country. In addition to loaning O'Neil's plaque, they had done the same with Satchel Paige's plaque,[76] loaned a wooden home plate that was made by Japanese-Americans at the Gila River Internment Camp, and loaned several of Jackie Robinson's artifacts, including his plaque, to both the Dodgers and the Jackie Robinson Museum.[77]

Two of the Hall of Fame's steps in 2022 would have enormous impact on the Hall's representation of Black baseball overall and the Negro Leagues in particular. They signaled an acknowledgment that the Hall needed to change with the times, something the Hall's vice president of communications, Jon Shestakofsky, made clear at the time O'Neil's plaque was loaned out. "Baseball has in some senses mirrored what's happened in America, what American society has gone through. In some ways it's led the way. But there are always parallels between what's happening in baseball and what's happening in America. This sport and this country have grown up side by side.... And these individuals that we celebrate ... each of them can help us better understand this country's own history and who we are as a society."[78]

One critical change was a restructuring of the Hall's Eras Committees. Announced in April 2022, the committees would be reduced from four to three, and the timeframes would be condensed to just two. There would be two committees for what the Hall now labeled the Contemporary Baseball Era, from 1980 to the present day. One committee would focus only on players from that period, while the other would focus on managers, umpires, and executives. The other timeframe, covering all of baseball history before 1980, was labeled the Classic Baseball Era, and its committee would consider the cases of everyone from that period, whether they be players, managers, executives, umpires, or other contributors to the game, including Negro Leaguers. Most significantly for supporters of the Negro Leagues, each of these committees would meet every three years, so there would no longer be a ten-year gap between meetings in which Negro Leagues candidates would be considered.[79]

It was the fifth restructuring of the former Veterans Committee in just over twenty years, but Rawitch explained that the amount of time between changes to the process wasn't a consideration when determining if it needed to evolve again. Rawitch had assumed his role after the last change to the process was implemented in 2016 and acknowledged that he brought a different perspective. "With new leadership comes new eyes and new perspective and new conversations," he said. "In talking to a number of board members and Hall of Famers and others who shared various perspectives, it was important obviously, from my standpoint, not to jump right into it when I got here, but to listen to a lot of people, see one of these processes through, [and] understand kind of how it goes."[80] In an interview with Jay Jaffe, he acknowledged that feedback and heightened interest regarding Negro Leagues and pre–Negro

Leagues Black baseball candidates played a role in the Hall's decision. "One of the first things that I recognized was that we couldn't wait until 2031 to look at some of these candidates," Rawitch said.[81]

The change was good news for proponents of the Negro Leagues in that candidates from Black baseball could now be considered more frequently. The bad news is that they would now be competing with every pre–1980 candidate of every race, color, ethnicity, and gender, for just eight slots on the ballot once every three years. "It does make it more challenging to get on a ballot, which I think is pretty obvious," said Rawitch. "The ballots not only will be a little bit smaller but will also cover a large period of time."[82] Election from that ballot will also be harder, as the members of the Classic Baseball Era Committee aren't permitted to vote for an unlimited number of candidates. They can only vote for three each year. Since there are 16 members of the committee, each voting for no more than three candidates, that means a maximum of 48 votes are cast. A candidate must receive 12 of them, or 75 percent of the voting members, to be elected.[83] Math therefore dictates that the maximum number of candidates that can be elected from each ballot is four, and then only if they each receive exactly twelve votes. It's far more likely that only one or two candidates will be elected each time. That was the case with the Early Baseball Era ballot in 2022, when only Fowler and O'Neil were elected, and it was the case in 2023 when the Contemporary Era committee elected only Fred McGriff, and it was the case again in 2024 when the non-player wing of the Contemporary Era committee elected only manager Jim Leyland. Fighting to be recognized with one of eight ballot slots from a pool of people covering a nearly 150-year period, and then hoping the 48 votes cast fall just the right way, isn't much of an improvement for candidates from Black baseball, but it's better having that chance once every three years instead of once every ten years.

A more concrete step announced by the Hall of Fame in 2022 was their plan to revamp the Hall's display on Black baseball. Labeled the Black Baseball Initiative, it is easily the Hall of Fame's largest initiative toward the goal of righting the wrongs in their previous representation of Black baseball's history, and how that story is told within the Hall of Fame's displays.[84]

As of April 2022, when the announcement of the initiative was made, there was scant mention of Black baseball players and leagues inside the museum except for the small, two-room "Ideals and Injustices" display that was dedicated to the subject. The history of the game's evolution was told in detail regarding White men, but the contributions of women, immigrants, and Black players was limited to a single small placard that noted "As segregation in baseball took hold in the later 1880s, African Americans carved out their own niche in the game by fielding independent barnstorming teams, like the Page Fence Giants, c. 1897." Besides the "Ideals and Injustices" display, the Hall dedicated more space and words to displaying the phony "Doubleday Baseball" and explaining the lie of the game's supposed origins in Cooperstown than were used to describe the role of Black people in the game's first hundred or more years.

Also problematic was the physical layout of the Ideals and Injustices display. Most of the museum's second floor is an open-concept design that starts at the origins of baseball and proceeds chronologically to the present day. Visitors essentially must walk through each display, from 19th-century artifacts into the hallway that begins the Baseball Timeline, with a dedicated Babe Ruth display and separate displays for women in baseball and Latin Americans that are all distinct yet still part of the path patrons must follow to get to the end. That's not the case with the Ideals and Injustices display. Its two rooms, which aren't much bigger than the space dedicated just to Ruth, are off the main Baseball Timeline hallway.[85] Patrons walking by must make a choice to step inside them. Walking by won't affect the rest of their visit at all, but they would have missed the only exhibit in the Hall of Fame dedicated to Black baseball. A very nice placard has been added since the unrest of 2020, noting the importance of the display "in light of recent events," and how much is yet to be accomplished in the battle against racism in society and in baseball. The problem is that the placard, which seeks to "call your special attention to this most important exhibit," is hung inside the exhibit itself. No patron can read it without having already made the decision to enter the exhibit. It's not drawing anyone in who wasn't already drawn.

Those flaws in the exhibit and the Hall's presentation of the history of Black baseball needed updating, particularly after the Negro Leagues were recognized as Major Leagues by Major League Baseball in 2020. The Black Baseball Initiative was launched in April 2022 to address those issues. "The National Baseball Hall of Fame's new initiative will provide greater depth to the stories of the Black baseball experience, including Black voices and interpretations, while incorporating new research that addresses society's evolving understanding of racism and its impact on the National Pastime—all while celebrating Black culture through the lens of baseball," said Rawitch in the Hall's press release announcing the initiative. Besides the new exhibit itself, the Hall also announced that stories about Black baseball would be integrated into the rest of the museum's existing exhibits, so that the dedicated exhibit

12. Another Effort, More Hope

would no longer be the only place in the museum where patrons could learn about Black baseball.[86]

The announcement also noted that an advisory board would be formed and would include representatives of Major League Baseball, the MLB Players Association, the Negro Leagues Baseball Museum, and Jackie Robinson Foundation and other organizations.[87] That board ultimately included people who were experts in the history of the Black baseball generally and the Negro Leagues in particular, some of whom, like Bob Kendrick, Larry Lester, and Joe Posnanski, had been critical of the Hall of Fame in the past for their handling of various aspects of Black baseball.[88] The initiative will also develop community outreach programs, and updates to the Hall of Fame's website and online exhibits, allowing them to tell the stories of Black baseball outside the walls of the Hall of Fame itself. That includes the development of virtual programs hosted on the museum's YouTube channel, part of Rawitch's commitment to expand the Hall's social media footprint.[89]

The timeline to complete the new exhibit and other changes was set at two years. In June 2023, Rawitch announced that the new exhibit would be named "The Souls of the Game: Voices of Black Baseball," a name taken from the book by W.E.B. Du Bois, *The Souls of Black Folk*.[90] "One of the main messages of Du Bois's book was that, in their status as free men and women, Black people needed to use all that was around them to invent, shape, and resurrect their own culture," said Dr. Gerald Early, a consultant to the Black Baseball Initiative. "By echoing Du Bois's book title, this exhibit emphasizes that message about the meaning of baseball for Black Americans. Baseball was not merely a sport for Blacks. It was an element, a brick, in building a culture. Baseball was about Blacks creating themselves anew as a free people, as Americans of African descent."[91] Rawitch added that everyone involved in the effort felt it was important to tell the story of Black baseball "through the voices and the words of those who have lived that experience."[92]

Part of the announcement noted that a principal donor to the new exhibit was the Yawkey Foundation, which had been established by the late Tom Yawkey and his wife, Jean.[93] No one involved mentioned the irony inherent in a display about Black baseball being funded by someone whose name had been removed from a street in Boston over his record in trying to keep Black players out of the Major Leagues. As with the cases of Frick, Garagiola, Feller, and others who had checkered histories regarding the integration of the game and the Hall of Fame, the involvement of the Yawkey Foundation represents another attempt at reputational redemption, even if the foundation's namesake was no longer living. These were all complex people, whose views about race and integration can't be encapsulated into a single act or period of time. Just as the Hall of Fame's representation of Black baseball has changed over time and continues to evolve, so, too, have the views and actions of many of the staunchest opponents of integrating baseball.

With the new administration at the Hall of Fame, and the Black Baseball Initiative they've launched, comes the hope that the Negro Leagues will finally be honored at the game's shrine in a manner befitting their importance. The hope that the story of Black baseball will be woven through the entire Hall of Fame instead of tucked into a room that visitors must consciously choose to enter. The hope that overlooked but deserving Negro Leagues players will finally be inducted, and the correct proportion of players from those leagues will finally be attained.

The Hall's statue of Satchel Paige currently sits outside on their grounds, behind the museum, literally facing one of the back doors he refused to go through (author's collection).

The hope that the great managers from the Negro Leagues, like Vic Harris and Dave Malarcher, will belatedly be recognized. The hope that Bob Motley, the great, flamboyant umpire, will properly join his brethren. The hope that the doors will be opened to remarkable players who excelled in other countries, like Sadaharu Oh, or the dozens of stars from Latin America whose greatness has not yet been recognized. The hope that the story of Cooperstown's homegrown Hall of Famer, Bud Fowler, will finally be truthfully told with the same vigor that the lie about Abner Doubleday was spread.

But, for now, it all remains just a hope. The Hall's beautiful statue to Satchel Paige is still outside, behind the museum, hidden from those who enter the Hall's main doors. Ol' Satch is captured mid-delivery, directly facing the literal back door to Cooperstown, about to throw his famous bee ball. Part of that hope is that one day soon he'll knock down that door, and the story of him and his fellow Negro Leaguers will finally be given its proper place inside.

Epilogue

THE INITIAL 35-YEAR DELAY by the Hall of Fame in recognizing players from the Negro Leagues has never fully been corrected. Had the decision in 1971 to finally admit Negro Leaguers been paired with a real plan, equity might have been achieved quickly. Instead that initial work was terminated prematurely, and the Veterans Committee that assumed the responsibility for properly recognizing the Negro Leagues simply didn't take that work seriously.

What followed was nearly two decades of the committee largely ignoring the Negro Leagues, choosing instead to continue packing the Hall of Fame with less talented White players and executives. When the Hall of Fame finally acted and mandated the annual election of at least one member of the Negro Leagues, the committee did the bare minimum. Some of its members and electors had the nerve to grumble at the perceived unfairness of being forced to elect players about whom they knew almost nothing because they hadn't taken the time to learn.

When the Hall of Fame tried one final dedicated effort to right the imbalance, the 2006 special committee that was formed devolved into factions, cut short their elections to avoid the impression of overreaching, and failed to elect anyone who was still alive to enjoy the honor. They even passed on the election of the Negro Leagues' most visible and beloved ambassador, Buck O'Neil, causing the widespread impression that they had failed to do their jobs.

And they had, of course. Even electing 17 new members from the Negro Leagues, nearly doubling Black baseball's representation in the Hall, they still failed to elect enough members to bring the total up to a representative proportion of the top professional players from that era. This situation was made worse by the Hall of Fame's subsequent decision to make individuals from the Negro Leagues ineligible for election for another 15 years after the committee's work was done.

The surest way to fix the systemic disproportion in the membership of the Hall of Fame is to have yet another special committee. It would be focused on the "Pre-Integration Era," as the Hall once sadly called it, that period from the beginning of professional baseball until its doors were finally broken back open for Black players in 1947. The committee would be comprised of historians and researchers and academics, like the 2006 Negro Leagues Special Committee.

Their task would be to identify everyone whose career took place primarily in that timeframe and deserves to be elected to the Hall of Fame. That would be every player, manager, umpire, executive, pioneer, journalist, broadcaster, and contributor. All Major Leagues would be included; American and National, Negro National and Negro American, the American Association and the Eastern Colored League. The Union Association and the second Negro National League. All of them. They would also consider the top leagues and teams that often aren't considered "major," but sometimes are. The traveling Black teams, the National Association, the House of David. The Society for American Baseball Research is currently undertaking an effort to review the top level of Black baseball that was played outside of the 1920–1948 window that was finally recognized as "major league" in 2020. It would make sense to wait until that effort is complete, so the committee would have more information and documentation to work with.

To ensure an equitable outcome, the committee would have an additional task: to have the final proportions of all the people elected from this period distributed across the various leagues and teams in proportion to the percentage of participants. For instance, if, as noted in Chapter 11, the proportion of rostered players in the White Major Leagues compared to the Negro Leagues was roughly two-to-one, then the number of Hall of Famers from that period should be distributed as close to that proportion as possible. If the proportion of players from the pre–Negro Leagues timeframe was 80-20 in favor of the White Major Leagues, then that should be the target proportion among the Hall of Famers from that period as well. This would include not only the individuals the committee elected, but also all current Hall of Famers from those time periods and leagues as well.

What I suspect would happen is that a great number of individuals from Black baseball and the Negro Leagues would be elected by the committee, not only because their proportions currently in the Hall of Fame are unfairly low, but also because the White leagues from this period have already been reviewed, and reviewed again, and picked over for decades. There will be some White players, managers and pioneers who deserve election but have somehow been passed over so far. Bad Bill Dahlen, for instance, or Doc Adams. But they will be few and far between compared to the new Black inductees who haven't remotely been afforded the same level of scrutiny.

Once the committee's work is done, the Hall of Fame should then close the books on this period. Maybe not permanently. In fact, probably not. New research is always being done that may unearth information that changes the way someone should be viewed. Who knows? Maybe someone will uncover a letter or diary that proves conclusively that Abner Graves was telling the truth all along, and Abner Doubleday should take his rightful place among the baseball pioneers enshrined in Cooperstown.

Those discoveries, however, would be rare. A new Era Committee that met only once every ten or twenty years should be sufficient to account for these outliers. Otherwise, the existing Era Committee structure could remain in place, changed only by the time periods they review. Both the Contemporary Era Committees would remain focused on the period from 1980 to the present. Over time, their starting point would shift away from 1980 to remain roughly forty or fifty years in the past, but otherwise they would be unchanged. The Classic Baseball Era Committee would shrink its focus to cover the years from 1947 through the point the Contemporary Era Committees took over. That makes their task far more manageable every three years. It also prevents their elections from again skewing the population of Hall of Famers from the period when separate Black teams and leagues had to be formed since they weren't welcome in the White Major Leagues.

Without an effort of this sort, it's unlikely the Hall of Fame will ever be able to boast of having a membership that includes a proportionate representation of Black players from the period before Jackie Robinson's debut. They will still be pushing the same myth that Stephen Clark and Alexander Cleland and Ford Frick pushed when the Hall's doors first opened in 1939. The myth that the White Major Leagues should have primacy of place in the new shrine, and that the Black players that bigotry forced into separate leagues aren't worthy of their fair share of the game's history.

Acknowledgments

IF YOU WRITE ABOUT BASEBALL, you probably owe a debt to the Society for American Baseball Research; SABR provides its members with writing opportunities they wouldn't find elsewhere, professional editing, a platform for their work, and research resources that are invaluable. All of this is particularly true for anyone researching the history of baseball, and the Negro Leagues in particular. It's likely that many veterans of the Negro Leagues were elected to the Hall of Fame primarily because of research done by dedicated members of SABR who found documentation of their careers and brought them to light. As a writer, but also as an advocate for the Negro Leagues and the proper telling of the history of Black baseball, I am indebted to SABR and its members. I am particularly grateful for the work done by Bill Nowlin in coordinating the SABR BioProject and two SABR book projects I've been lucky enough to collaborate upon, and John Fredland for his coordination of the SABR Games Project. Working on those SABR projects has allowed me to keep my research skills fresh and have my work read and reviewed by trusted baseball writers. They've made me a better writer and researcher, and it's appreciated.

Thank you to Joe Posnanski for being generous with his time in speaking to me about the book, and for giving me and the book a shout-out in one of his newsletter entries. His input was invaluable, and the exposure he provided for the book and my other writing by mentioning it to his enormous audience was something I will never be able to repay.

John Shestakofsky at the National Baseball Hall of Fame and Museum was very helpful in providing background information about the Hall of Fame's ongoing efforts related to their displays about Black baseball and the Negro Leagues. He shared articles and other materials about the Black Baseball Initiative that pointed me in interesting directions I hadn't anticipated. He also gave his perspective on the past steps the Hall of Fame had taken regarding the Negro Leagues, and how those steps informed the Hall's current leadership in their ongoing efforts to get those stories right. His input made for a more complete book than would otherwise have been the case, and I appreciate it.

Gary Mitchem at McFarland reached out to me about twenty years ago because I'd written several online pieces about one of his favorite players, Jim Rice. He offered me the chance to write a biography of Rice, an opportunity I promptly flubbed as the rest of my life intervened in my hopes to be a writer. When I reached back out to him in 2022 to see if he remembered me and would be interested in giving me a second chance, he was more welcoming and helpful than I could have dreamed. It's only through his willingness to give me not just one but two chances that this book became possible. I will always owe him more thanks than I could ever hope to adequately convey.

Have you ever been driving, following turn-by-turn GPS directions, and wondered to yourself how far we've come from the days of paper maps and road atlases from the American Automobile Association? If you're old enough to know what I'm talking about, then let me tell you that same feeling applies to baseball research since the creation of Baseball-Reference.com. The folks who built and maintain that site are the baseball equivalent of the rocket scientists who put the satellites into orbit for GPS systems to use. Baseball-Reference.com provides an unmatched service to all writers, historians, and just plain fans of baseball, and has saved people like me hundreds of hours of research time. If you see a statistic cited in these pages, or a Hall of Fame voting result, it came from Baseball-Reference. They are the gold standard for baseball stats, another ancient reference that dates me.

Finally, my family is the most important part of my life. They have not only provided me with the love and support needed to write this book, and the encouragement that I could do it, but also gave me a love of baseball that made me want to write about it in the first place. From my parents, Joe and Ann White, letting me stay up late to watch Game Six of the 1975 World Series, to my aunt, Mary Miller, bringing me to my first ballgame at Fenway Park. From playing ball with my older brother, Joe, to coaching my younger brother, Rich. From being scorekeeper for my son Sam's teams, and a fan for my daughters' softball teams. (Katie and Katie; yes, they're both named Katie.) From getting a Mookie Betts jersey for my birthday from my sister Jeannie and her husband Stu, to traveling the country to watch games in every Major League ballpark with my beloved wife, Shelley. My love for my family, and their love for me, has been the foundation for my love of baseball. That love is baked into these pages.

As usual, though all these folks provided immense support and guidance, any errors or omissions in the book are mine alone. There is not enough love in the world to stop me from fat-fingering a keyboard.

Chapter Notes

Chapter 1

1. George B. Kirsch, *Baseball in Blue and Gray: The National Pastime during the Civil War* (Princeton: Princeton University Press, 2003), x–xi.

2. Brian Martin, *Baseball's Creation Myth: Adam Ford, Abner Graves and the Cooperstown Story* (Jefferson, NC: McFarland, 2013), location 244.

3. John Thorn, *Baseball in the Garden of Eden: The Secret History of the Early Game* (New York: Simon & Schuster, 2011), 6–7.

4. James A. Vlasich, *A Legend for the Legendary: The Origin of the Baseball Hall of Fame* (Bowling Green: Bowling Green State University Popular Press, 1990), 133.

5. Victor Salvatore, "The Man Who Didn't Invent Baseball," *American Heritage*, June/July 1983, https://www.americanheritage.com/man-who-didnt-invent-baseball.

6. Salvatore, "The Man Who Didn't Invent Baseball."

7. Salvatore, "The Man Who Didn't Invent Baseball."

8. Thorn, *Baseball in the Garden of Eden: The Secret History of the Early Game*, 294.

9. Salvatore, "The Man Who Didn't Invent Baseball."

10. Vlasich, *A Legend for the Legendary*, 20.

11. National Park Service, "A Brief History," *NPS.gov*, https://www.nps.gov/poex/learn/historyculture/index.htm.

12. Salvatore, "The Man Who Didn't Invent Baseball."

13. Martin, *Baseball's Creation Myth*, location 244.

14. Martin, *Baseball's Creation Myth*, location 244.

15. Martin, *Baseball's Creation Myth*, location 271.

16. Martin, *Baseball's Creation Myth*, location 276.

17. Thorn, *Baseball in the Garden of Eden: The Secret History of the Early Game*, 3.

18. Martin, *Baseball's Creation Myth*, location 2244.

19. Martin, *Baseball's Creation Myth*, location 2388.

20. Thorn, *Baseball in the Garden of Eden: The Secret History of the Early Game*, 294–296.

21. Jay Jaffe, *The Cooperstown Casebook: Who's in the Baseball Hall of Fame, Who Should Be In, and Who Should Pack Their Plaques* (New York: Thomas Dunne, 2017), 29.

22. Brian McKenna, "Bud Fowler," *SABR.org*, https://sabr.org/bioproj/person/Bud-Fowler/.

23. That figure that hasn't changed substantially in the last 160 years, with the 2020 Census indicating that only 3 percent of the village's 1,794 residents are Black.

24. McKenna, "Bud Fowler."

25. McKenna, "Bud Fowler."

26. McKenna, "Bud Fowler."

Chapter 2

1. John George Taylor Spink, *Judge Landis and 25 Years of Baseball*, 4th Printing (Binghamton: Vail-Ballou Press, 1947), 104.

2. Jerome Holtzman, *No Cheering in the Press Box*, Expanded ed. (New York: Henry Holt, 1995), 54.

Notes—Chapter 3

3. Todd Peterson, ed., *The Negro Leagues Were Major Leagues: Historians Reappraise Black Baseball* (Jefferson, NC: McFarland, 2020), 83.

4. Ford C. Frick, *Games, Asterisks, and People: Memoirs of a Lucky Fan* (New York: Crown, 1973), 202.

5. Chris Lamb, *Conspiracy of Silence: Sportswriters and the Long Campaign to Desegregate Baseball* (Lincoln: University of Nebraska Press, 2012), 48.

6. Holtzman, *No Cheering in the Press Box*, 211.

7. Holtzman, *No Cheering in the Press Box*, 198.

8. Holtzman, *No Cheering in the Press Box*, 316–317.

9. Lamb, *Conspiracy*, 3.

10. Lamb, *Conspiracy*, 52.

11. "Tributes Paid Walt Johnson and Carl Hubbell," *The Sporting News*, February 15, 1934, 8.

12. John Graf, et al., *From Rube to Robinson: SABR's Best Articles on Black Baseball* (Phoenix: Society for American Baseball Research, 2020).

13. Wendell Smith, "Cincinnati Reds' Manager, Players Laud Negro Stars," *Pittsburgh Courier*, July 15, 1939, 13.

14. Frick, *Games, Asterisks, and People*, 94.

15. Frick, *Games, Asterisks, and People*, ix–x.

16. Wendell Smith, "General Public Must Be Changed," *Pittsburgh Courier*, February 25, 1939, 1 and 16.

17. Holtzman, *No Cheering in the Press Box*, 17–19.

18. Holtzman, *No Cheering in the Press Box*, 54.

19. Holtzman, *No Cheering in the Press Box*, 311.

20. Holtzman, *No Cheering in the Press Box*, 334.

21. Holtzman, *No Cheering in the Press Box*, 363.

22. John B. Holway, *Blackball Stars: Negro League Pioneers* (Westport, CT: Meckler, 1988), 24.

23. John George Taylor Spink, "Three and One," *The Sporting News*, June 7, 1934, 4.

24. Edgar G. Brands, "Between Innings," *The Sporting News*, June 18, 1931, 4.

25. Edgar G. Brands, "Between Innings," *The Sporting News*, August 25, 1932, 4.

26. Spink, *Judge Landis and 25 Years of Baseball*, 60.

27. Spink, *Judge Landis and 25 Years of Baseball*, 192.

Chapter 3

1. Lawrence D. Hogan, *Shades of Glory: The Negro Leagues and the Story of African-American Baseball* (Washington, D.C.: National Geographic Society, 2006), 46.

2. Benjamin Hill, "Full Circle: Bud Fowler Set for Hall Enshrinement," *MILB.com*, February 23, 2022, https://www.milb.com/news/bud-fowler-baseball-pioneer-and-hall-of-famer.

3. Thomas Kern, "John Henry 'Pop' Lloyd," *SABR.org*, https://sabr.org/bioproj/person/pop-lloyd/.

4. Alex Coffey, "Buck Leonard and Josh Gibson Are Elected to the Hall of Fame," *Baseballhall.org*, https://baseballhall.org/discover-more/stories/inside-pitch/buck-leonard-josh-gibson-elected-to-hof.

5. Jane Leavy, *The Big Fella: Babe Ruth and the World He Created* (New York: HarperCollins, 2018), 180.

6. Joe Posnanski, *The Baseball 100* (New York: Avid Reader Press, 2021), 707.

7. Posnanski, *The Baseball 100*, 707.

8. Posnanski, *The Baseball 100*, 724–735.

9. Spink, *Judge Landis*, 156–163.

10. Posnanski, *The Baseball 100*, 634.

11. Frank A. Young, "Dandridge as Good as Mel Ott at His Best," *Chicago Defender*, September 24, 1938, 9.

12. Young, "Dandridge."

13. Young, "Dandridge."

14. John Lardner, "Negro Ball Players Able Despite Major League Ban," *Edmonton Journal*, November 23, 1939, 7.

15. "Robeson Selects Colored All-Stars," *New York Daily News*, June 29, 1939, 126.

16. Cumberland Posey, "Cum Posey Turns Back Colorful Pages of Negro Baseball and Lists 8 of the Greatest Sepia Ball Clubs of All Time," *Pittsburgh Courier*, January 20, 1940, 17.

17. Lardner, "Negro Ball Players Able Despite Major League Ban."

Notes—Chapter 3

18. Leavy, *The Big Fella*, 319–320.

19. Associated Press, "Baseball's Black Pioneers Get 'Tip of the Cap' to Salute 100-Year Anniversary of Negro Leagues," *ESPN.com*, June 29, 2020, https://www.espn.com/mlb/story/_/id/29382314/baseball-black-pioneers-given-tip-cap-salute-100-year-anniversary-negro-leagues.

20. Smith, "General Public Must Be Changed."

21. Wendell Smith, "'No Need for Color Ban in Big Leagues'—Pie Traynor," *Pittsburgh Courier*, September 2, 1939, 16.

22. Donald Spivey, *If You Were Only White: The Life of Leroy "Satchel" Paige* (Columbia: University of Missouri Press, 2012), 358–359.

23. Smith, "General Public Must Be Changed."

24. Wendell Smith, "Owners Must Solve Color Problem in Majors—Stengel," *Pittsburgh Courier*, August 26, 1939, 16.

25. Frick, *Games, Asterisks, and People*, 94.

26. Wendell Smith, "Smitty's Sport Spurts," *Pittsburgh Courier*, December 10, 1938, 16.

27. Holtzman, *No Cheering in the Press Box*, 316–317.

28. Larry Lester, "Can You Read, Judge Landis?" *SABR.org*, https://sabr.org/journal/article/can-you-read-judge-landis/.

29. Holtzman, *No Cheering in the Press Box*, 315–316.

30. Frick, *Games, Asterisks, and People*, 94–95.

31. Holtzman, *No Cheering in the Press Box*, 316.

32. Lester, "Can You Read, Judge Landis?"

33. Lester, "Can You Read, Judge Landis?"

34. Hogan, *Shades of Glory*, 332.

35. Lester, "Can You Read, Judge Landis?"

36. John George Taylor Spink, "No Good From Raising Race Issue," *The Sporting News*, August 6, 1942, 4.

37. Neil Lanctot, *Campy: The Two Lives of Roy Campanella* (New York: Simon & Schuster, 2011), 86.

38. Associated Press, "Moguls Quiet on Landis' Negro Rule," *Dayton Journal-Herald*, July 18, 1942, 9.

39. John Lardner, "Landis Dumps Negro Play Into Major Bosses' Laps," *Omaha Evening World-Herald*, July 29, 1942, 16.

40. Hogan, *Shades of Glory*, 328.

41. Hogan, *Shades of Glory*, 329.

42. Lanctot, *Campy*, 85.

43. Lanctot, *Campy*, 85.

44. Lanctot, *Campy*, 86–87.

45. Lanctot, *Campy*, 80–81.

46. Joe Williams, "What Goes On?" *Pittsburgh Press*, July 27, 1942, 17.

47. Jaffe, *Cooperstown Casebook*, 96.

48. Bill Surface, "The Last Days of Rogers Hornsby," *The Saturday Evening Post*, June 15, 1963, 72.

49. Matt Cox, "Keep Baseball Going," *Baseballhall.org*, 2009, https://baseballhall.org/discover-more/stories/shortstops/keep-baseball-going.

50. Mark Z. Aaron and Bill Nowlin, eds., *Who's on First: Replacement Players in World War II* (Phoenix: Society for American Baseball Research, 2015), location 221.

51. Aaron and Nowlin, *Who's on First*, location 222.

52. Aaron and Nowlin, *Who's on First*, location 239.

53. Bill Veeck with Ed Linn, *Veeck as in Wreck: The Autobiography of Bill Veeck* (Chicago: University of Chicago Press, 2012), 171.

54. Veeck and Linn, *Veeck as in Wreck*, 171.

55. Veeck and Linn, *Veeck as in Wreck*, 171.

56. Veeck and Linn, *Veeck as in Wreck*, 171.

57. Larry Gerlach, David Jordan, and John Rossi, "A Baseball Myth Exploded: Bill Veeck and the 1943 Sale of the Phillies," *The National Pastime* 18 (1998), available at *SABR.org*, https://sabr.org/research/article/a-baseball-myth-exploded-bill-veeck-and-the-1943-sale-of-the-phillies/.

58. Jules Tygiel, "Revisiting Bill Veeck and the 1943 Phillies," *The Baseball Research Journal* (2006), 109.

59. Jaffe, *Cooperstown Casebook*, 380.

60. Jules Tygiel, *Baseball's Great Experiment: Jackie Robinson and His Legacy*

(New York: Oxford University Press, 2008), 182–185.

61. Jaffe, *Cooperstown Casebook*, 91.

62. Jaffe, *Cooperstown Casebook*, 91.

63. Tygiel, *Baseball's Great Experiment*, 42.

64. National Archives, "Executive Order 8802: Prohibition of Discrimination in the Defense Industry (1941)," *Archives.org*, https://www.archives.gov/milestone-documents/executive-order-8802.

65. Euell A. Nielsen, "The Double V Campaign (1942–1945)," *Blackpast.org*, July 1, 2020, https://www.blackpast.org/african-american-history/events-african-american-history/the-double-v-campaign-1942-1945/.

66. Tygiel, *Baseball's Great Experiment*, 43.

67. Glenn Stout, "Tryout and Fallout: Race, Jackie Robinson, and the Red Sox," *Massachusetts Historical Review* 6 (2004): 11–37, available at *Glennstout.com*, https://glennstout.com/tryout-and-fallout-race-jackie-robinson-and-the-red-sox/.

68. Tygiel, *Baseball's Great Experiment*, 43.

69. Howard Bryant, *Shut Out: A Story of Race and Baseball in Boston* (New York: Routledge, 2002), 37.

70. Bryant, *Shut Out*, 37.

71. Bryant, *Shut Out*, 38.

72. Bryant, *Shut Out*, 29.

73. Stout, "Tryout and Fallout."

74. Bryant, *Shut Out*, 28–29.

75. Bryant, *Shut Out*, 31.

76. Stout, "Tryout and Fallout."

77. Tygiel, *Baseball's Great Experiment*, 43–44.

78. Tygiel, *Baseball's Great Experiment*, 44.

79. Larry Whiteside, "The First to Play," *Boston Globe*, July 22, 1979, 41.

80. Whiteside, "The First to Play."

81. Whiteside, "The First to Play."

82. Hy Hurwitz, "Red Sox Sign Dolf Camilli; Metkovich May Play Outfield," *Boston Globe*, June 17, 1945, 20.

83. Hogan, *Shades of Glory*, 331.

84. Hogan, *Shades of Glory*, 342.

85. Hogan, *Shades of Glory*, 343.

86. Jeff Obermeyer, "The Business of Baseball During World War II," *SABR.org*, https://sabr.org/journal/article/the-business-of-baseball-during-world-war-ii/.

87. Obermeyer, "The Business of Baseball."

88. Murray Polner, *Branch Rickey: A Biography* (Jefferson, NC: McFarland, 2007), 171.

89. John Paul Hill, "Commissioner A.B. 'Happy' Chandler and the Integration of Major League Baseball: A Reassessment," *NINE, A Journal of Baseball History and Culture* 19, no. 1 (Fall 2010): 37.

90. Hogan, *Shades of Glory*, 343.

91. "The Ford C. Frick Award: A Disgraceful and Unnecessary Reminder of Major League Baseball's Racist Past," *Boomsalad.com*, August 26, 2021, http://www.boomsalad.com/english/nonfiction/fordfrickaward/.

92. Cox, "Keep Baseball Going."

93. He was also Joe Cronin's pseudo father-in-law. His niece, Mildred, who was being raised by Griffith and his wife after her parents' deaths, married his star player in 1934.

94. Bart Barnes, "Crusading Sportswriter Sam Lacy, 99, Dies," *Washington Post*, May 10, 2003, https://www.washingtonpost.com/archive/local/2003/05/10/crusading-sportswriter-sam-lacy-99-dies/14a5394b-cfa0-4b9a-85f2-87dda21976be/?utm_term=.ca781e1d0749.

95. Brad Snyder, "When Segregation Doomed Baseball in Washington," *Washington Post*, February 16, 2003, https://www.washingtonpost.com/archive/sports/2003/02/16/when-segregation-doomed-baseball-in-washington/90dfcd24-7414-4de9-affd-518faba3cd87/.

96. Kevin Hennessy, "Calvin Griffith," *SABR.org*, https://sabr.org/bioproj/person/calvin-griffith/.

Chapter 4

1. Frick, *Games, Asterisks, and People*, 97.

2. Tygiel, *Baseball's Great Experiment*, 186.

3. Frick, *Games, Asterisks, and People*, 97.

4. Harold Parrott, *The Lords of Baseball: A Wry Look at a Side of the Game*

Notes—Chapter 4

the Fan Seldom Sees—the Font Office (Atlanta: Longstreet Press, 2001), 242.

5. Tygiel, *Baseball's Great Experiment*, 182–183.

6. Tygiel, *Baseball's Great Experiment*, 202–204.

7. John George Taylor Spink, "The Negro Player Steps on the Scales," *The Sporting News*, May 21, 1947, 14.

8. Gordon Cobbledick, "Jockeys Ride Every Rookie," *The Sporting News*, May 21, 1947, 14.

9. Jonathan Eig, *Opening Day: The Story of Jackie Robinson's First Season* (New York: Simon & Schuster, 2007), 75.

10. Cobbledick, "Jockeys Ride Every Rookie."

11. Editorial, "Once Again, That Negro Question," *The Sporting News*, July 16, 1947, 16.

12. John George Taylor Spink "Two Ill-Advised Moves," *The Sporting News*, July 14, 1948, 8.

13. Spink, "Two Ill-Advised Moves."

14. Spink, "Two Ill-Advised Moves."

15. Gordon (Red) Marston, "Boston Debate—Pro and Con!" *The Sporting News*, August 4, 1948, 36.

16. Eig, *Opening Day*, 67.

17. "Dixie Action on Negroes Needed," *The Sporting News*, July 16, 1947, 15.

18. "The History of Baseball and Civil Rights in America," *Basbeallhall.org*, https://baseballhall.org/civilrights.

19. Arthur Daley, "Play Ball!" *New York Times*, April 15, 1947, 31.

20. Arthur Daley, "Opening Day at Ebbets Field," *New York Times*, April 16, 1947, 32.

21. Eig, *Opening Day*, 60.

22. Eig, *Opening Day*, 52.

23. Rick Swaine, *The Integration of Major League Baseball: A Team by Team History* (Jefferson, NC: McFarland, 2009), 6.

24. Burton W. Folsom, "The Costs of Segregation to the Detroit Tigers," *Fee. org*, https://fee.org/articles/the-costs-of-segregation-to-the-detroit-tigers/.

25. Bryant, *Shut Out*, 3.

26. Dan Cichalski, "April 14, 1955: Elston Howard integrates the Yankees," *SABR.org*, https://sabr.org/gamesproj/game/april-14-1955-elston-howard-integrates-the-yankees/.

27. Cichalski, "April 14, 1955."

28. Adrian Burgos, Jr., *Playing America's Game: Baseball, Latinos, and the Color Line* (Berkeley: University of California Press, 2007), 144.

29. Harvey Frommer, "Casey Stengel Remembered: A Baseball Icon and a Yankee Immortal." *Bleacherreport.com*, October 14, 2011, https://bleacherreport.com/articles/890508-casey-stengel-remembered-a-baseball-icon-and-a-yankee-immortal.

30. Swaine, *The Integration of Major League Baseball*, 122.

31. Ken Smith, *Baseball's Hall of Fame*, rev. ed. (New York: Grosset & Dunlap, 1970), 76.

32. Bill James, *Whatever Happened to the Hall of Fame? Baseball, Cooperstown, and the Politics of Glory* (New York: Simon & Schuster, 1995), 41.

33. Jaffe, *Cooperstown Casebook*, 91.

34. Dan Daniel, "Writers and League Heads to Confer on MV Balloting," *The Sporting News*, December 21, 1949, 16.

35. "An Extra Grand Grin—15 Grand," *The Sporting News*, December 21, 1949, 5.

36. Terry Bohn, "Happy Chandler," *SABR.org*, https://sabr.org/bioproj/person/happy-chandler/.

37. "Black Pioneer Jackie Robinson Dead," *The Sporting News*, November 11, 1972, 35.

38. "Wakefield Ruling Cost Job, Chandler Declares," *The Sporting News*, August 15, 1951, 7.

39. Holtzman, *No Cheering in the Press Box*, 201.

40. Bohn, "Happy Chandler."

41. Frank Graham, Jr., "Frick Favors Spitter Return," *The Sporting News*, November 2, 1949, 10.

42. Joe Posnanski, *Why We Love Baseball: A History in 50 Moments* (New York: Dutton, 2023), 153.

43. Eig, *Opening Day*, 94.

44. Eig, *Opening Day*, 63.

45. Warren Corbett, "Ford Frick," *SABR.org*, https://sabr.org/bioproj/person/ford-frick/.

46. United Press, "Making Players Ineligible is Blacklist Frick Admits," *St. Louis Post-Dispatch*, July 31, 1951, 29.

47. Parrott, *The Lords of Baseball*, 250.

48. Editorial, "Stop, Look and Listen, Jackie," *The Sporting News*, May 2, 1951, 12.

49. Lanctot, *Campy*, 247.

50. Lanctot, *Campy*, 249.

51. Smith, "General Public Must Be Changed."

52. Frick, *Games, Asterisks, and People*, 102.

53. David Bohmer, "Ford Frick and Jackie Robinson: The Enabler," *SABR.org*, https://sabr.org/journal/article/ford-frick-and-jackie-robinson-the-enabler/.

54. John Paul Hill, "Commissioner A.B. 'Happy' Chandler and the Integration of Major League Baseball: A Reassessment," *NINE, A Journal of Baseball History and Culture* 19, no. 1 (Fall 2010): 31.

55. PFC Frederick M. Leigh, "Colored GIs Distinguish Selves in Bombay Meet," *Baltimore Afro-American*, May 5, 1945, 18.

56. Tygiel, *Baseball's Great Experiment*, 295.

57. "Bavasi Berates Bombers," *New York Times*, December 3, 1952, 47.

58. Jackie Robinson, *I Never Had It Made* (New York: HarperCollins, 1995), 101.

59. Bohmer, "Ford Frick and Jackie Robinson."

60. Eig, *Opening Day*, 220.

61. Phil S. Dixon, *The Dizzy and Daffy Dean Barnstorming Tour: Race, Media, and America's National Pastime* (Lanham, MD: Rowman & Littlefield, 2019), location 51.

62. Wendell Smith, "St. Louis Pilot, Players Friendly, Helpful to Jackie," *Pittsburgh Courier*, June 21, 1947, 14.

63. Smith, "St. Louis Pilot."

64. Eig, *Opening Day*, 229.

65. "Buck O'Neil Award," *Baseball hall.org*, https://baseballhall.org/discover-more/awards/890.

66. Paula Boivin, "Garagiola Embodies Award He Will Receive," *Arizona Republic*, July 24, 2014, C1.

67. Eig, *Opening Day*, 266.

68. Eig, *Opening Day*, 46.

69. Eig, *Opening Day*, 211.

70. Eig, *Opening Day*, 211.

71. Eig, *Opening Day*, 75.

72. John George Taylor Spink, "Rookie of the Year ... Jackie Robinson," *The Sporting News*, September 17, 1947, 3.

73. Lanctot, *Campy*, 208.

74. Scott Simon, *Jackie Robinson and the Integration of Baseball* (Hoboken: John Wiley & Sons, 2002), 93.

75. Eric Nusbaum, "The Story Behind Jackie Robinson's Moving Testimony Before the House Un-American Activities Committee," *Time.com*, March 24, 2020, https://time.com/5808543/jackie-robinson-huac/.

76. Johnny Smith, "Jackie Robinson Was Asked to Denounce Paul Roberson. Instead, He Went after Jim Crow," *Andscape.com*, April 15, 2019, https://andscape.com/features/jackie-robinson-was-asked-to-denounce-paul-robeson-before-huac-instead-he-went-after-jim-crow/.

77. Eig, *Opening Day*, 272.

78. Luke Epplin, *Our Team: The Epic Story of Four Men and the World Series That Changed Baseball* (New York: Flatiron Books, 2021), 27–28.

79. Epplin, *Our Team*, 47.

80. Epplin, *Our Team*, 48.

81. Spivey, *If You Were Only White*, 403–404.

82. Jack Curry, "Bob Feller: Lots of Words, Plus a Ride to the Airport," *NYTimes.com*, June 23, 2008, https://archive.nytimes.com/bats.blogs.nytimes.com/2008/06/23/bob-feller-lots-of-words-plus-a-ride-to-the-airport/.

83. Posnanski, *Baseball 100*, 315.

84. Jack Curry, "Going Back, Back, Back to 1939," *NYTimes.com*, June 23, 2008, https://www.nytimes.com/2008/06/23/sports/baseball/23allstar.html.

85. Posnanski, *Baseball 100*, 309.

86. Epplin, *Our Team*, 86.

87. Dennis Manoloff, "Bob Feller at 91: 'Living legend? It's a term I respect and appreciate,'" *Cleveland.com*, April 4, 2010, https://www.cleveland.com/tribe/2010/04/bob_feller_at_91_living_legend.html.

88. Manoloff, "Bob Feller at 91."

89. Manoloff, "Bob Feller at 91."

90. Posnanski, *Baseball 100*, 309.

91. Epplin, *Our Team*, 86.

92. Vincent X. Flaherty, "Feller Doubts Robinson Future," *Akron Beacon Journal*, October 27, 1945, 12.

93. Steve George, "250,000 See Feller-Paige Teams Play," *The Sporting News*, October 30, 1946, 9.

94. Epplin, *Our Team*, 139.

95. Epplin, *Our Team*, 138.

Notes—Chapter 5

96. Epplin, *Our Team*, 137.

97. Epplin, *Our Team*, 177.

98. Hy Hurwitz, "Anti-Feller Bloc Grows; Red Sox Join," *Boston Globe*, July 13, 1948, 18.

99. Oscar Fraley, "Feller Saddest Man in Series," *Wichita Falls Times*, October 12, 1948, 11.

100. Epplin, *Our Team*, 290.

101. Simon, *Jackie Robinson and the Integration of Baseball*, 154.

102. Bob Feller with Edward Linn, "The Trouble with the Hall of Fame," *The Saturday Evening Post*, January 27, 1962, 49–50.

103. Feller and Linn, "The Trouble with the Hall of Fame," 50.

104. Feller and Linn, "The Trouble with the Hall of Fame," 51.

105. Feller and Linn, "The Trouble with the Hall of Fame," 50–51.

106. Sec Taylor, "Sittin' in with the Athletes," *Des Moines Register*, February 1, 1961, 12.

107. Jim Murray, "Feller Wanted In, But His Way," *Arizona Republic*, January 28, 1962, 46.

108. Ed Nichols, "Paige, Ineligible, Deserves to Be in Hall," *The Salisbury Daily Times*, February 2, 1962, 14.

109. Walter L. Johns, "Sports Sputterings," *The Hammond Times*, February 7, 1962, 47.

110. David Condon, "In the Wake of the News," *Chicago Tribune*, July 9, 1963, 39.

111. Feller and Linn, "The Trouble with the Hall of Fame," 51.

Chapter 5

1. Ben Bradlee, Jr., *The Kid: The Immortal Life of Ted Williams* (New York: Little, Brown, 2013), 504.

2. Bradlee, *The Kid*, 504.

3. Bradlee, *The Kid*, 504.

4. James, *Whatever Happened to the Hall of Fame?*, 185.

5. Bradlee, *The Kid*, 503.

6. Drew Silva, "Throwback: Ted Williams' Hall of Fame Speech." *NBCSports.com*, July 27, 2104, https://www.nbcsports.com/mlb/news/throwback-ted-williams-hall-of-fame-speech.

7. "'The Splendid Splinter' Is En-shrined in Cooperstown," YouTube video, 3:00, posted by MLB, December 12, 2013, https://youtu.be/Yi8ukM_NCf4?si=O1GmTqqq9yup7mJ5.

8. Bradlee, *The Kid*, 508.

9. Joe Posnanski, "Ted and Satchel," *Joeposnanski.substack.com*, October 10, 2021, https://joeposnanski.substack.com/p/ted-and-satchel.

10. Bryant, *Shut Out*, 66.

11. Bradlee, *The Kid*, 509.

12. "Ted Williams (Part One of Three)," YouTube video, 14:19, posted by MyyyClips, September 21, 2010, https://youtu.be/DeiNQqMyQ_k?si=jOovhlRAp6t5Z-um.

13. Joe McGuff, "Sporting Comment," *Kansas City Star*, July 26, 1966, 11.

14. Will McDonough, "Ted Awes Cooperstown Crowd," *Boston Globe*, July 26, 1966, 1.

15. Jerry Nason, "Joss Deserves Place in 'Hall,'" *Boston Globe*, July 27, 1966, 29.

16. Nason, "Joss Deserves Place in 'Hall.'"

17. Francis Storrs, "Boston's Best Feuds," *BostonMagazine.com*, December 28, 2009, https://www.bostonmagazine.com/2009/12/28/bostons-best-feuds/.

18. Bradlee, *The Kid*, 506.

19. Bradlee, *The Kid*, 506.

20. Bradlee, *The Kid*, 507.

21. Shirley Povich, "This Morning...," *Washington Post*, July 26, 1966) B1.

22. Dick Young, "Young Ideas," *The Sporting News*, August 6, 1966, 14.

23. Bud Burns, "Splinter Group, Led by Ted, Seeks Hall Shift," *Nashville Tennessean*, July 31, 1966, 5-C.

24. "Ted Williams Strikes Again," *The Vancouver Sun*, August 3, 1966, 5.

25. David Condon, "In the Wake of the News," *Chicago Tribune*, January 21, 1967, 45.

26. Ric Roberts, "Ted Urges Naming Josh, Satch to Shine," *Pittsburgh Courier*, August 6, 1966, 15.

27. "Williams Wants Paige, Gibson Named to 'Hall,'" *Alexandria News Leader*, August 14, 1966, 8.

28. Wendell Smith, "Sports Beat," *Pittsburgh Courier*, January 21, 1967, 15.

29. Joseph Durso, "Frick, in Last Year, Warns Big Leagues," *New York Times*, January 3, 1965, 2.

30. Dan Daniel, "Writers and League

Notes—Chapter 5

Heads to Confer on MV Balloting," *The Sporting News*, December 21, 1949, 16.

31. Condon, "In the Wake of the News."

32. Stan Isaacs, "Satchel Paige Belongs in the Hall of Fame," *Newsday*, January 23, 1967, 83.

33. Steve Jacobson, "The Voting Doesn't Always Do Justice," *Newsday*, March 1, 1967, 158.

34. "Indianapolis Clowns Here Wednesday," *Burlington Daily Times-News*, May 23, 1967, 10.

35. David Condon, "In the Wake of the News," *Chicago Tribune*, June 26, 1967, 61.

36. David Condon, "In the Wake of the News," *Chicago Tribune*, April 20, 1968, 71.

37. "Pioneering Rube Foster 'Saved' Major Leagues," *Pittsburgh Courier*, May 18, 1968, 15.

38. "Two Great Eras of Marvels Preceded Robinson's Years," *Pittsburgh Courier*, May 18, 1968, 15.

39. A.S. "Doc" Young, "Season for Nostalgia," *Chicago Defender*, May 17, 1967, 28.

40. Claude E. Harrison, Jr., "Josh Gibson Rated No. One Slugger by Satchel Paige," *Philadelphia Tribune*, September 3, 1968, 16.

41. Sheep Jackson, "From the Sidelines," *Cleveland Call and Post*, April 27, 1968, 9B.

42. Obituary, "C.C. Johnson Spink of the Sporting News Dies," *St. Louis Post-Dispatch*, March 27, 1992, 3A.

43. Leonard Koppett, "Baseball's Bias is Subtle, Disturbing," *The Sporting News*, March 21, 1970, 4.

44. Editorial, "Jackie's Voice Missed at Cooperstown," *The Sporting News*, August 12, 1967, 14.

45. Dick Young, "Young Ideas," *New York Daily News*, July 26, 1966, 55.

46. Young, "Young Ideas," *The Sporting News*, August 6, 1966, 14.

47. Dick Young, "Young Ideas," *New York Daily News*, September 1, 1965, C26.

48. Dick Young, "Young Ideas," *New York Daily News*, November 11, 1965, 116.

49. Dick Young, "Young Ideas," *New York Daily News*, November 26, 1965, C26.

50. Dick Young, "Young Ideas," *New York Daily News*, December 3, 1965, 101.

51. Dick Young, "Young Ideas," *New York Daily News*, December 19, 1965), 37C.

52. Dick Young, "Young Ideas," *New York Daily News*, January 13, 1966, 62.

53. Dana Mozley, "Revised Rule to Open Door to Fame Hall for Stengel," *New York Daily News*, January 31, 1966, 46.

54. Dick Young, "Young Ideas," *New York Daily News*, February 6, 1966, 31.

55. Dick Young, "First Division for Mets? Why Not? Barks Casey," *New York Daily News*, March 5, 1966, 27.

56. Dick Young, "Young Ideas," *New York Daily News*, March 6, 1966, 137.

57. Dick Young, "Special Vote Places Casey in Fame Hall," *New York Daily News*, March 9, 1966, C26.

58. Dick Young, "Young Ideas," *New York Daily News*, March 9, 1966, C30.

59. Dick Young, "Young Ideas," *New York Daily News*, March 12, 1966, 52.

60. Dick Young, "Young Ideas," *New York Daily News*, April 2, 1966, 33.

61. Dick Young, "Young Ideas," *New York Daily News*, April 17, 1966, 151.

62. Dick Young, "Young Ideas," *New York Daily News*, April 20, 1966, C26.

63. Eig, *Opening Day*, 199–200.

64. Lanctot, *Campy*, 168.

65. Lanctot, *Campy*, 168.

66. Lanctot, *Campy*, 358.

67. Robinson, *I Never Had It Made*, 93.

68. Eig, *Opening Day*, 201.

69. David Maraniss, *Clemente: The Passion and Grace of Baseball's Last Hero* (New York: Simon & Schuster, 2006, Kindle), 248.

70. Eig, *Opening Day*, 201.

71. Young, "Young Ideas," April 20, 1966.

72. Burgos, *Playing America's Game*, 144.

73. Smith, "'Owners Must Solve Color Problem in Majors—Stengel."

74. Frommer, "Casey Stengel Remembered."

75. Steven Goldman, "On Jackie Robinson Day, the Yankees must answer for Jim Crow Baseball," *Pinstripealley.com*, April 15, 2013, https://www.pinstripealley.com/2013/4/15/4228172/jackie-robinson-day-new-york-yankees-vic-power-elston-howard.

76. Young, "Young Ideas," April 20, 1966.

Notes—Chapter 6

77. Young, "Young Ideas," July 26, 1966.

78. Dick Young, "Young Ideas," *New York Daily News*, August 17, 1968, 31.

79. Dick Young, "Jackie, Feller in Racial Debate," *New York Daily News*, July 23, 1969, 89.

80. Associated Press, "Negro Hall-of-Famers Possibilities Extended," *Indianapolis Star*, July 29, 1969, 21.

81. Dick Young, "Campy, 'The Man,' Hoyt, Coveleski Deck the Hall," *New York Daily News*, July 29, 1969, 58.

82. Dick Young, "Young Ideas," *New York Daily News*, July 30, 1969, 81.

83. Young, "Young Ideas," July 30, 1969.

84. Bowie Kuhn, *Hardball: The Education of a Baseball Commissioner* (Lincoln: University of Nebraska Press, 1997), 3–7.

85. Kuhn, *Hardball*, 12–13.

86. Kuhn, *Hardball*, 16–17.

87. Kuhn, *Hardball*, 15.

88. Bob Luke, *Willie Wells: "El Diablo" of the Negro Leagues* (Austin: University of Texas Press, 2007), location 1965.

89. Kuhn, *Hardball*, 109.

90. Kuhn, *Hardball*, 110.

91. Bob Broeg, "New Book Traces History of Black Baseball," *St. Louis Post-Dispatch*, April 26, 1970, 2E.

92. Stan Isaacs, "The First Black Manager: Who? When?" *Newsday*, April 24, 1970, 49.

93. Robert Peterson, *Only the Ball Was White: A History of Legendary Black Players and All-Black Professional Teams* (New York: Oxford University Press, 1970), 253.

94. Peterson, *Only the Ball Was White*, 253.

95. Peterson, *Only the Ball Was White*, 254.

96. Peterson, *Only the Ball Was White*, 254.

97. Peterson, *Only the Ball Was White*, 254.

98. Kuhn, *Hardball*, 109.

99. Kuhn, *Hardball*, 110.

100. Jackie Robinson, *Baseball Has Done It* (Brooklyn: IG Publishing, 2005), 101.

101. Kuhn, *Hardball*, 110.

102. Kuhn, *Hardball*, 110.

103. Luke, *Willie Wells*, 107.

104. Gabe Buonauro, "How Wide Will Hall of Fame Open Its Gates?" *The Record*, July 3, 1970, B-7.

105. Luke, *Willie Wells*, 111.

106. John B. Holway, *Black Giants* (Springfield, VA: Lord Fairfax Press, 2010, Kindle), 7.

107. Buonauro, "How Wide Will Hall of Fame Open Its Gates?"

108. Robinson, *Baseball Has Done It*, 111.

109. Luke, *Willie Wells*, 111.

110. Steven R. Greenes, *Negro Leaguers and the Hall of Fame: The Case for Inducting 24 Overlooked Ballplayers* (Jefferson, NC: McFarland, 2020, Kindle), 20.

111. Greenes, *Negro Leaguers and the Hall of Fame*, 21.

Chapter 6

1. Luke, *Willie Wells*, 111.

2. Kuhn, *Hardball*, 110.

3. Holway, *Black Giants*, 7.

4. Joseph Durso, "Baseball to Admit Negro Stars," *New York Times*, February 4, 1971, 42.

5. Luke, *Willie Wells*, 112.

6. Buonauro, "How Wide Will Hall of Fame Open Its Gates?"

7. Holway, *Black Giants*, 6.

8. Phil Pepe, "Old Negro Greats Get Crack at Hall of Fame," *New York Daily News*, February 4, 1971, 91.

9. Associated Press, "Old Negro Stars Become Eligible for Baseball Shrine," *Hartford Courant*, February 4, 1971, 24.

10. Luke, *Willie Wells*, 112.

11. "Satch, Josh & Co. ... Color 'Em Great," *New York Daily News*, February 4, 1971, 12.

12. Associated Press, "Old Negro Stars Become Eligible For Baseball Shrine."

13. Greenes, *Negro Leaguers and the Hall of Fame*, 25.

14. Phil Pepe, "Ol' Satch Makes Hall of Fame, Natch," *New York Daily News*, February 10, 1971, C26.

15. Pepe, "Ol' Satch Makes Hall of Fame, Natch."

16. Dick Young, "Young Ideas," *New York Daily News*, February 4, 1971, 23C.

17. Arthur Daley, "Sport of the Times," *New York Times*, February 10, 1971, 52.

18. Luke, *Willie Wells*, 114.

194 Notes—Chapter 7

19. Milton Gross, "Jackie Robinson Raps Plan to Add Old Negroes to Hall," *Omaha World-Herald*, February 5, 1971, 25.

20. Gross, "Jackie Robinson Raps Plan to Add Old Negroes to Hall."

21. Joe McGuff, "Sporting Comment," *Kansas City Star*, February 9, 1971, 7.

22. Editorial, "'Old Satch' Joins the Stars," *Detroit Free Press*, February 15, 1971, 6.

23. Hal Wood, "Satch Makes It by Back Door," *The Honolulu Advertiser*, February 10, 1971, 53.

24. Jim Murray, "Back Door to Hall of Fame," *Modesto Bee*, February 16, 1971, 18.

25. Pepe, "Ol' Satch Makes Hall of Fame, Natch."

26. William Weinbaum, "50 Years Ago, Major League Baseball Stumbled Before Inducting Satchel Paige to the Hall of Fame," *Andscape.com*, August 9, 2021, https://andscape.com/features/50-years-ago-major-league-baseball-stumbled-before-inducting-satchel-paige-into-the-hall-of-fame/.

27. Hogan, *Shades of Glory*, xviii.

28. Kuhn, *Hardball*, 110–111.

29. Red Smith, "Racism Hasn't Disappeared from Baseball's Memory," *Hartford Courant*, February 24, 1971, 29.

30. David Condon, "In the Wake of the News," *Chicago Tribune*, February 5, 1971, 49.

31. Kuhn, *Hardball*, 110.

32. "BL-175.2003, Folder 1, Fancorr_1971_02_23," *Basbeallhall.org*, https://baseballhall.org/discover-more/digital-collection/1543.

33. Charles T. Grigsby, "Whitney Young Was Killed, Too," *Boston Globe*, April 5, 1971, 14.

34. Robert Peterson, "Josh Gibson Was the Equal of Babe Ruth, But," *New York Times*, April 11, 1971, SM12.

35. Ira Berkow, "Hall of Shame—Wynn," *Abilene Reporter-News*, April 14, 1971, 9-A.

36. Robin Miller, "Jackie Robinson 'Fights' Drugs," *Indianapolis Star*, April 17, 1971, 28.

37. Dick Young, "Young Ideas," *New York Daily News*, June 11, 1971, 83.

38. James, *Whatever Happened to the Hall of Fame?*, 188.

39. United Press, "Hall of Fame to Move Satchel Paige into Its Regular Lineup Next Month," *Evansville Press*, July 7, 1971, 34.

40. Spivey, *If You Were Only White*, 663.

41. Larry Tye, *Satchel: The Life and Times of an American Legend* (New York: Random House, 2009), 269–270.

Chapter 7

1. James, *Whatever Happened to the Hall of Fame?*, 162–163.

2. Mark Armour and Daniel R. Levitt, "Baseball Demographics, 1947–2016," *SABR.org*, https://sabr.org/bioproj/topic/baseball-demographics-1947-2016/.

3. Luke, *Willie Wells*, 107.

4. Luke, *Willie Wells*, 112.

5. "Too Few Black Baseball Greats in Hall: Powell," *Chicago Daily Defender*, August 12, 1972, 41.

6. "Junk Negro Shrine Vote, Says Young," *The Sporting News*, March 15, 1975, 51.

7. Luke, *Willie Wells*, 118.

8. Luke, *Willie Wells*, 119.

9. John Holway, "Shutting the Door on Negro League Stars," *New York Times*, July 31, 1977, 151.

10. Holway, *Blackball Stars*, viii.

11. Holway, *Black Giants*, 7.

12. Luke, *Willie Wells*, 119.

13. Greenes, *Negro Leaguers and the Hall of Fame*, 25.

14. Holway, *Black Giants*, 8.

15. "Junk Negro Shrine Vote, Says Young."

16. Greenes, *Negro Leaguers and the Hall of Fame*, 26.

17. Holway, "Shutting the Door on Negro League Stars."

18. "Satch, Josh & Co. ... Color 'Em Great."

19. Jim Smith, "Limit Set on Negro Leagues' Famers," *Newsday*, February 4, 1977, 92.

20. Dick Young, "Young Ideas," *New York Daily News*, August 9, 1977, 55.

21. Bill Nack, "Nine Is Not Nearly Enough for Recognition of Blacks," *Newsday*, August 11, 1977, 129.

22. Young, "Young Ideas," August 9, 1977.

Notes—Chapter 8

23. Jack Lang, "Treaty by Hall Voters," *The Sporting News*, February 17, 1973, 39.

24. James, *Whatever Happened to the Hall of Fame?*, 165.

25. C.C. Johnson Spink, "We Believe...," *The Sporting News*, September 1, 1977, 14.

26. Bob Broeg, "Doubting Writer Hopes Mize Is All Through As Hitter," *St. Louis Post-Dispatch*, August 14, 1977, 2B.

27. Associated Press, "Hall of Fame Picks Might Be Changed," *Hartford Courant*, August 8, 1977, 47.

28. Associated Press, "Hall Restricts Entries," *Oakland Tribune*, October 4, 1977, 26.

29. Associated Press, "Hall Restricts Entries."

30. Greenes, *Negro Leaguers and the Hall of Fame*, 33.

31. John Holway, "Blacks Losers Only at Hall of Fame," *Boston Globe*, August 4, 1978, 14–15.

Chapter 8

1. Peterson, *Only the Ball Was White*, 223.

2. Lanctot, *Campy*, 25.

3. Dandridge batted .362 for Minneapolis in 1949, played multiple infield positions, and was right-handed. He was never promoted. His teammate, Jack Hughes, batted .348 for Minneapolis in 1949, also played multiple infield positions, and was right-handed. He was promoted to the Giants the following year. In 1950, Dandridge batted .311 for the Millers while fellow right-handed infielder Davey Williams batted .280, yet it was Williams who was promoted to the Giants the following year and spent five seasons in New York. In 1951, Dandridge hit .324 in Minneapolis without receiving a promotion, while teammate Bobby Hofman batted .291 and was brought up New York the next season. In 1952, his average slipped to .291, which was still better than teammates Billy Gardner and Ron Samford, both of whom were eventually promoted to the big leagues.

4. "Satch, Josh & Co. ... Color 'Em Great."

5. Will Grimsley, "Should Hall of Fame include Rizzuto?" *Sioux City Journal*, May 15, 1983, 10.

6. Holway, "Blacks Losers Only at Hall of Fame."

7. Herbert Sparrow, "Cooperstown Neglecting Black Stars," *Owensboro-Messenger-Inquirer*, June 25, 1980, 13.

8. Associated Press, "Black Baseball Players Basking in Limelight That Once Evaded Them," *Charlotte News*, June 25, 1980, 53.

9. Associated Press, "Hall of Fame a Dream for Negro League Star Page," *Owensboro Messenger-Inquirer*, August 12, 1979, 32.

10. Jay Weiner, "Negro Leagues' Players Overlooked," *Newsday*, January 13, 1980, 268.

11. Lanctot, *Campy*, 178.

12. Holway, "Blacks Losers Only at Hall of Fame."

13. Holway, "Blacks Losers Only at Hall of Fame."

14. United Press, "Irvin, Paige Top Negro All-Star Team," *Newport News Daily Press*, June 27, 1982, 38.

15. Holway, "Blacks Losers Only at Hall of Fame."

16. Vlasich, *A Legend for the Legendary*, 203–204.

17. Buck O'Neil, with Steve Wulf and David Conrads, *I Was Right on Time: My Journey From the Negro Leagues to the Majors* (New York: Simon & Schuster, 1996), 40.

18. O'Neil, *I Was Right on Time*, 26.

19. O'Neil, *I Was Right on Time*, 141.

20. O'Neil, *I Was Right on Time*, 5.

21. Bill Ford, "Negro Leagues Find Fame in Greenup, Ky," *Cincinnati Enquirer*, June 20, 1979, 51.

22. Ford, "Negro Leagues Find Fame in Greenup, Ky."

23. D.G. FitzMaurice, "Past and Future: Black Baseball Stars from Another Era Gather in Greenup to Relive Old Times," *Lexington Herald-Leader*, July 4, 1979, 1.

24. Associated Press, "Memorable Time for Forgotten Stars," *Honolulu Star-Bulletin*, July 4, 1979, 46.

25. D.G. FitzMaurice, "Negro League Reunion Will Honor Greenup's Thomas," *Lexington Herald-Leader*, July 1, 1979, 24.

26. Associated Press, "Love of Baseball Draws Old Timers," *Nashville Tennessean*, July 6, 1979, 56.

Notes—Chapter 9

27. Tovia Smith, "Boston Changes 'Yawkey Way' to 'Jersey Street' After Concerns Over Racist Legacy," *NPR.org*, April 26, 2018, https://www.npr.org/2018/04/26/605851052/boston-red-sox-want-to-strike-former-owners-name-off-street-sign.

28. United Press, "Klein, Yawkey in Hall of Fame," *Philadelphia Daily News*, March 12, 1980, 63.

29. United Press, "Focus on Manley at Players Reunion," *Nashville Tennessean*, June 17, 1980, 10.

30. Herbert Sparrow, "Limelight Finally Finds Negro League Star," *Owensboro Messenger-Inquirer*, June 25, 1980, 15.

31. Sparrow, "Cooperstown Neglecting Black Stars."

32. Associated Press, "Black baseball Players Basking in Limelight That Once Evaded Them."

33. Herbert Sparrow, "Negro Baseball Hall of Fame proposed," *Biloxi-Gulfport Sun Herald*, June 25, 1980, 43.

34. United Press, "Irvin, Paige Top Negro All-Star Team."

35. Associated Press, "Black Baseball Players Honor Forgotten Generation," *Miami Herald*, November 7, 1980, 96.

36. Associated Press, "Negro Baseball Hall of History to open," *Hanford Sentinel*, April 27, 1981, 8.

37. Associated Press, "Black Baseball Players Honor Forgotten Generation."

38. Owen Canfield, "Mays Says Thanks to Black Leagues," *Hartford Courant*, June 25, 1981, 67.

39. Canfield, "Mays Says Thanks to Black Leagues."

40. Associated Press, "Negro League Museum Starts in White Woman's Cottage," *Birmingham Post-Herald*, June 21, 1982, B7.

41. Associated Press, "Kuhn Vows to Keep Negro Leagues Fight," *Salisbury Daily Times*, November 5, 1983, 11.

42. Associated Press, "Kuhn Vows to Keep Negro Leagues Fight."

43. Associated Press, "Negro League Hall of History heading for Cooperstown," *Kansas City Times*, June 20, 1988, D-5.

44. Associated Press, "Negro League Hall of History heading for Cooperstown."

45. Kuhn, *Hardball*, 112.

46. Brian Burnes, "At the old ballpark," *Kansas City Star*, April 2, 1984, 1 and 5.

47. Editorial, "Jazz and More," *Kansas City Star*, September 19, 1985, 18.

48. Burnes, "At the Old Ballpark."

49. Don Wade, "In Memories Yet Green...," *Kansas City Times*, April 6, 1985, C1 and C3.

50. James Kuhnhenn, "City Gets Grant to Boost Jazz District," *Kansas City Times*, June 12, 1986, 22.

51. O'Neil, *I Was Right on Time*, 88.

52. O'Neil, *I Was Right on Time*, 75–76.

Chapter 9

1. "Ted Williams (Part One of Three)," YouTube video.

2. Ritter Collett, "Black Promoter Ends Retirement," *Dayton Journal Herald*, May 20, 1986, 19.

3. O'Neil, *I Was Right on Time*, 238.

4. O'Neil, *I Was Right on Time*, 226–227.

5. Burnes, "At the Old Ballpark."

6. Ward W. Triplett, III, "Men Find Heroes in Research of Negro Leagues," *Kansas City Star*, December 31, 1985, 46.

7. Ford, "Negro Leagues Find Fame in Greenup, Ky."

8. Burns later updated *Baseball* with two additional episodes released in 2010.

9. Richard Sandomir, "Hits, Runs and Memories," *New York Times*, September 18, 1994, 2–1.

10. Jennifer L. Stevenson, "Buck O'Neil Not Only Talks a Good Game," *Tampa Bay Times*, September 18, 1994, 1F.

11. Larry Shores, "Baseball—Looking for Answers," *Muncie Star*, September 24, 1994, 8A.

12. Editorial, "Finding Our Story," *Ventura County Star*, September 29, 1994, D1.

13. Bill Chastain, "Voice of Baseball," *Tampa Tribune*, October 1, 1994, 1.

14. Ray Routhier, "Burns' Boner: 'Baseball' Forgot to Touch Home," *Portland Press Herald*, October 2, 1994, 12E.

15. Bob Keisser, "Anchor Cries Foul Ball," *Newport News Daily Press*, October 1, 1994) B6.

Notes—Chapter 10

16. *Baseball*, directed by Ken Burns, National Endowment for the Humanities, 1994, Episode 4, 30:52.

17. Gail Pennington, "Ken Burns' 'Baseball': That's a Winner (Sort Of)," *St. Louis Post-Dispatch*, October 6, 1994, 6G.

18. "On Good Clean Fun, Long Hair and So Forth...," *Des Moines Register*, October 9, 1994, 11D.

19. Jim Auchmutey, "'Being Around Him Just Makes You Feel Better,'" *Atlanta Journal*, September 21, 1994, D4.

20. "New Museum Pitches Flavor of Negro Leagues," *Arizona Republic*, September 22, 1994, D2.

21. Kate Bailey, "Baseball Documentary Brings New Interest in Negro Leagues Museum," *Anniston Star*, December 18, 1994, 30.

22. Bailey, "Baseball Documentary Brings New Interest in Negro Leagues Museum."

23. Paula Span, "Ratings to Boost 'Baseball' Gear," *Philadelphia Inquirer*, October 6, 1994) E1 and E4.

24. Charles Strouse, "Recalling Segregation in Baseball," *Indianapolis Star*, October 4, 1994, 37.

25. Alan Robinson, "'Like We Invented the Game,'" *Raleigh News and Observer*, October 2, 1994, 26.

26. Jeff Plass, "ESPN Program Assesses Negro League's Legacy," *Bangor Daily News*, October 15, 1994, 103.

27. Luke, *Willie Wells*, 129.

28. "Gil, Roger Given Better Shot at Hall," *New York Daily News*, February 19, 1995, 76.

29. Dave Johnson, "19th Century Baseball, Negro League Get Crack at Fame," *Evansville Courier and Press*, March 5, 1995) 20.

30. Thomas Stinson, "PBS Series May Have Rekindled Negro Leagues Interest," *Atlanta Constitution*, February 5, 1995, 62.

31. Johnson, "19th Century Baseball, Negro League Get Crack at Fame."

32. O'Neil, *I Was Right on Time*, 6.

33. Stinson, "PBS Series May Have Rekindled Negro Leagues Interest."

34. Holway, *Black Giants*, 11.

35. Greenes, *Negro Leaguers and the Hall of Fame*, 37.

36. "Satch, Josh & Co. ... Color 'Em Great."

37. O'Neil, *I Was Right on Time*, 6.

38. Stan Baumgartner, "Pennock's Death Casts Shadow Over NL Meeting," *Philadelphia Inquirer*, February 1, 1948, 31–32.

39. "Gil, Roger Given Better Shot at Hall."

40. John Kekis, "Black Players Focus of New Hall Exhibit," *Elmira Star-Gazette*, June 10, 1997, 5.

41. Associated Press, "Baseball Hall Honors Blacks," *Binghamton Press and Sun-Bulletin*, June 13, 1997, 20.

42. Holway, *Black Giants*, 13.

43. Luke, *Willie Wells*, 130.

44. Holway, *Blackball Stars*, 339.

45. Joe Donnelly, "A Moving Tribute," *Newsday*, July 2, 1993, 239.

Chapter 10

1. Luke, *Willie Wells*, 130.

2. Associated Press, "Mazeroski Finally Makes It Into Hall," *Newsday*, March 7, 2001, 76.

3. Jon Heyman, "O's Shed No Tears in Loss of Belle," *Newsday*, March 11, 2001, 38.

4. Roger Neuman, "Veterans Committee Does Injustice to Baseball Hall of Fame," *Elmira Star-Gazette*, March 9, 2001, 4.

5. Jeff Jacobs, "Hey, Time to Call a Tech," *Hartford Courant*, March 10, 2001, C10.

6. "Voice of the People," *New York Daily News*, March 19, 2001, 32.

7. "Sound Off," *St. Louis Post-Dispatch*, March 25, 2001, 54.

8. Jaffe, *Cooperstown Casebook*, 58–59.

9. Associated Press, "Hall of Fame Revamps Voting, All Balloting to Be Revealed," *Olathe News*, August 7, 2001, B3.

10. Associated Press, ""Hall of Fame Revamps Voting, All Balloting to Be Revealed."

11. Jack O'Connell, "Sensible Shakeup at Hall," *Hartford Courant*, August 7, 2001, C1 and C5.

12. O'Connell, "Sensible Shakeup at Hall."

13. Associated Press, "Hall of Fame to Study Black Baseball History," *Dayton Daily News*, July 21, 2000, 13.

14. Hogan, *Shades of Glory*, xx.

15. National Baseball Hall of Fame Press Release, "National Baseball Hall of Fame and Museum Selects Research Team to Complete African-American Baseball History Study," *Web.archive.org*, February 14, 2001, https://web.archive.org/web/20010618112844/http://baseballhalloffame.org/whats_new/press_releases/pr2001_02_19.htm.

16. Greenes, *Negro Leaguers and the Hall of Fame*, 42.

17. National Baseball Hall of Fame, "A Brief History of Elections of Negro Leagues Candidates," *Web.archive.org*, https://web.archive.org/web/20060228193953/http://www.baseballhalloffame.org/hofers_and_honorees/negro_lg_overview.htm.

18. Hogan, *Shades of Glory*, xx.

19. Hogan, *Shades of Glory*, xxii.

20. Greenes, *Negro Leaguers and the Hall of Fame*, 43.

21. Negro League Baseball Players Association, "Transcript of Negro Leagues, Pre-Negro Leagues Special Election Results Announcement," *NLBPA.com*, February 27, 2006, http://www.nlbpa.com/news/febuary-27-2006.html.

22. Greenes, *Negro Leaguers and the Hall of Fame*, 232.

23. "Satch, Josh & Co. ... Color 'Em Great."

24. Leavy, *The Big Fella*, 180.

25. Dave Anderson, "Sports of the Times; Those Not in Hall Who Should Be by Now," *New York Times*, March 13, 2002, D3.

26. Kevin Murphy, "White House Salutes Legends," *Kansas City Star*, March 31, 2001, D8.

27. Joe Posnanski, "Let's Get Behind Buck," *Kansas City Star*, May 17, 2001, D1 and D6.

28. Steve Penn, "The Hall. O'Neil. It's Time," *Kansas City Star*, July 5, 2005, B1.

29. Randy Covitz, "Did Feud Sabotage Buck's Bid for Hall?" *Kansas City Star*, May 7, 2006, 1 and 10.

30. Covitz, "Did Feud Sabotage Buck's Bid for Hall?"

31. Dan Margolies, "Suit Filed Over Missing Tapes," *Greensboro News & Record*, May 16, 2004, C6.

32. Dan Margolies, "Case of the Miss-ing Tapes Takes a Few New Twists," *Kansas City Star*, October 25, 2005, D15.

33. Covitz, "Did Feud Sabotage Buck's Bid for Hall?"

34. Dan Margolies, "Baseball Museum Prevails in Suit," *Kansas City Star*, February 9, 2006, C1 and C8.

35. Greenes, *Negro Leaguers and the Hall of Fame*, 46.

36. Greenes, *Negro Leaguers and the Hall of Fame*, 46.

37. Greenes, *Negro Leaguers and the Hall of Fame*, 46.

38. Covitz, "Did Feud Sabotage Buck's Bid for Hall?"

39. Covitz, "Did Feud Sabotage Buck's Bid for Hall?"

40. Joe Posnanski, "After Shock, an Outcry of O'Neil," *Kansas City Star*, March 5, 2006, C1 and C13.

41. Posnanski, "After Shock, an Outcry of O'Neil."

42. Covitz, "Did Feud Sabotage Buck's Bid for Hall?"

43. Covitz, "Did Feud Sabotage Buck's Bid for Hall?"

44. Covitz, "Did Feud Sabotage Buck's Bid for Hall?"

45. Greenes, *Negro Leaguers and the Hall of Fame*, 47.

46. Larry Lester and officials with the Negro Leagues Baseball Museum were contacted and asked to be interviewed for this book. Each declined to do so.

47. Greenes, *Negro Leaguers and the Hall of Fame*, 54.

Chapter 11

1. Covitz, "Did Feud Sabotage Buck's Bid for Hall?"

2. Jaffe, *Cooperstown Casebook*, 59.

3. Joe Posnanski, "The Pre-Integration Committee," *NBCSports.com*, October 27, 2015, https://sportsworld.nbcsports.com/the-pre-integration-committee/.

4. Anthony Rieber, "Oops! Major League Baseball's 500,000th Error," *Newsday*, September 16, 2012, A64–65.

5. Pete Grathoff, "Museum to Celebrate Buck on His Birthday," *Kansas City Star*, November 7, 2011, B2.

6. National Baseball Hall of Fame, "2016 Pre-Integration Committee Candidates," *Baseballhall.org*, https://

Notes—Chapter 11

baseballhall.org/discover-more/stories/pre-integration/2016-candidates.

7. Ryan Whirty, "HOF: No More Negro Leaguers, and No Changes to Policy," *Homeplatedontmove.wordpress.com*, https://homeplatedontmove.wordpress.com/2016/01/14/hof-no-more-negro-leaguers-and-no-changes-to-policy/.

8. Greenes, *Negro Leaguers and the Hall of Fame*, 386.

9. National Baseball Hall of Fame, "Buck O'Neil Award," *Basbeallhall.org*, https://baseballhall.org/discover-more/awards/890.

10. Boivin, "Garagiola Embodies Award He Will Receive."

11. John Kekis, "Robinson Honored with New Plaque," *SanDiegoUnionTribune.com*, June 25, 2008, https://www.sandiegouniontribune.com/sdut-robinson-honored-new-hall-fame-plaque-2008jun25-story.html.

12. National Baseball Hall of Fame, "Jackie Robinson," *Basbeallhall.org*, https://baseballhall.org/hall-of-famers/robinson-jackie.

13. "Library Hosts Baseball History," *Casper Star-Tribune*, November 8, 2009, 20.

14. Lori Holcomb, "Exhibit Showcases Negro Baseball Leagues," *Battle Creek Enquirer*, March 19, 2009, 22.

15. Cody Thorn, "Exhibit Highlights African-American Baseball Experience," *St. Joseph News-Press*, May 18, 2011, A1 and A3.

16. Shawn Windsor, "Exhibit Is Home Run for Harper Woods," *Detroit Free Press*, November 3, 2010, 15.

17. Tom Archdeacon, "Sinclair Community College Capture Spirit of Negro Leagues," *Dayton Daily News*, January 31, 2014, C1 and C4.

18. Nate Taylor, "A Comeback for Negro Leagues Museum," *New York Times*, August 24, 2013, D1.

19. Mike Hendricks, "A Squeeze Play," *Kansas City Star*, July 7, 2013, A1 and A12.

20. Tyler Kepner, "Another Shutout in Electing Members of the Baseball Hall of Fame," *New York Times*, February 29, 2007).

21. National Baseball Hall of Fame Press Release, "Two Managers, Three Executives Comprise Class of 2008," *Web.archive.org*, December 3, 2007, https://web.archive.org/web/20071204185637/http://web.baseballhalloffame.org/news/article.jsp?ymd=20071203&content_id=5714&vkey=hof_pr.

22. National Baseball Hall of Fame Press Release, "Joe Gordon Elected to Baseball Hall of Fame by Vets' Committee," *Web.archive.org*, https://web.archive.org/web/20081211121742/http://www.hofmag.com/content/view/1314/190/.

23. Lou Cappetta, "Who's In? Evaluating the 2010 Baseball Hall of Fame Ballot," *Bleacherreport.com*, January 2, 2010, https://bleacherreport.com/articles/318561-whos-in-evaluating-the-2010-baseball-hall-of-fame-ballot.

24. Tim Kurkjian, "New HOF Ballot Eying Those Left Behind," *ESPN.com*, November 19, 2010, https://www.espn.com/mlb/columns/story?columnist=kurkjian_tim&id=5820675.

25. Sun-Times Wire, "White Sox Legend Miñoso on Hall of Fame Ballot for 2012," *Chicago.suntimes.com*, November 3, 2011, https://chicago.suntimes.com/news/2011/11/3/18548047/white-sox-legend-minoso-on-hall-of-fame-ballot-for-2012.

26. "10 Finalists Named for Baseball Hall of Fame's 2013 Pre-Integration Era Ballot," *SABR.org*, November 1, 2012, https://sabr.org/latest/10-finalists-named-for-baseball-hall-of-fames-2013-pre-integration-era-ballot/.

27. National Baseball Hall of Fame Press Release, "Cox, LaRussa, Torre Elected to Hall of Fame," *Web.archive.org*, December 9, 2013, https://web.archive.org/web/20131212121956/http://baseballhall.org/news/press-releases/cox-la-russa-torre-elected-hall-fame.

28. Associated Press, "All Golden Era Candidates Fall Short," *ESPN.com*, December 8, 2014, https://www.espn.com/mlb/story/_/id/11999830/all-10-golden-era-candidates-fall-short-hall-fame-induction.

29. Jay Jaffe, "Pre-Integration Era Vote Again Shows Flaws in Hall of Fame's Process," *SI.com*, December 7, 2015, https://www.si.com/mlb/2015/12/07/hall-of-fame-veterans-committee-pre-integration-era-vote.

30. Jaffe, "Pre-Integration Era Vote Again Shows Flaws in Hall of Fame's Process."

31. Posnanski, "The Pre-Integration Committee."

32. Ryan Whirty, "Posnanski: Hall of Fame Is 'Tone Deaf,'" *Homeplatedontmove.com*, https://homeplatedontmove. wordpress.com/2016/02/03/posnanski-hall-of-fame-is-tone-deaf/.

33. Ryan Whirty, "KC's Father-Son Battery Made Baseball History 75 Years Ago," *Kansas City Star*, February 14, 2016, 7B.

34. National Baseball Hall of Fame, "Hall of Famer Ozzie Smith Elected to Board of Directors; Era Committees Restructured," *Basbeallhall.org*, July 23, 2016, https://baseballhall.org/discover-more/news/hall-of-fame-announcements.

Chapter 12

1. De'Zhon Grace, Carolyn Johnson and Treva Reid, "Racial Inequality and COVID-19," *Greenlining.org*, May 4, 2020, https://greenlining.org/2020/racial-inequality-and-covid-19/.

2. Richard A. Oppel, Jr., Derrick Bryson Taylor, and Nicholas Bogel-Burroughs, "What to Know About Breonna Taylor's Death," *NYTimes.com*, December 13, 2023, https://www.nytimes.com/article/breonna-taylor-police.html.

3. "George Floyd: What Happened in the Final Moments of His Life," *BBC.com*, July 15, 2020, https://www.bbc.com/news/world-us-canada-52861726.

4. "'I Can't Breathe!' Video of Fatal Arrest Shows Minneapolis Officer Kneeling on George Floyd's Neck for Several Minutes," *CBSNews.com*, May 26, 2020, https://www.cbsnews.com/minnesota/news/george-floyd-man-dies-after-being-arrested-by-minneapolis-police-fbi-called-to-investigate/.

5. Emily Olson, "Antifa, Boogaloo Boys, White Nationalists: Which extremists Showed Up to the U.S. Black Lives Matter Protests?" *ABC.net.au*, June 27, 2020, https://www.abc.net.au/news/2020-06-28/antifa-boogaloo-extremists-at-us-floyd-protests/12388260.

6. "Roger Goodell Issues Statement on Death of George Floyd, Nationwide Protests," *NFL.com*, May 30, 2020, https://www.nfl.com/news/roger-goodell-issues-statement-on-killing-of-george-floyd-nationwide-protests.

7. "Adam Silver, "NBA Teams Express Outrage After George Floyd's Death," *NBA.com*, https://www.nba.com/news/nba-teams-respond-tragic-death-george-floyd.

8. "NHL Statement on Calls for Racial Justice," *NHL.com*, May 31, 2020, https://www.nhl.com/news/national-hockey-league-statement-on-calls-for-racial-justice-317076670.

9. James Wagner, "A League's First Comment, at Last," *New York Times*, June 4, 2020, B7.

10. Wagner, "A League's First Comment, at Last."

11. Armour and Levitt, "Baseball Demographics, 1947–2016."

12. Wagner, "A League's First Comment, at Last."

13. Bob Nightengale, "Adam Jones on MLB's lack of Kaepernick Protest: 'Baseball Is a White Man's Sport,'" *USA Today*, September 12, 2016, https://www.usatoday.com/story/sports/mlb/columnist/bob-nightengale/2016/09/12/adam-jones-orioles-colin-kaepernick-white-mans-sport/90260326/.

14. Nate Scott, "A Night of Protest: Where NBA, WNBA, MLS, and MLB Stand After Players Boycott Games," *USAToday.com*, August 27, 2020, https://ftw.usatoday.com/2020/08/nba-wnba-mls-mlb-protests.

15. Scott, "A night of Protest: Where NBA, WNBA, MLS, and MLB Stand After Players Boycott Games."

16. ESPN News Services, "Astros Manager Dusty Baker 'Proud of This Generation' as Houston, Oakland Protest," *ESPN.com*, August 28, 2020, https://www.espn.com/mlb/story/_/id/29762453/oakland-athletics-houston-astros-call-game.

17. Joel Sherman, "Vets Vote Him In, But ... No Way Maz Deserves Hall," *New York Post*, March 7, 2021, https://nypost.com/2001/03/07/vets-vote-him-in-but-no-way-maz-deserves-hall/.

18. Matt Kelly, "Era Committee Elections Rescheduled to 2021," *MLB.com*,

Notes—Chapter 12 201

August 24, 2020, https://www.mlb.com/news/hall-of-fame-era-committee-elections-rescheduled-to-2021.

19. Dan Kelly, "Negro Leagues 100th Anniversary Celebration," *Kansas City Star*, February 13, 2020, B6.

20. Associated Press, "Honoring the Icons," *St. Joseph News-Press*, February 14, 2020, C1 and C2.

21. Kelly, "Negro Leagues 100th Anniversary Celebration."

22. Jack Harris, "A Story of Triumph," *Carlisle Sentinel*, August 22, 2020, C8.

23. "Tipping Your Cap," *Tipping YourCap.com*, https://www.tippingyourcap.com/.

24. Ben Walker, "MVP Plaque Presenters to Discuss Landis' Name on MLB Trophy," Associated Press, July 2, 2020, https://apnews.com/article/82cdd84723ffb741e885d4795afc09f3.

25. Associated Press, "Congressional Group Wants Landis Name Pulled from MVP Plaque." *USAToday.com*, August 4, 2020, https://www.usatoday.com/story/sports/mlb/2020/08/04/congressional-group-wants-landis-name-pulled-from-mvp-plaque/112813382/.

26. Matt Kelly, "Landis' Name to Be Removed from MVP Trophies," *MLB. com*, October 2, 2020, https://www.mlb.com/news/kenesaw-mountain-landis-name-removed-mvp-trophies.

27. Bob Nightengale, "Opinion: It's Time to Remove J.G. Taylor Spink's Name Off Baseball Writer's Award Over His Racist Views," *USA Today*, July 1, 2020, https://www.usatoday.com/story/sports/mlb/columnist/bob-nightengale/2020/07/01/j-g-taylor-spink-baseball-writers-award-racism/5356572002/.

28. Dan Schlossberg, "Writers Remove J.G. Taylor Spink Name from Prestigious Award After Research Reveals Racist Tendencies," *Forbes*, February 5, 2021, https://www.forbes.com/sites/danschlossberg/2021/02/05/writers-remove-jg-taylor-spink-name-from-prestigious-award-after-research-reveals-racist-tendencies/?sh=2f17a44e1e17.

29. Tyler Kepner, "Baseball Rights a Wrong by Adding Negro Leagues to Official Records," *New York Times*, December 17, 2020, A1.

30. Vahe Gregorian, "How the Negro Leagues Purged MLB Bias," *Kansas City Star*, December 27, 2020, B1 and B3.

31. Anthony Castrovince, "MLB Adds Negro Leagues to Official Records," *MLB.com*, December 16, 2020, https://www.mlb.com/news/negro-leagues-given-major-league-status-for-baseball-records-stats.

32. MLB Press Release, "MLB Officially Designates the Negro Leagues as 'Major League,'" *MLB.com*, December 16, 2020, https://www.mlb.com/press-release/press-release-mlb-officially-designates-the-negro-leagues-as-major-league.

33. Christian Red, "Baseball's Recognition of Negro Leagues 'Long Overdue' to Heirs and Supporters," *NBCNews.com*, December 18, 2020, https://www.nbcnews.com/news/nbcblk/baseball-s-recognition-negro-leagues-long-overdue-heirs-supporters-n1251704.

34. Gregorian, "How the Negro Leagues Purged MLB Bias."

35. Bridget Condon, "'We've Always Been Somebody': Negro League Families Say MLB Recognition 'Long Overdue,'" *ABC11.com*, February 15, 2021, https://abc11.com/baseball-negro-league-leagues-players/10334088/.

36. Clinton Yates, "MLB Elevating the Status of the Negro Leagues Is the Problem, Not the Solution," *Andscape.com*, December 16, 202o, https://andscape.com/features/mlb-elevating-the-status-of-negro-leagues-is-the-problem-not-the-solution/.

37. MLB Press Release, "MLB Officially Designates the Negro Leagues as 'Major League.'"

38. Gary Ashwill, "Building the Seamheads Negro Leagues Database," *Baseball-Reference.com*, https://www.baseball-reference.com/articles/building-the-seamheads-negro-league-database-gary-ashwill.shtml.

39. Stephen J. Nesbitt, "The Negro Leagues Are Major Leagues—But Merging Their Stats Has Been Anything but Seamless," *The Athletic*, May 11, 2023, https://theathletic.com/4503613/2023/05/11/negro-leagues-statistics-mlb-records/.

40. James Wagner, "Baseball Reference Adds Negro Leagues Statistics,

202   Notes—Chapter 12

Rewriting Its Record Book," *New York Times*, June 16, 2021, B10.

41. Dave Appelman, "Negro Leagues Data Is Now Available on FanGraphs!" *FanGraphs.com*, February 14, 2023, https://blogs.fangraphs.com/negro-leagues-data-is-now-available-on-fangraphs/.

42. Nesbitt, "The Negro Leagues Are Major Leagues—But Merging Their Stats Has Been Anything but Seamless."

43. Nesbitt, "The Negro Leagues Are Major Leagues—But Merging Their Stats Has Been Anything but Seamless."

44. Anthony Castrovince, "The Ongoing Search Through History to Give Negro Leaguers Their Due," *MLB.com*, November 6, 2023, https://www.mlb.com/news/mlb-working-to-add-negro-leagues-stats-to-record.

45. J.P. Hoornstra, "'Elevating' the Negro Leagues Requires More Than Numbers—an Apology Is Appropriate," *Lexington Herald-Leader*, December 25, 2020, B3.

46. National Baseball Hall of Fame Press Release, "Tim Mead to Step Down as President of National Baseball Hall of Fame and Museum," *Baseballhall.org*, April 16, 2021, https://baseballhall.org/news/tim-mead-to-step-down-as-president-of-national-baseball-hall-of-fame-and-museum.

47. National Baseball Hall of Fame Press Release, "Josh Rawitch Named President of the National Baseball Hall of Fame and Museum," *Baseballhall.org*, June 28, 2021, https://baseballhall.org/news/josh-rawitch-named-hall-of-fame-president.

48. Dominic Ramirez, Jr., "Wife, Parents of Late MLB Player Skaggs File Lawsuits," *Fort Worth Star-Telegram*, June 30, 2021, 6A.

49. As of this writing the lawsuits are still ongoing, delayed by pretrial motions related to evidence in the case.

50. Alden Gonzalez, "MLB Moving 2021 All-Star Game from Atlanta Over Georgia Voting Law," *ESPN.com*, April 2, 2021, https://www.espn.com/mlb/story/_/id/31183822/mlb-moving-all-star-game-atlanta-georgia-voting-law.

51. MLB Press Release, "MLB Statement Regarding 2021 All-Star Game," *MLB.com*, April 2, 2021, https://www.mlb.com/press-release/press-release-mlb-statement-regarding-2021-all-star-game.

52. Sean Lahman, "As Negro Leagues Teams Get 'Major' Status, How Baseball Is Reckoning with Past Inequities," *DemocratandChronicle.com*, March 31, 2021, https://www.democratandchronicle.com/story/sports/2021/03/31/black-major-league-baseball-legacy-hall-fame-and-cooperstown/4668662001/.

53. Lahman, "As Negro Leagues Teams Get 'Major' Status, How Baseball Is Reckoning with Past Inequities."

54. Dan Shaughnessy, "Tom Has Won This Year, But Back Off on Bill," *Boston Globe*, January 3, 2021, C1 and C7.

55. National Baseball Hall of Fame, "Tom Yawkey, Executive, Class of 1980," *Baseballhall.org*, https://baseballhall.org/hall-of-famers/yawkey-tom.

56. Tyler Kepner, "The Hall of Fame Tries to Contextualize Baseball's Racist Past," *New York Times*, December 21, 2020, https://www.nytimes.com/2020/12/21/sports/baseball/hall-of-fame.html.

57. Kepner, "The Hall of Fame Tries to Contextualize Baseball's Racist Past."

58. Kepner, "The Hall of Fame Tries to Contextualize Baseball's Racist Past."

59. Steve Henson, "Rawitch Ascends to Hall Heaven," *Los Angeles Times*, September 7, 2021, B8 and B10.

60. David Moriah, "Collector Josh Rawitch Relishes Dream Job as President of Baseball's Hall of Fame," *Sportscollectorsdigest.com*, March 31, 2023, https://sportscollectorsdigest.com/news/baseball-hall-of-fame-president-josh-rawitch-cards-memorabilia-mlb.

61. Henson, "Rawitch Ascends to Hall Heaven."

62. Ronald Blum, "Jackie Robinson Museum Opens After 14 Years of Planning," *Fort Worth Star-Telegram*, July 27, 2022, B3.

63. "Rawitch Announcement," *MLB.com* video, 1:19, posted by MLB Film-Room, January 25, 2022, https://www.mlb.com/es/video/anuncio-de-rawitch.

64. Steve Henson, "Dodgers Honor Jarrín Before 110th Win," *Los Angeles Times*, October 2, 2022, D1.

65. Tim Booth, "Ichiro Reflects on Career," *Longview Daily News*, August 30, 2022, B3.

Notes—Chapter 12

66. Vahe Gregorian, "NLBM Awaits Verdict on O'Neil for Hall of Fame," *Kansas City Star*, December 5, 2021, B1 and B7.

67. Gregorian, "NLBM Awaits Verdict on O'Neil for Hall of Fame."

68. Anthony Castrovince, "Buck, Gil, Minnie Among 6 Elected to Hall," *MLB.com*, January 25, 2022, https://www.mlb.com/news/2021-hall-of-fame-committee-election-results.

69. Renée Graham, "Bring Them Their Flowers Now, While They're Living," *Boston Globe*, July 31, 2022, K7.

70. Bill Shaikin, "Forget Frick. It's Time for Scully's Name on Award," *Los Angeles Times*, October 8, 2022, DD1.

71. Joe Posnanski, "Brilliant Reader Challenges: Dogs, Journeymen, Dumb Lyrics and More," *Joeblogs.joeposnanski. com*, June 22, 2023,https://joeblogs. joeposnanski.com/p/brilliant-reader-challenges-dogs.

72. National Baseball Hall of Fame Press Release, "Hall of Fame Restructures Era Committee, Frick Award Voting," *Baseballhall.org*, April 22, 2022 https://baseballhall.org/news/hall-of-fame-restructures-era-committee-frick-award-voting.

73. Shaikin, "Forget Frick. It's Time for Scully's Name on Award."

74. There is no indication as of early 2024 that Frick's name will be removed from the award. The most recent recipient, Joe Castiglione, was announced in December 2023 with no mention of consideration being given to changing the award's name.

75. Vahe Gregorian, "Why O'Neil's Hall of Fame Plaque Stands for Much More," *Kansas City Star*, August 14, 2022, B1 and B9.

76. Mike Hendricks, "'A Great Day' as Project Unveiled to Restore Satchel Paige Home in Kansas City," *Kansascity.com*, August 11, 2021, https://www.kansascity.com/news/local/article253368638.html.

77. Evan Gerike, "Loans Take Cooperstown Magic Throughout the World," *Basebabllhall.org*, https://baseballhall.org/discover/loans-take-cooperstown-magic-throughout-the-world.

78. Gregorian, "Why O'Neil's Hall of Fame Plaque Stands for Much More."

79. National Baseball Hall of Fame Press Release, "Hall of Fame Restructures Era Committee, Frick Award Voting."

80. Jay Jaffe, "The Hall of Fame Shakes Up Its Era Committee System Yet Again," *Fangraphs.com*, April 26, 2022, https://blogs.fangraphs.com/the-hall-of-fame-shakes-up-its-era-committee-system-yet-again/.

81. Jaffe, "The Hall of Fame Shakes Up Its Era Committee System Yet Again."

82. Jaffe, "The Hall of Fame Shakes Up Its Era Committee System Yet Again."

83. National Baseball Hall of Fame, "Eras Committees," *Basbeallhall.org*, https://baseballhall.org/hall-of-fame/election-rules/era-committees.

84. National Baseball Hall of Fame, "Museum Initiative to Highlight Story of Black Baseball," *Basbeallhall.org*, April 15, 2022, https://baseballhall.org/news/museum-initiative-to-highlight-story-of-black-baseball.

85. National Baseball Hall of Fame, "Museum Floor Plan," *Basbeallhall. org*, https://baseballhall.org/visit/museum-map.

86. National Baseball Hall of Fame, "Museum Initiative to Highlight Story of Black Baseball."

87. National Baseball Hall of Fame, "Museum Initiative to Highlight Story of Black Baseball."

88. National Baseball Hall of Fame, "Meet the Team," *Basbeallhall.org*, https://baseballhall.org/The-Black-Baseball-Initiative/Meet-the-Team.

89. National Baseball Hall of Fame, "Education and Outreach," *Basbeallhall. org*, https://baseballhall.org/The-Black-Baseball-Initiative/Education-and-Outreach.

90. Dan Cichalski, "Hall of Fame Reveals Name of New Black Baseball Exhibit: 'The Souls of the Game,'" *MLB.com*, June 19, 2023, https://www.mlb.com/news/baseball-hall-of-fame-announces-new-black-baseball-exhibit.

91. National Baseball Hall of Fame Press Release, "The Souls of the Game Exhibit Will Celebrate Black Baseball and How It Shaped America," *Baseball hall.org*, June 19, 2023, https://baseballhall.org/news/the-souls-of-the-game-exhibit-to-debut-in-spring-2024.

92. Cichalski, "Hall of Fame Reveals

Name of New Black Baseball Exhibit: 'The Souls of the Game.'"

93. "The Souls of the Game: Voices of Black Baseball," *YawkeyFoundation.org*, June 27, 2023, https://yawkeyfoundation.org/the-souls-of-the-game-voices-of-black-baseball/.

Bibliography

Books

Aaron, Mark Z., and Bill Nowlin, eds. *Who's on First: Replacement Players in World War II*. Phoenix: Society for American Baseball Research, 2015. Kindle.

Bjarkman, Peter C., and Bill Nowlin, eds. *Cuban Baseball Legends: Baseball's Alternative Universe*. Phoenix: Society for American Baseball Research, 2016. Kindle.

Bradlee, Ben, Jr. *The Kid: The Immortal Life od Ted Williams*. New York: Little, Brown, 2013.

Bruns, Roger. *Negro Leagues Baseball*. Santa Barbara: ABC-CLIO, 2012.

Bryant, Howard. *Shut Out: A Story of Race and Baseball in Boston*. New York: Routledge, 2002.

Burgos, Adrian, Jr. *Playing America's Game: Baseball, Latinos, and the Color Line*. Berkeley: University of California Press, 2007. Kindle.

Daniels, Eddie. *The Baseball Hall of Fame Corrected*. 2015. Self-published. Kindle.

Dickson, Paul. *Bill Veeck: Baseball's Greatest Maverick*. New York: Bloomsbury, 2012.

Dixon, Phil S. *The Dizzy and Daffy Dean Barnstorming Tour: Race, Media, and America's National Pastime*. Lanham, MD: Rowman & Littlefield, 2019. Kindle.

Eig, Jonathan. *Opening Day: The Story of Jackie Robinson's First Season*. New York: Simon & Schuster, 2007.

Epplin, Luke. *Our Team: The Epic Story of Four Men and the World Series That Changed Baseball*. New York: Flatiron Books, 2021.

Forman, Sean, and Cecilia M. Tan, eds. *The Negro Leagues Are Major Leagues: Essays and Research for Overdue Recognition*. Phoenix: Society for American Baseball Research, 2021.

Frick, Ford C. *Games, Asterisks, and People: Memoirs of a Lucky Fan*. New York: Crown, 1973.

Graf, John, et al. *From Rube to Robinson: SABR's Best Articles on Black Baseball*. Phoenix: Society for American Baseball Research, 2020. Kindle.

Greenes, Steven R. *Negro Leaguers and the Hall of Fame: The Case for Inducting 24 Overlooked Ballplayers*. Jefferson, NC: McFarland, 2020. Kindle.

Grigsby, Daryl Russell. *Celebrating Ourselves: African-Americans and the Promise of Baseball*. Indianapolis: Dog Ear Publishing, 2010. Kindle.

Hernández, Lou. *The Rise of the Latin American Baseball Leagues, 1947–1961: Cuba, the Dominican Republic, Mexico, Nicaragua, Panama, Puerto Rico and Venezuela*. Jefferson, NC: McFarland, 2011. Kindle.

Hogan, Lawrence D. *Shades of Glory: The Negro Leagues and the Story of African-American Baseball*. Washington, D.C.: National Geographic Society, 2006.

Holtzman, Jerome. *No Cheering in the Press Box*. Expanded ed. New York: Henry Holt, 1995.

Holway, John B. *Black Giants*. Springfield, VA: Lord Fairfax Press, 2010. Kindle.

Holway, John B. *Blackball Stars: Negro League Pioneers*. Westport, CT: Meckler Books, 1988.

Jaffe, Jay. *The Cooperstown Casebook:*

Who's in the Baseball Hall of Fame, Who Should Be In, and Who Should Pack Their Plaques. New York: Thomas Dunne, 2017.

James, Bill. *Whatever Happened to the Hall of Fame? Baseball, Cooperstown, and the Politics of Glory.* New York: Simon & Schuster, 1995.

Johnson, Susan E. *When Women Played Hardball.* Seattle: Seal Press, 1994. Kindle.

Kirsch, George B. *Baseball in Blue and Gray: The National Pastime During the Civil War.* Princeton: Princeton University Press, 2003. Kindle.

Kuhn, Bowie. *Hardball: The Education of a Baseball Commissioner.* Lincoln: University of Nebraska Press, 1997.

Lamb, Chris. *Conspiracy of Silence: Sportswriters and the Long Campaign to Desegregate Baseball.* Lincoln: University of Nebraska Press, 2012. Kindle.

Lanctot, Neil. *Campy: The Two Lives of Roy Campanella.* New York: Simon & Schuster, 2011.

Leavy, Jane. *The Big Fella: Babe Ruth and the World He Created.* New York: HarperCollins, 2018.

Luke, Bob. *Willie Wells: "El Diablo" of the Negro Leagues.* Austin: University of Texas Press, 2007. Kindle.

Maraniss, David. *Clemente: The Passion and Grace of Baseball's Last Hero.* New York: Simon & Schuster, 2006. Kindle.

Martin, Brian. *Baseball's Creation Myth: Adam Ford, Abner Graves and the Cooperstown Story.* Jefferson, NC: McFarland, 2013. Kindle.

Moore, Joseph Thomas. *Larry Doby: The Struggle of the American League's First Black Player.* Mineola, NY: Dover, 2011.

O'Neil, Buck, with Steve Wulf and David Conrads. *I Was Right on Time: My Journey from the Negro Leagues to the Majors.* New York: Simon & Schuster, 1996.

Parrott, Harold. *The Lords of Baseball: A Wry Look at a Side of the Game the Fan Seldom Sees—the Font Office.* Atlanta: Longstreet Press, 2001.

Peterson, Robert. *Only the Ball Was White: A History of Legendary Black Players and All-Black Professional Teams.* New York: Oxford University Press, 1970.

Peterson, Todd, ed. *The Negro Leagues Were Major Leagues: Historians Reappraise Black Baseball.* Jefferson, NC: McFarland, 2020. Kindle.

Pietrusza, David. *Judge and Jury: The Life and Times of Judge Kenesaw Mountain Landis.* South Bend, IN: Diamond Communications, 1998. Kindle.

Polner, Murray. *Branch Rickey: A Biography.* Jefferson, NC: McFarland, 2007.

Posnanski, Joe. *The Baseball 100.* New York: Avid Reader Press, 2021.

Posnanski, Joe. *Why We Love Baseball: A History in 50 Moments.* New York: Dutton, 2023.

Robinson, Jackie. *Baseball Has Done It.* Brooklyn: IG Publishing, 2005.

Robinson, Jackie. *I Never Had It Made.* New York: HarperCollins, 1995.

Ruck, Rob. *Raceball: How the Major Leagues Colonized the Black and Latin Game.* Boston: Beacon, 2012. Kindle.

Simon, Scott. *Jackie Robinson and the Integration of Baseball.* Hoboken: John Wiley & Sons, 2002.

Smith, Ken. *Baseball's Hall of Fame.* Revised. New York: Grosset & Dunlap, 1970.

Spink, John George Taylor. *Judge Landis and 25 Years of Baseball.* 4th Printing. Binghamton: Vail-Ballou Press, 1947.

Spivey, Donald. *If You Were Only White: The Life of Leroy "Satchel" Paige.* Columbia: University of Missouri Press, 2012. Kindle.

Swaine, Rick. *The Integration of Major League Baseball: A Team by Team History.* Jefferson, NC: McFarland, 2009. Kindle.

Swift, Tom. *Chief Bender's Burden: The Silent Struggle of a Baseball Star.* Lincoln: University of Nebraska Press, 2008.

Thorn, John. *Baseball in the Garden of Eden: The Secret History of the Early Game.* New York: Simon & Schuster, 2011. Kindle.

Tiant, Luis, and Saul Wisnia. *Son of Havana: A Baseball Journey From Cuba to the Big Leagues and Back.* New York: Diversion Books, 2019.

Tye, Larry. *Satchel: The Life and Times of an American Legend.* New York: Random House, 2009.

Tygiel, Jules. *Baseball's Great Experiment: Jackie Robinson and His Legacy.*

New York: Oxford University Press, 2008.

Veeck, Bill, with Ed Linn. *Veeck As in Wreck: The Autobiography of Bill Veeck.* Chicago: University of Chicago Press, 2012. Kindle.

Vlasich, James A. *A Legend for the Legendary: The Origin of the Baseball Hall of Fame.* Bowling Green: Bowling Green State University Popular Press, 1990.

Whiting, Robert. *You Gotta Have Wa: When Two Cultures Collide on the Baseball Diamond.* New York: Macmillan, 1989. Kindle.

Newspapers and Periodicals

Anderson, Dave. "Sports of The Times; Those Not in Hall Who Should Be by Now." *New York Times*, March 13, 2002, D3.

Archdeacon, Tom. "Sinclair Community College Capture Spirit of Negro Leagues." *Dayton Daily News*, January 31, 2014, C1 and C4.

Associated Press. "Baseball Hall Honors Blacks." *Binghamton Press and Sun-Bulletin*, June 13, 1997, 20.

Associated Press. "Black Baseball Players Basking in Limelight That Once Evaded Them." *Charlotte News*, June 25, 1980, 53.

Associated Press. "Black Baseball Players Honor Forgotten Generation." *Miami Herald*, November 7, 1980, 96.

Associated Press. "Hall of Fame a Dream for Negro League Star Page." *Owensboro Messenger-Inquirer*, August 12, 1979, 32.

Associated Press. "Hall of Fame Picks Might Be Changed." *Hartford Courant*, August 8, 1977, 47.

Associated Press. "Hall of Fame Revamps Voting, all Balloting to Be Revealed." *Olathe News*, August 7, 2001, B3.

Associated Press. "Hall of Fame to Study Black Baseball History." *Dayton Daily News*, July 21, 2000, 13.

Associated Press. "Hall Restricts Entries." *Oakland Tribune*, October 4, 1977, 26.

Associated Press. "Honoring the Icons." *St. Joseph News-Press*, February 14, 2020, C1 and C2.

Associated Press. "Kuhn Vows to Keep Negro Leagues Fight." *Salisbury Daily Times*, November 5, 1983, 11.

Associated Press. "Love of Baseball Draws Old Timers." *Nashville Tennessean*, July 6, 1979, 56.

Associated Press. "Mazeroski Finally Makes It Into Hall." *Newsday*, March 7, 2001, 76.

Associated Press. "Memorable Time for Forgotten Stars." *Honolulu Star-Bulletin*, July 4, 1979, 46.

Associated Press. "Moguls Quiet on Landis' Negro Rule." *Dayton Journal-Herald*, July 18, 1942, 9.

Associated Press. "Negro Baseball Hall of History to Open." *Hanford Sentinel*, April 27, 1981, 8.

Associated Press. "Negro Hall-of-Famers Possibilities Extended." *Indianapolis Star*, July 29, 1969, 21.

Associated Press. "Negro League Hall of History heading for Cooperstown." *Kansas City Times*, June 20, 1988, D-5.

Associated Press. "Negro League Museum Starts in White Woman's Cottage." *Birmingham Post-Herald*, June 21, 1982, B7.

Associated Press. "Old Negro Stars Become Eligible for Baseball Shrine." *Hartford Courant*, February 4, 1971, 24.

Auchmutey, Jim. "'Being Around Him Just Makes You Feel Better.'" *Atlanta Journal*, September 21, 1994, D4.

Bailey, Kate. "Baseball Documentary Brings New Interest in Negro Leagues Museum." *Anniston Star*, December 18, 1994, 30.

Baumgartner, Stan. "Pennock's Death Casts Shadow Over NL Meeting." *Philadelphia Inquirer*, February 1, 1948, 31–32.

"Bavasi Berates Bombers." *New York Times*, December 3, 1952, 47.

Benson, Ted. "'League Open to Negroes' Says Frick, League Prexy." *Chicago Defender*, August 29, 1936, 13.

Berkow, Ira. "Hall of Shame—Wynn." *Abilene Reporter-News*, April 14, 1971, 9-A.

"Bishop Sheil Joins Fight Against Major League Color Barrier." *Michigan Chronicle*, June 13, 1942, 21.

"Black Pioneer Jackie Robinson Dead." *The Sporting News*, November 11, 1972, 35.

Blum, Ronald. "Jackie Robinson Museum Opens After 14 years of Planning." *Fort Worth Star-Telegram*, July 27, 2022, B3.

Boivin, Paula. "Garagiola Embodies Award He Will Receive." *Arizona Republic*, July 24, 2014, C1.

Booth, Tim. "Ichiro Reflects on Career." *Longview Daily News*, August 30, 2022, B3.

Brands, Edgar G. "Between Innings." *The Sporting News*, June 18, 1931, 4.

Brands, Edgar G. "Between Innings." *The Sporting News*, August 25, 1932, 4.

Broeg, Bob. "Doubting Writer Hopes Mize Is All Through as Hitter." *St. Louis Post-Dispatch*, August 14, 1977, 2B.

Broeg, Bob. "New Book Traces History of Black Baseball." *St. Louis Post-Dispatch*, April 26, 1970, 2E.

Buonauro, Gabe. "How Wide Will Hall of Fame Open Its Gates?" *The Record*, July 3, 1970, B-7.

Burnes, Brian. "At the Old Ballpark." *Kansas City Star*, April 2, 1984, 1 and 5.

Burns, Bud. "Splinter Group, Led by Ted, Seeks Hall Shift." *Nashville Tennessean*, July 31, 1966, 5-C.

Canfield, Owen. "Mays Says Thanks to Black Leagues." *Hartford Courant*, June 25, 1981, 67.

Chastain, Bill. "Voice of Baseball." *Tampa Tribune*, October 1, 1994, 1.

Cobbledick, Gordon. "Jockeys Ride Every Rookie." *The Sporting News*, May 21, 1947, 14.

Collett, Ritter. "Black Promoter Ends Retirement." *Dayton Journal Herald*, May 20, 1986, 19.

Condon, David. "In the Wake of the News." *Chicago Tribune*, July 9, 1963, 39.

Condon, David. "In the Wake of the News." *Chicago Tribune*, January 21, 1967, 45.

Condon, David. "In the Wake of the News." *Chicago Tribune*, June 26, 1967, 61.

Condon, David. "In the Wake of the News." *Chicago Tribune*, April 20, 1968, 71.

Condon, David. "In the Wake of the News." *Chicago Tribune*, August 21, 1968, 69.

Condon, David. "In the Wake of the News." *Chicago Tribune*, February 5, 1971, 49.

Covitz, Randy. "Did Feud Sabotage Buck's Bid for Hall?" *Kansas City Star*, May 7, 2006, 1 and 10.

Daley, Arthur. "Opening Day at Ebbets Field." *New York Times*, April 16, 1947, 32.

Daley, Arthur. "Play Ball!" *New York Times*, April 15, 1947, 31.

Daley, Arthur. "Sport of The Times." *New York Times*, February 10, 1971, 52.

Daniel, Dan. "Writers and League Heads to Confer on MV Balloting." *The Sporting News*, December 21, 1949, 16.

"Dixie Action on Negroes Needed." *The Sporting News*, July 16, 1947, 15.

Donnelly, Joe. "A Moving Tribute." *Newsday*, July 2, 1993, 239.

Durso, Joseph. "Baseball to Admit Negro Stars." *New York Times*, February 4, 1971, 42.

Durso, Joseph. "Frick, in Last Year, Warns Big Leagues." *New York Times*, January 3, 1965, 2.

Editorial. "Finding Our Story." *Ventura County Star*, September 29, 1994, D1.

Editorial. "Jackie's Voice Missed at Cooperstown." *The Sporting News*, August 12, 1967, 14.

Editorial. "Jazz and More." *Kansas City Star*, September 19, 1985, 18.

Editorial. "'Old Satch' Joins the Stars." *Detroit Free Press*, February 15, 1971, 6.

Editorial. "Once Again, That Negro Question." *The Sporting News*, July 16, 1947, 16.

Editorial. "Robinson Should Be Player— Not Crusader." *The Sporting News*, December 10, 1952, 12.

Editorial. "Stop, Look and Listen, Jackie." *The Sporting News*, May 2, 1951, 12.

"An Extra Grand Grin—15 Grand." *The Sporting News*, December 21, 1949, 5.

Feller, Bob, with Edward Linn. "The Trouble With the Hall of Fame." *Saturday Evening Post*, January 27, 1962, 49–52.

FitzMaurice, D.G. "Negro League Reunion Will Honor Greenup's Thomas." *Lexington Herald-Leader*, July 1, 1979, 24.

FitzMaurice, D.G. "Past and Future: Black Baseball Stars From Another Era Gather in Greenup to Relive Old

Bibliography

Times." *Lexington Herald-Leader*, July 4, 1979, 1.

Flaherty, Vincent X. "Feller Doubts Robinson Future." *Akron Beacon Journal*, October 27, 1945, 12.

Ford, Bill. "Negro Leagues Find Fame in Greenup, Ky." *Cincinnati Enquirer*, June 20, 1979, 51.

Fraley, Oscar. "Feller Saddest Man in Series." *Wichita Falls Times*, October 12, 1948, 11.

George, Steve. "250,000 See Feller-Paige Teams Play." *The Sporting News*, October 30, 1946, 9.

"Gil, Roger Given Better Shot at Hall." *New York Daily News*, February 19, 1995, 76.

Graham, Frank, Jr. "Frick Favors Spitter Return." *The Sporting News*, November 2, 1949, 10.

Graham, Frank, Jr. "When Baseball Went to War." *Sports Illustrated*, April 17, 1967, 78.

Graham, Renée. "Bring Them Their Flowers Now, While They're Living." *Boston Globe*, July 31, 2022, K7.

Grathoff, Pete. "Museum to Celebrate Buck on His Birthday." *Kansas City Star*, November 7, 2011, B2.

Gregorian, Vahe. "How the Negro Leagues Purged MLB Bias." *Kansas City Star*, December 27, 2020, B1 and B3.

Gregorian, Vahe. "NLBM Awaits Verdict on O'Neil for Hall of Fame." *Kansas City Star*, December 5, 2021, B1 and B7.

Gregorian, Vahe. "Why O'Neil's Hall of Fame plaque Stands for Much More." *Kansas City Star*, August 14, 2022, B1 and B9.

Grigsby, Charles T. "Whitney Young Was Killed, Too." *Boston Globe*, April 5, 1971, 14.

Grimsley, Will. "Should Hall of Fame Include Rizzuto?" *Sioux City Journal*, May 15, 1983, 10.

Gross, Milton. "Jackie Robinson Raps Plan to Add Old Negroes to Hall." *Omaha World-Herald*, February 5, 1971, 25.

Harris, Jack. "A Story of Triumph." *Carlisle Sentinel*, August 22, 2020, C8.

Harrison, Claude E., Jr. "Josh Gibson Rated No. One Slugger By Satchel Paige." *Philadelphia Tribune*, September 3, 1968, 16.

Hendricks, Mike. "A Squeeze Play." *Kansas City Star*, July 7, 2013, A1 and A12.

Henson, Steve. "Dodgers Honor Jarrín Before 110th Win." *Los Angeles Times*, October 2, 2022, D1.

Henson, Steve. "Rawitch Ascends to Hall Heaven." *Los Angeles Times*, September 7, 2021, B8 and B10.

Heyman, Jon. "O's Shed No Tears in Loss of Belle." *Newsday*, March 11, 2001, 38.

Hill, John Paul. "Commissioner A.B. 'Happy' Chandler and the Integration of Major League Baseball: A Reassessment." *NINE, A Journal of Baseball History and Culture* 19, no. 1 (Fall 2010): 28–51.

Holcomb, Lori. "Exhibit Showcases Negro Baseball Leagues." *Battle Creek Enquirer*, March 19, 2009, 22.

Holway, John. "Blacks Losers Only at Hall of Fame." *Boston Globe*, August 4, 1978, 14–15.

Holway, John. "Shutting the Door on Negro League Stars." *New York Times*, July 31, 1977, 151.

Hoornstra, J.P. "'Elevating' the Negro Leagues Requires More Than Numbers—an Apology Is Appropriate." *Lexington Herald-Leader*, December 25, 2020, B3.

Hurwitz, Hy. "Anti-Feller Bloc Grows; Red Sox Join." *Boston Globe*, July 13, 1948, 18.

Hurwitz, Hy. "Red Sox Sign Dolf Camilli; Metkovich May Play Outfield." *Boston Globe*, June 17, 1945, 20.

"Indianapolis Clowns Here Wednesday." *Burlington Daily Times-News*, May 23, 1967, 10.

Isaacs, Stan. "The First Black Manager: Who? When?" *Newsday*, April 24, 1970, 49.

Isaacs, Stan. "Satchel Paige Belongs in the Hall of Fame." *Newsday*, January 23, 1967, 83.

Jackson, Sheep. "From the Sidelines." *Cleveland Call and Post*, April 27, 1968, 9B.

Jacobs, Jeff. "Hey, Time to Call a Tech." *Hartford Courant*, March 10, 2001, C10.

Jacobson, Steve. "The Voting Doesn't Always Do Justice." *Newsday*, March 1, 1967, 158.

Johns, Walter L. "Sports Sputterings." *The Hammond Times*, February 7, 1962, 47.

Johnson, Dave. "19th Century Baseball, Negro League Get Crack at Fame." *Evansville Courier and Press*, March 5, 1995, 20.

"Junk Negro Shrine Vote, Says Young." *The Sporting News*, March 15, 1975, 51.

Keisser, Bob. "Anchor Cries Foul Ball." *Newport News Daily Press*, October 1, 1994, B6.

Kekis, John. "Black Players Focus of New Hall Exhibit." *Elmira Star-Gazette*, June 10, 1997, 5.

Kelly, Dan. "Negro Leagues 100th Anniversary Celebration." *Kansas City Star*, February 13, 2020, B6.

Kepner, Tyler. "Baseball Rights a Wrong by Adding Negro Leagues to Official Records." *New York Times*, December 17, 2020, A1.

Koppett, Leonard. "Baseball's Bias Is Subtle, Disturbing." *The Sporting News*, March 21, 1970, 4.

Kuhnhenn, James. "City Gets Grant to Boost Jazz District." *Kansas City Times*, June 12, 1986, 22.

Lang, Jack. "Treaty by Hall Voters." *The Sporting News*, February 17, 1973, 39.

Lardner, John. "Landis Dumps Negro Play Into Major Bosses' Laps." *Omaha Evening World-Herald*, July 29, 1942, 16.

Lardner, John. "Negro Ball Players Able Despite Major League Ban." *Edmonton Journal*, November 23, 1939, 7.

Leigh, PFC Frederick M. "Colored GIs Distinguish Selves in Bombay Meet." *Baltimore Afro-American*, May 5, 1945, 18.

"Library Hosts Baseball History." *Casper Star-Tribune*, November 8, 2009, 20.

Lipman, Dave. "This Was Cool Papa: Better Paid Than Satch, Faster Than Owens." *St. Louis Post-Dispatch*, March 3, 1963, 77.

"MacPhail Has a Tough Sell." *Hartford Courant*, July 23, 2000, E8.

Margolies, Dan. "Baseball Museum Prevails in Suit." *Kansas City Star*, February 9, 2006, C1 and C8.

Margolies, Dan. "Case of the Missing Tapes Takes a Few New Twists." *Kansas City Star*, October 25, 2005, D15.

Margolies, Dan. "Suit Filed Over Missing Tapes." *Greensboro News & Record*, May 16, 2004, C6.

Marston, Gordon (Red). "Boston Debate—

Pro and Con!" *The Sporting News*, August 4, 1948, 36.

McDonough, Will. "Ted Awes Cooperstown Crowd." *Boston Globe*, July 26, 1966, 1.

McGuff, Joe. "Sporting Comment." *Kansas City Star*, February 9, 1971, 7.

McGuff, Joe. "Sporting Comment." *Kansas City Star*, July 26, 1966, 11.

Miller, Robin. "Jackie Robinson 'Fights' Drugs." *Indianapolis Star*, April 17, 1971, 28.

Monroe, Al. "It's News to Me." *Chicago Defender*, February 5, 1938, 9.

Moses, Al. "Beating the Gun." *Phoenix Index*, July 19, 1941, 6.

Mozley, Dana. "Revised Rule to Open Door to Fame Hall for Stengel." *New York Daily News*, January 31, 1966, 46.

Murphy, Kevin. "White House Salutes Legends." *Kansas City Star*, March 31, 2001, D8.

Murray, Jim. "Back Door to Hall of Fame." *Modesto Bee*, February 16, 1971, 18.

Murray, Jim. "Feller Wanted In, But His Way." *Arizona Republic*, January 28, 1962, 46.

Nack, Bill. "Nine Is Not Nearly Enough for Recognition of Blacks." *Newsday*, August 11, 1977, 129.

Nason, Jerry. "Joss Deserves Place in 'Hall.'" *Boston Globe*, July 27, 1966, 29.

Neuman, Roger. "Veterans Committee Does Injustice to Baseball Hall of Fame." *Elmira Star-Gazette*, March 9, 2001, 4.

"New Agreement Curbs Veto by Commissioner." *The Sporting News*, February 8, 1945, 4.

"New Museum Pitches Flavor of Negro Leagues." *Arizona Republic*, September 22, 1994, D2.

"New Shrine Rules Could Spell Peace." *The Sporting News*, October 15, 1977, 7.

Nichols, Ed. "Paige, Ineligible, Deserves to Be in Hall." *Salisbury Daily Times*, February 2, 1962, 14.

Obituary. "C.C. Johnson Spink of the Sporting News Dies." *St. Louis Post-Dispatch*, March 27, 1992, 3A.

O'Connell, Jack. "Sensible Shakeup at Hall." *Hartford Courant*, August 7, 2001, C1 and C5.

"On Good Clean Fun, Long Hair and So Forth...." *Des Moines Register*, October 9, 1994, 11D.

Bibliography

Penn, Steve. "The Hall. O'Neil. It's Time." *Kansas City Star*, July 5, 2005, B1.

Pennington, Gail. "Ken Burns' 'Baseball': That's a Winner (Sort Of)." *St. Louis Post-Dispatch*, October 6, 1994, 6G.

Pepe, Phil. "Ol' Satch Makes Hall of Fame, Natch." *New York Daily News*, February 10, 1971, C26.

Pepe, Phil. "Old Negro Greats Get Crack at Hall of Fame." *New York Daily News*, February 4, 1971, 91.

Peterson, Robert. "Josh Gibson Was the Equal of Babe Ruth, But...." *New York Times*, April 11, 1971, SM12.

"Pioneering Rube Foster 'Saved' Major Leagues." *Pittsburgh Courier*, May 18, 1968, 15.

Plass, Jeff. "ESPN Program Assesses Negro League's Legacy." *Bangor Daily News*, October 15, 1994, 103.

Posey, Cumberland. "Cum Posey Turns Back Colorful Pages of Negro Baseball and Lists 8 of the Greatest Sepia Ball Clubs of All Time." *Pittsburgh Courier*, January, 20, 1940, 17.

Posnanski, Joe. "After Shock, an Outcry of O'Neil." *Kansas City Star*, March 5, 2006, C1 and C13.

Posnanski, Joe. "Let's Get Behind Buck." *Kansas City Star*, May 17, 2001, D1 and D6.

Povich, Shirley. "This Morning..." *Washington Post*, July 26, 1966, B1.

Ramirez, Dominic, Jr. "Wife, Parents of Late MLB Player Skaggs File Lawsuits." *Fort Worth Star-Telegram*, June 30, 2021, 6A.

Rieber, Anthony. "Oops! Major League Baseball's 500,000th Error." *Newsday*, September 16, 2012, A64–65.

Roberts, Ric. "Ted Urges Naming Josh, Satch to Shine." *Pittsburgh Courier*, August 6, 1966, 15.

"Robeson Selects Colored All-Stars." *New York Daily News*, June 29, 1939, 126.

Robinson, Alan. "'Like We Invented the Game.'" *Raleigh News and Observer*, October 2, 1994, 26.

Routhier, Ray. "Burns' Boner: 'Baseball' Forgot to Touch Home." *Portland Press Herald*, October 2, 1994, 12E.

Sandomir, Richard. "Hits, Runs and Memories." *New York Times*, September 18, 1994, 2–1.

"Satch, Josh & Co ... Color 'Em Great." *New York Daily News*, February 4, 1971, 12.

Shaikin, Bill. "Forget Frick. It's Time for Scully's Name on Award." *Los Angeles Times*, October 8, 2022, DD1.

Shaughnessy, Dan. "Tom Has Won This Year, but Back Off on Bill." *Boston Globe*, January 3, 2021, C1 and C7.

Shores, Larry. "Baseball—Looking for Answers." *Muncie Star*, September 24, 1994, 8A.

Smith, Jim. "Limit Set on Negro Leagues' Famers." *Newsday*, February 4, 1977, 92.

Smith, Red. "Racism Hasn't Disappeared from Baseball's Memory." *Hartford Courant*, February 24, 1971, 29.

Smith, Wendell. "Cincinnati Reds' Manager, Players Laud Negro Stars." *Pittsburgh Courier*, July 15, 1939, 13.

Smith, Wendell. "General Public Must Be Changed." *Pittsburgh Courier*, February 25, 1939, 1 and 16.

Smith, Wendell. "'No Need for Color Ban in Big Leagues'—Pie Traynor." *Pittsburgh Courier*, September 2, 1939, 16.

Smith, Wendell. "'Owners Must Solve Color Problem In Majors—Stengel." *Pittsburgh Courier*, August 26, 1939, 16.

Smith, Wendell. "St. Louis Pilot, Players Friendly, Helpful to Jackie." *Pittsburgh Courier*, June 21, 1947, 14.

Smith, Wendell. "Smitty's Sport Spurts." *Pittsburgh Courier*, December 10, 1938, 16.

Smith, Wendell. "Sports Beat." *Pittsburgh Courier*, January 21, 1967, 15.

"Sound Off." *St. Louis Post-Dispatch*, March 25, 2001, 54.

Span, Paula. "Ratings to Boost 'Baseball' Gear." *Philadelphia Inquirer*, October 6, 1994, E1 and E4.

Sparrow, Herbert. "Cooperstown Neglecting Black Stars." *Owensboro Messenger-Inquirer*, June 25, 1980, 13.

Sparrow, Herbert. "Limelight Finally Finds Negro League Star." *Owensboro Messenger-Inquirer*, June 25, 1980, 15.

Sparrow, Herbert. "Negro Baseball Hall of Fame Proposed." *Biloxi-Gulfport Sun Herald*, June 25, 1980, 43.

Spink, C.C. Johnson. "We Believe..." *The Sporting News*, September 1, 1977, 14.

Spink, John George Taylor. "The Negro Player Steps on the Scales." *The Sporting News*, May 21, 1947, 14.

Spink, John George Taylor. "No Good from Raising Race Issue." *The Sporting News*, August 6, 1942, 4.

Spink, John George Taylor. "Rookie of the Year ... Jackie Robinson." *The Sporting News*, September 17, 1947, 3.

Spink, John George Taylor. "Three and One." *The Sporting News*, June 7, 1934, 4.

Spink, John George Taylor. "Two Ill-Advised Moves." *The Sporting News*, July 14, 1948, 8.

Spink, John George Taylor. "Writers Manage to Dig Up Kick for Happy." *The Sporting News*, December 21, 1949, 6.

Stevenson, Jennifer L. "Buck O'Neil Not Only Talks a Good Game." *Tampa Bay Times*, September 18, 1994, 1F.

Stinson, Thomas. "PBS Series May Have Rekindled Negro Leagues Interest." *Atlanta Constitution*, February 5, 1995, 62.

Strouse, Charles. "Recalling Segregation in Baseball." *Indianapolis Star*, October 4, 1994, 37.

Surface, Bill. "The Last Days of Rogers Hornsby." *Saturday Evening Post*, June 15, 1963, 72.

Talbert, Ted. "Negro League Reunion Shows Ex-Projects Kid Old Legends Live." *Detroit Free Press*, July 29, 1980, 1D and 3D.

Taylor, Nate. "A Comeback for Negro Leagues Museum." *New York Times*, August 24, 2013, D1.

Taylor, Sec. "Sittin' in with the Athletes." *Des Moines Register*, February 1, 1961, 12.

"Ted Williams Strikes Again." *Vancouver Sun*, August 3, 1966, 5.

Thorn, Cody. "Exhibit Highlights African-American Baseball Experience." *St. Joseph News-Press*, May 18, 2011, A1 and A3.

"Too Few Black Baseball Greats in Hall: Powell." *Chicago Daily Defender*, August 12, 1972, 41.

"Tributes Paid Walt Johnson and Carl Hubbell." *The Sporting News*, February 15, 1934, 8.

Triplett, Ward W., III. "Men Find Heroes in Research of Negro Leagues." *Kansas City Star*, December 31, 1985, 46.

"Two Great Eras of Marvels Preceded Robinson's Years." *Pittsburgh Courier*, May 18, 1968, 15.

Tygiel, Jules. "Revisiting Bill Veeck and the 1943 Phillies." *Baseball Research Journal* (2006), 109.

United Press. "Focus on Manley at Players Reunion." *Nashville Tennessean*, June 17, 1980, 10.

United Press. "Hall of Fame to Move Satchel Paige Into Its Regular Lineup Next Month." *Evansville Press*, July 7, 1971, 34.

United Press. "Hall of History Planned for Black Baseball Stars." *Hartford Courant*, November 7, 1980, 101.

United Press. "Irvin, Paige Top Negro All-Star Team." *Newport News Daily Press*, June 27, 1982, 38.

United Press. "Klein, Yawkey in Hall of Fame." *Philadelphia Daily News*, March 12, 1980, 63.

United Press. "Making Players Ineligible Is Blacklist Frick Admits." *St. Louis Post-Dispatch*, July 31, 1951, 29.

"Voice of the People." *New York Daily News*, March 19, 2001, 32.

Wade, Don. "In Memories Yet Green...." *Kansas City Times*, April 6, 1985, C1 and C3.

Wagner, James. "Baseball Reference Adds Negro Leagues Statistics, Rewriting Its Record Book." *New York Times*, June 16, 2021, B10.

Wagner, James. "A League's First Comment, at Last." *New York Times*, June 4, 2020, p. B7.

"Wakefield Ruling Cost Job, Chandler Declares." *The Sporting News*, August 15, 1951, 7.

Walker, Ben. "Reconciling a Dark Past." *Atlanta Journal-Constitution*, July 1, 2020, C5.

Washington, Chester. "Build on Ballyhoo." *Pittsburgh Courier*, January 29, 1938, 16.

Washington, Chester. "He's Sez." *Pittsburgh Courier*, January 29, 1938, 16.

Weiner, Jay. "Negro Leagues' Players Overlooked." *Newsday*, January 13, 1980, 268.

Whirty, Ryan. "KC's Father-Son Battery Made Baseball History 75 Years Ago." *Kansas City Star*, February 14, 2016, 7B.

Whiteside, Larry. "The First to Play." *Boston Globe*, July 22, 1979, 41.

Williams, Joe. "What Goes On?" *Pittsburgh Press*, July 27, 1942, 17.

"Williams Wants Paige, Gibson Named to 'Hall.'" *Alexandria News Leader*, August 14, 1966, 8.

Bibliography

Windsor, Shawn. "Exhibit Is Home Run for Harper Woods." *Detroit Free Press,* November 3, 2010, 15.

Wood, Hal. "Satch Makes It by Back Door." *Honolulu Advertiser,* February 10, 1971, 53.

Young, A.S. "Doc." "Season for Nostalgia." *Chicago Defender,* May 17, 1967, 28.

Young, Dick. "Campy, 'The Man,' Hoyt, Coveleski Deck the Hall." *New York Daily News,* July 29, 1969, 58.

Young, Dick. "First Division for Mets? Why Not? Barks Casey." *New York Daily News,* March 5, 1966, 27.

Young, Dick. "Jackie, Feller in Racial Debate." *New York Daily News,* July 23, 1969, 89.

Young, Dick. "Special Vote Places Casey in Fame Hall." *New York Daily News,* March 9, 1966, C26.

Young, Dick. "Young Ideas." *New York Daily News,* September 1, 1965, C26.

Young, Dick. "Young Ideas." *New York Daily News,* November 11, 1965, 116.

Young, Dick. "Young Ideas." *New York Daily News,* November 26, 1965, C26.

Young, Dick. "Young Ideas." *New York Daily News,* December 3, 1965, 101.

Young, Dick. "Young Ideas." *New York Daily News,* December 19, 1965, 37C.

Young, Dick. "Young Ideas." *New York Daily News,* January 13, 1966, 62.

Young, Dick. "Young Ideas." *New York Daily News,* January 25, 1966, 53.

Young, Dick. "Young Ideas." *New York Daily News,* February 6, 1966, 31.

Young, Dick. "Young Ideas." *New York Daily News,* March 6, 1966, 137.

Young, Dick. "Young Ideas." *New York Daily News,* March 9, 1966, C30.

Young, Dick. "Young Ideas." *New York Daily News,* March 12, 1966, 52.

Young, Dick. "Young Ideas." *New York Daily News,* April 2, 1966, 33.

Young, Dick. "Young Ideas." *New York Daily News,* April 17, 1966, 151.

Young, Dick. "Young Ideas." *New York Daily News,* April 20, 1966, C26.

Young, Dick. "Young Ideas." *New York Daily News,* July 26, 1966, 55.

Young, Dick. "Young Ideas." *New York Daily News,* August 17, 1968, 31.

Young, Dick. "Young Ideas." *New York Daily News,* July 30, 1969, 81.

Young, Dick. "Young Ideas." *New York Daily News,* February 4, 1971, 23C.

Young, Dick. "Young Ideas." *New York Daily News,* June 11, 1971, 83.

Young, Dick. "Young Ideas." *New York Daily News,* August 9, 1977, 55.

Young, Dick. "Young Ideas." *The Sporting News,* August 6, 1966, 14.

Young, Frank A. "Dandridge as Good as Mel Ott at His Best." *Chicago Defender,* September 24, 1938, 9.

Internet

"Adam Silver, NBA Teams Express Outrage After George Floyd's Death." *NBA.com.* Retrieved January 11, 2024, from https://www.nba.com/news/nba-teams-respond-tragic-death-george-floyd.

Appelman, Dave. "Negro Leagues Data Is Now Available on FanGraphs!" *Fan Graphs.com,* February 14, 2023. Retrieved December 21, 2023, from https://blogs.fangraphs.com/negro-leagues-data-is-now-available-on-fangraphs/.

Armour, Mark, and Daniel R. Levitt. "Baseball Demographics, 1947–2016." *SABR.org.* Retrieved October 11, 2023, from https://sabr.org/bioproj/topic/baseball-demographics-1947-2016/.

Ashwill, Gary. "Building the Seamheads Negro Leagues Database." *Baseball-Reference.com.* Retrieved December 21, 2023, from https://www.baseball-reference.com/articles/building-the-seamheads-negro-league-database-gary-ashwill.shtml.

Associated Press. "All Golden Era Candidates Fall Short." *ESPN.com,* December 8, 2014. Retrieved December 6, 2023, from https://www.espn.com/mlb/story/_/id/11999830/all-10-golden-era-candidates-fall-short-hall-fame-induction.

Associated Press. "Baseball's Black Pioneers Get 'Tip of the Cap' to Salute 100-Year Anniversary of Negro Leagues." *ESPN.com,* June 29, 2020. Retrieved August 2, 2023, from https://www.espn.com/mlb/story/_/id/29382314/baseball-black-pioneers-given-tip-cap-salute-100-year-anniversary-negro-leagues.

Associated Press. "BBWAA Removes Ex–MLB Commissioner Kenesaw

Mountain Landis' Name from MVP Awards." *ESPN.com*, October 2, 2020. Retrieved December 15, 2023, from https://www.espn.com/mlb/story/_/id/30024685/bbwaa-removes-ex-mlb-commissioner-kenesaw-mountain-landis-name-mvp-awards.

Associated Press. "Congressional Group Wants Landis Name Pulled from MVP Plaque." *USAToday.com*, August 4, 2020. Retrieved December 19, 2023, from https://www.usatoday.com/story/sports/mlb/2020/08/04/congressional-group-wants-landis-name-pulled-from-mvp-plaque/112813382/.

Barnes, Bart. "Crusading Sportswriter Sam Lacy, 99, Dies." *Washington Post*, May 10, 2023. Retrieved August 16, 2023, from https://www.washingtonpost.com/archive/local/2003/05/10/crusading-sportswriter-sam-lacy-99-dies/14a5394b-cfa0-4b9a-85f2-87dda21976be/?utm_term=.ca781e1d0749.

Bohmer, David. "Ford Frick and Jackie Robinson: The Enabler." *SABR.org*. Retrieved August 31, 2020, from https://sabr.org/journal/article/ford-frick-and-jackie-robinson-the-enabler/.

Bohn, Terry. "Happy Chandler." *SABR.org*. Retrieved August 28, 2023, from https://sabr.org/bioproj/person/happy-chandler/.

Cappetta, Lou. "Who's In? Evaluating the 2010 Baseball Hall of Fame Ballot." *Bleacherreport.com*, January 2, 2010. Retrieved December 6, 2023, from https://bleacherreport.com/articles/318561-whos-in-evaluating-the-2010-baseball-hall-of-fame-ballot.

Castrovince, Anthony. "Buck, Gil, Minnie Among 6 Elected to Hall." *MLB.com*, January 25, 2022. Retrieved January 2, 2024, from https://www.mlb.com/news/2021-hall-of-fame-committee-election-results.

Castrovince, Anthony. "MLB Adds Negro Leagues to Official Records." *MLB.com*, December 16, 2020. Retrieved December 20, 2023, from https://www.mlb.com/news/negro-leagues-given-major-league-status-for-baseball-records-stats.

Castrovince, Anthony. "The Ongoing Search Through History to Give Negro Leaguers Their Due." *MLB.com*, November 6, 2023. Retrieved December 21, 2023, from https://www.mlb.com/news/mlb-working-to-add-negro-leagues-stats-to-record.

Cichalski, Dan. "April 14, 1955: Elston Howard Integrates the Yankees." *SABR.org*, February 17, 2022. Retrieved January 9, 2024, from https://sabr.org/gamesproj/game/april-14-1955-elston-howard-integrates-the-yankees/.

Cichalski, Dan. "Hall of Fame Reveals Name of New Black Baseball Exhibit: 'The Souls of the Game.'" *MLB.com*, June 19, 2023. Retrieved January 5, 2024, from https://www.mlb.com/news/baseball-hall-of-fame-announces-new-black-baseball-exhibit.

Clark, Dave. "Kenesaw Mountain Landis' Name Removed from Major League Baseball's MVP Awards." *Cincinnati Enquirer*, October 2, 2020. Retrieved April 17, 2023, from https://www.cincinnati.com/story/sports/mlb/reds/2020/10/02/kenesaw-mountain-landis-name-removed-mlbs-mvp-awards/3594308001/.

Coffey, Alex. "Buck Leonard and Josh Gibson Are Elected to the Hall of Fame." *Baseballhall.org*. Retrieved January 9, 2024, from https://baseballhall.org/discover-more/stories/inside-pitch/buck-leonard-josh-gibson-elected-to-hof.

Condon, Bridget. "'We've Always Been Somebody': Negro League Families Say MLB Recognition 'Long Overdue.'" *ABC11.com*, February 15, 2021. Retrieved August 3, 2023, from https://abc11.com/baseball-negro-league-leagues-players/10334088/.

"Constitution." *BBWAA.com*. Retrieved August 1, 2023, from https://bbwaa.com/constitution/.

Corbett, Warren. "Ford Frick." *SABR.org*. Retrieved August 29, 2023, from https://sabr.org/bioproj/person/ford-frick/.

Cox, Joe. "Happy Helping? Inside Commissioner Chandler's Role in Jackie Robinson's Great Quest." *SABR.org*. Retrieved August 28, 2023, from https://sabr.org/journal/article/happy-helping-inside-commissioner-chandlers-role-in-jackie-robinsons-great-quest/#calibre_link-1281.

Bibliography

Cox, Matt. "Keep Baseball Going." *Baseballhall.org*, 2009. Retrieved August 9, 2023, from https://baseballhall.org/discover-more/stories/short-stops/keep-baseball-going.

Curry, Jack. "Bob Feller: Lots of Words, Plus a Ride to the Airport." *NYTimes.com*, June 23, 2008. Retrieved September 6, 2023, from https://archive.nytimes.com/bats.blogs.nytimes.com/2008/06/23/bob-feller-lots-of-words-plus-a-ride-to-the-airport/.

Curry, Jack. "Going Back, Back, Back to 1939." *NYTimes.com*, June 23, 2008. Retrieved September 6, 2023, from https://www.nytimes.com/2008/06/23/sports/baseball/23allstar.html.

Dreier, Peter. "'White Fragility' Gets Jackie Robinson's Story Wrong." *Boston Review*, February 8, 2021. Retrieved June 22, 2023, from https://www.bostonreview.net/articles/peter-dreier-getting-jackie-robinsons-story-wrong/.

Dreier, Peter. "Will MLB Confront Its Racist History?" *DissentMagazine.org*, July 22, 2020. Retrieved August 31, 2023, from https://www.dissentmagazine.org/online_articles/will-the-mlb-confront-its-racist-history/.

ESPN News Services. "Astros Manager Dusty Baker 'Proud of This Generation' as Houston, Oakland Protest." *ESPN.com*, August 28, 2020. Retrieved January 11, 2024, from https://www.espn.com/mlb/story/_/id/29762453/oakland-athletics-houston-astros-call-game.

Fertig, Todd. "Legacy: Negro League Experience a Blend of Beauty, Tragedy." *CJOnline.com*, March 12, 2016. Retrieved August 3, 2023, from https://www.cjonline.com/story/sports/2016/03/12/legacy-negro-league-experience-blend-beauty-tragedy/16597752007/.

Folsom, Burton W. "The Costs of Segregation to the Detroit Tigers." *Fee.org*, December 1, 2023. Retrieved August 23, 2023, from https://fee.org/articles/the-costs-of-segregation-to-the-detroit-tigers/.

"The Ford C. Frick Award: A Disgraceful and Unnecessary Reminder of Major League Baseball's Racist Past." *Boomsalad.com*. Retrieved August 31, 2023, from http://www.boomsalad.com/english/nonfiction/fordfrickaward/.

Frommer, Harvey. "Casey Stengel Remembered: A Baseball Icon and a Yankee Immortal." *Bleacherreport.com*, October 14, 2022. Retrieved August 22, 2023, from https://bleacherreport.com/articles/890508-casey-stengel-remembered-a-baseball-icon-and-a-yankee-immortal.

"George Floyd: What Happened in the Final Moments of His Life." *BBC.com*. Retrieved January 11, 2024, from https://www.bbc.com/news/world-us-canada-52861726.

Gerike, Evan. "Loans Take Cooperstown Magic Throughout the World." *Baseballhall.org*, 2022. Retrieved January 3, 2024, from https://baseballhall.org/discover/loans-take-cooperstown-magic-throughout-the-world.

Gerlach, Larry, David Jordan, and John Rossi. "A Baseball Myth Exploded: Bill Veeck and the 1943 Sale of the Phillies." Originally published in *The National Pastime* 18 (1998). Retrieved August 10, 2023, from https://sabr.org/research/article/a-baseball-myth-exploded-bill-veeck-and-the-1943-sale-of-the-phillies/.

Goldman, Steven. "On Jackie Robinson Day, the Yankees Must Answer for Jim Crow Baseball." *Pinstripealley.com*, April 15, 2013. Retrieved August 23, 2023, from https://www.pinstripealley.com/2013/4/15/4228172/jackie-robinson-day-new-york-yankees-vic-power-elston-howard.

Gonzalez, Alden. "MLB Moving 2021 All-Star Game from Atlanta Over Georgia Voting Law." *ESPN.com*, April 2, 2021. Retrieved December 28, 2023, from https://www.espn.com/mlb/story/_/id/31183822/mlb-moving-all-star-game-atlanta-georgia-voting-law.

Gordon, David J. "Racial Parity in the Hall of Fame." *SABR.org*, 2018. Retrieved August 28, 2023, from https://sabr.org/journal/article/racial-parity-in-the-hall-of-fame/.

Grace, De'Zhon, Carolyn Johnson, and Treva Reid (2020, May 4). "Racial Inequality and COVID-19." *Greenlining.org*, May 4, 2020. Retrieved January 11, 2024, from https://greenlining.org/2020/racial-inequality-and-covid-19/.

Hendricks, Mike. "'A Great Day' as Project

Unveiled to Restore Satchel Paige Home in Kansas City." *Kansascity.com*, August 11, 2021. Retrieved January 3, 2024, from https://www.kansascity.com/news/local/article253368638.html.

Hennessy, Kevin. "Calvin Griffith." *SABR.org*. Retrieved August 16, 2023, from https://sabr.org/bioproj/person/calvin-griffith/.

Henson, Steve. "Eric Kay's Appeal Denied in Fentanyl Case That Killed Angels Pitcher Tyler Skaggs." *LATimes.com*, November 16, 2023. Retrieved December 27, 2023, from https://www.latimes.com/sports/story/2023-11-16/eric-kay-appeal-denied-tyler-skaggs-death-fentanyl-angels.

Hill, Benjamin. "Full Circle: Bud Fowler Set for Hall Enshrinement." *MILB.com*, February 23, 2022. Retrieved July 31, 2023, from https://www.milb.com/news/bud-fowler-baseball-pioneer-and-hall-of-famer.

Hughson, Callum. "Adolfo 'Dolf' Luque: The Pride of Havana." *Mopupduty.com*, November 3, 2010. Retrieved September 21, 2023, from http://mopupduty.com/adolfo-dolf-luque-the-pride-of-havana/.

"'I Can't Breathe!' Video of Fatal Arrest Shows Minneapolis Officer Kneeling in George Floyd's Neck for Several Minutes." *CBSNews.com*, May 26, 2020. Retrieved January 11, 2024, from https://www.cbsnews.com/minnesota/news/george-floyd-man-dies-after-being-arrested-by-minneapolis-police-fbi-called-to-investigate/.

Jaffe, Jay. "The Hall of Fame Shakes Up Its Era Committee System Yet Again." *Fangraphs.com*, April 26, 2022. Retrieved January 3, 2024, from https://blogs.fangraphs.com/the-hall-of-fame-shakes-up-its-era-committee-system-yet-again/.

Jaffe, Jay. "Pre-Integration Era Vote Again Shows Flaws in Hall of Fame's Process." *SI.com*, December 7, 2015. Retrieved December 5, 2023, from https://www.si.com/mlb/2015/12/07/hall-of-fame-veterans-committee-pre-integration-era-vote.

Jaffe, Jay. "Upcoming Early Baseball Era Committee Ballot Will Give Negro Leagues Candidates Another Shot at Hall of Fame." *Fangraphs.com*, August 9, 2021. Retrieved January 4, 2024, from https://blogs.fangraphs.com/upcoming-early-baseball-era-committee-ballot-will-give-negro-leagues-candidates-another-shot-at-hall-of-fame/.

Jenkinson, Bill. "Babe Ruth and the Issue of Race." *Baberuthcentral.com*, 2009, updated 2016. Retrieved August 28, 2023, from http://www.baberuthcentral.com/babe-ruth-and-the-issue-of-race-bill-jenkinson/.

Kekis, John. "Robinson Honored with New Plaque." *SanDiegoUnionTribune.com*, June 25, 2008. Retrieved January 11, 2024, from https://www.sandiegouniontribune.com/sdut-robinson-honored-new-hall-fame-plaque-2008jun25-story.html.

Kelly, Matt. "Era Committee Elections Rescheduled to 2021." *MLB.com*, August 24, 2020. Retrieved December 14, 2023, from https://www.mlb.com/news/hall-of-fame-era-committee-elections-rescheduled-to-2021.

Kelly, Matt. "Innovations of the Negro League." *MLB.com*. Retrieved August 28, 2023, from https://www.mlb.com/history/negro-leagues/features/negro-league-innovations.

Kelly, Matt. "Landis' Name to Be Removed from MVP Trophies." *MLB.com*, October 2, 2020. Retrieved April 17, 2023, from https://www.mlb.com/news/kenesaw-mountain-landis-name-removed-mvp-trophies.

Kepner, Tyler. "Another Shutout in Electing Members of the Baseball Hall of Fame." *New York Times*, February 28, 2007. Retrieved January 11, 2024, from https://www.nytimes.com/2007/02/28/sports/28iht-BASE.4752502.html.

Kepner, Tyler. "The Hall of Fame Tries to Contextualize Baseball's Racist Past." *New York Times*, December 21, 2020. Retrieved, June 14, 2023, from https://www.nytimes.com/2020/12/21/sports/baseball/hall-of-fame.html.

Kepner, Tyler. "'This Is American History': The Hall of Fame Reconsiders Race." *New York Times*, April 14, 2022. Retrieved, June 14, 2023, from https://www.nytimes.com/2022/04/14/sports/baseball/jackie-robinson-hall-of-fame.html.

Bibliography

Kern, Thomas. "John Henry 'Pop' Lloyd." *SABR.org*. Retrieved January 9, 2024, from https://sabr.org/bioproj/person/pop-lloyd/.

Kurkjian, Tim. "New HOF Ballot Eying Those Left Behind." *ESPN.com*, November 19, 2010. Retrieved December 6, 2023, from https://www.espn.com/mlb/columns/story?columnist=kurkjian_tim&id=5820675.

Lahman, Sean. "As Negro Leagues Teams Get 'Major' Status, How Baseball Is Reckoning with Past Inequities." *DemocratandChronicle.com*, March 31, 2021. Retrieved December 28, 2023, from https://www.democratandchronicle.com/story/sports/2021/03/31/black-major-league-baseball-legacy-hall-fame-and-cooperstown/4668662001/.

Lamb, Chris. "J.G. Taylor Spink's Racist Baseball Legacy Lasted Decades, but in the End, Truth Won." *USA Today*, March 13, 2021. Retrieved April 13, 2023, from https://www.usatoday.com/story/sports/2021/03/13/jg-taylor-spinks-racist-baseball-legacy-lasted-years/6939295002/.

Lee, Michael. "The Negro Leagues Museum, After a Year of Loss, Counts Its 'Merger' with MLB as a Ain." *Washington Post*, January 5, 2021. Retrieved June 14, 2023, from https://www.washingtonpost.com/sports/2021/01/05/negro-leagues-museum-major-league-baseball/.

Lee, Michael. "Once Shut Out of the Hall of Fame, These Black Ballplayers Are Getting Another Shot." *Washington Post*, December 4, 2021. Retrieved June 14, 2023, from https://www.washingtonpost.com/sports/2021/12/04/baseball-hall-fame-negro-leagues/.

Lester, Larry. "Can You Read, Judge Landis?" *SABR.org*, Fall 2008. Retrieved January 9, 2024, from https://sabr.org/journal/article/can-you-read-judge-landis/.

Manoloff, Dennis. "Bob Feller at 91: 'Living Legend? It's a Term I Respect and Appreciate.'" *Cleveland.com*, April 4, 2010. Retrieved September 7, 2023, from https://www.cleveland.com/tribe/2010/04/bob_feller_at_91_living_legend.html.

McKenna, Brian. "Bud Fowler." *SABR.org*. Retrieved January 8, 2024, from https://sabr.org/bioproj/person/Bud-Fowler/.

Miglio, Alexander. "Baseball's Hall of Fame Voters Have Forgotten What the Hall Is All About." *Bleacher report.com*, January 10, 2013. Retrieved August 28, 2023, from https://bleacherreport.com/articles/1479706-baseballs-hall-of-fame-voters-forget-what-the-hall-is-about.

MLB Press Release. "MLB Officially Designates the Negro Leagues as 'Major League.'" *MLB.com*, December 16, 2020. Retrieved December 21, 2023, from https://www.mlb.com/press-release/press-release-mlb-officially-designates-the-negro-leagues-as-major-league.

MLB Press Release. "MLB Statement Regarding 2021 All-Star Game." *MLB.com*, April 2, 2021. Retrieved December 28, 2023, from https://www.mlb.com/press-release/press-release-mlb-statement-regarding-2021-all-star-game.

Moriah, David. "Collector Josh Rawitch Relishes Dream Job as President of Baseball's Hall of Fame." *Sports collectorsdigest.com*, March 31, 2023. Retrieved December 29, 2023, from https://sportscollectorsdigest.com/news/baseball-hall-of-fame-president-josh-rawitch-cards-memorabilia-mlb.

National Archives. "Executive Order 8802: Prohibition of Discrimination in the Defense Industry (1941)." *Archives.org*. Retrieved August 11, 2023, from https://www.archives.gov/milestone-documents/executive-order-8802.

National Baseball Hall of Fame. "BL-175. 2003, Folder 1, Fancorr_1971 _02_23." *Baseballhall.org*. Retrieved October 9, 2023, from https://baseballhall.org/discover-more/digital-collection/1543.

National Baseball Hall of Fame. "A Brief History of Elections of Negro Leagues Candidates." *Web.archive.org*. Retrieved November 22, 2023, from https://web.archive.org/web/20060228193953/http://www.baseballhalloffame.org/hofers_and_honorees/negro_lg_overview.htm.

National Baseball Hall of Fame. "Buck

Bibliography

O'Neil Award." *Baseballhall.org*. Retrieved September 1, 2023, from https://baseballhall.org/discover-more/awards/890.

National Baseball Hall of Fame. "Education and Outreach." *Baseballhall.org*. Retrieved January 5, 2024, from https://baseballhall.org/The-Black-Baseball-Initiative/Education-and-Outreach.

National Baseball Hall of Fame. "Eras Committees." *Baseballhall.org*. Retrieved January 4, 2024, from https://baseballhall.org/hall-of-fame/election-rules/era-committees.

National Baseball Hall of Fame. "Hall of Famer Ozzie Smith Elected to Board of Directors; Era Committees Restructured." *Baseballhall.org*, July 23, 2016. Retrieved December 8, 2023, from https://baseballhall.org/discover-more/news/hall-of-fame-announcements.

National Baseball Hall of Fame. "The History of Baseball and Civil Rights in America." *Baseballhall.org*. Retrieved August 22, 2023, from https://baseballhall.org/civilrights.

National Baseball Hall of Fame. "Jackie Robinson." *Baseballhall.org*. Retrieved December 8, 2023, from https://baseballhall.org/hall-of-famers/robinson-jackie.

National Baseball Hall of Fame. "Meet the Team." *Baseballhall.org*. Retrieved January 1, 2024, from https://baseballhall.org/The-Black-Baseball-Initiative/Meet-the-Team.

National Baseball Hall of Fame. "Museum Floor Plan." *Baseballhall.org*. Retrieved January 5, 2024, from https://baseballhall.org/visit/museum-map.

National Baseball Hall of Fame. "Museum Initiative to Highlight Story of Black Baseball." *Baseballhall.org*, April 15, 2022. Retrieved January 4, 2024, from https://baseballhall.org/news/museum-initiative-to-highlight-story-of-black-baseball.

National Baseball Hall of Fame. "President and Leadership Team." *Baseballhall.org*. Retrieved December 29, 2023, from https://baseballhall.org/about-the-hall/staff/staff-directory.

National Baseball Hall of Fame. "Tom Yawkey, Executive, Class of 1980." *Baseballhall.org*. Retrieved December 28, 2023, from https://baseballhall.org/hall-of-famers/yawkey-tom.

National Baseball Hall of Fame. "2016 Pre-Integration Committee Candidates." *Baseballhall.org*. Retrieved December 1, 2023, from https://baseballhall.org/discover-more/stories/pre-integration/2016-candidates.

National Baseball Hall of Fame. "Voting Rules History." *Baseballhall.org*. Retrieved August 22, 2023, from https://baseballhall.org/hall-of-famers/rules/voting-rules-history.

National Baseball Hall of Fame Press Release. "Cox, LaRussa, Torre Elected to Hall of Fame." *Web.archive.org*, December 9, 2013. Retrieved December 6, 2023, from https://web.archive.org/web/20131212121956/http://baseballhall.org/news/press-releases/cox-la-russa-torre-elected-hall-fame.

National Baseball Hall of Fame Press Release. "Hall of Fame Restructures Era Committee, Frick Award Voting." *Baseballhall.org*, April 22, 2022. Retrieved January 3, 2024, from https://baseballhall.org/news/hall-of-fame-restructures-era-committee-frick-award-voting.

National Baseball Hall of Fame Press Release. "Joe Gordon Elected to Baseball Hall of Fame by Vets' Committee." *Web.archive.org*. Retrieved December 6, 2023, from https://web.archive.org/web/20081211121742/http://www.hofmag.com/content/view/1314/190/.

National Baseball Hall of Fame Press Release. "Josh Rawitch Named President of the National Baseball Hall of Fame and Museum." *Baseballhall.org*, June 28, 2021. Retrieved December 27, 2023, from https://baseballhall.org/news/josh-rawitch-named-hall-of-fame-president.

National Baseball Hall of Fame Press Release. "National Baseball Hall of Fame and Museum Selects Research Team to Complete African-American Baseball History Study." *Web.archive.org*, February 14, 2021. Retrieved November 22, 2023, from https://web.archive.org/web/20010618112844/http://baseballhalloffame.org/whats_new/press_releases/pr2001_02_19.htm.

Bibliography

National Baseball Hall of Fame Press Release. "The Souls of the Game Exhibit Will Celebrate Black Baseball and How It Shaped America." *Baseballhall.org*, June 19, 2021. Retrieved January 5, 2024, from https://baseballhall.org/news/the-souls-of-the-game-exhibit-to-debut-in-spring-2024.

National Baseball Hall of Fame Press Release. "Tim Mead to Step Down as President of National Baseball Hall of Fame and Museum." *Baseballhall.org*, April 16, 2021. Retrieved December 27, 2023, from https://baseballhall.org/news/tim-mead-to-step-down-as-president-of-national-baseball-hall-of-fame-and-museum.

National Baseball Hall of Fame Press Release. "Two Managers, Three Executives Comprise Class of 2008." *Web.archive.org*, December 3, 2007. Retrieved December 6, 2023, from https://web.archive.org/web/20071204185637/http://web.baseball halloffame.org/news/article.jsp?ymd=20071203&content_id=5714&vkey=hof_pr.

Negro League Baseball Players Association. "Transcript of Negro Leagues, Pre-Negro Leagues Special Election Results Announcement." *NLBPA.com*, February 27, 2006. Retrieved November 23, 2023, from http://www.nlbpa.com/news/febuary-27-2006.html.

Nesbitt, Stephen J. "The Negro Leagues Are Major Leagues—but Merging Their Stats Has Been Anything but Seamless." *The Athletic*, May 11, 2023. Retrieved May 29, 2023, from https://theathletic.com/4503613/2023/05/11/negro-leagues-statistics-mlb-records/.

"NHL Statement on Calls for Racial Justice." *NHL.com*. Retrieved January 11, 2024, from https://www.nhl.com/news/national-hockey-league-statement-on-calls-for-racial-justice-317076670.

Nielsen, Euell A. "The Double V Campaign (1942–1945)." *Blackpast.org*, July 1, 2020. Retrieved August 11, 2023, from https://www.blackpast.org/african-american-history/events-african-american-history/the-double-v-campaign-1942-1945/.

Nightengale, Bob (2016, September 12). "Adam Jones on MLB's Lack of Kaeper-nick Protest: 'Baseball Is a White Man's Sport.'" *USA Today*, September 12, 2016. Retrieved December 14, 2023, from https://www.usatoday.com/story/sports/mlb/columnist/bob-nightengale/2016/09/12/adam-jones-orioles-colin-kaepernick-white-mans-sport/90260326/.

Nightengale, Bob. "Opinion: It's Time to Remove J.G. Taylor Spink's Name Off Baseball Writer's Award Over His Racist Views." *USA Today*, July 1, 2020. Retrieved April 13, 2023, from https://www.usatoday.com/story/sports/mlb/columnist/bob-nightengale/2020/07/01/j-g-taylor-spink-baseball-writers-award-racism/5356572002/.

Nusbaum, Eric. "The Story Behind Jackie Robinson's Moving Testimony Before the House Un-American Activities Committee." *Time.com*, March 24, 2020. Retrieved October 9, 2023, from https://time.com/5808543/jackie-robinson-huac/.

Obermeyer, Jeff. "The Business of Baseball During World War II." *SABR.org*. Retrieved January 9, 2024, from https://sabr.org/journal/article/the-business-of-baseball-during-world-war-ii/.

Olson, Emily. "Antifa, Boogaloo Boys, White Nationalists: Which Extremists Showed Up to the US Black Lives Matter Protests?" *ABC.net.au*, June 27, 2020. Retrieved January 11, 2024, from https://www.abc.net.au/news/2020-06-28/antifa-boogaloo-extremists-at-us-floyd-protests/12388260.

Oppel, Richard A., Jr., Derrick Bryson Taylor, and Nicholas Bogel-Burroughs. "What to Know About Breonna Taylor's Death." *NYTimes.com*, December 13, 2023. Retrieved January 11, 2024, from https://www.nytimes.com/article/breonna-taylor-police.html.

Poindexter, Owen. "MLB's Move to 'Elevate' the Negro Leagues Risks Diminishing Them." *Slate.com*, December 23, 2020. Retrieved December 20, 2023, from https://slate.com/culture/2020/12/negro-leagues-major-league-baseball-record-books-complications.html.

Posnanski, Joe. "Brilliant Reader Challenges: Dogs, Journeymen, Dumb Lyrics and More." *Joeblogs.joeposnanski.com*, June 22, 2023. Retrieved

January 2, 2024, from https://joeblogs.joeposnanski.com/p/brilliant-reader-challenges-dogs.

Posnanski, Joe. "The Pre-Integration Committee." *NBCSports.com*, October 7, 2015. Retrieved June 20, 2023, from https://sportsworld.nbcsports.com/the-pre-integration-committee/.

Posnanski, Joe. "Ted and Satchel." *Joeposnanski.substack.com*, October 10, 2021. Retrieved June 20, 2023, from https://joeposnanski.substack.com/p/ted-and-satchel.

Posnanski, Joe. "Time for a Hall of Fame Stand." *NBCSports.com*, December 26, 2013. Retrieved June 20, 2023, from https://mlb.nbcsports.com/2013/12/26/time-for-a-hall-of-fame-stand/.

"Rawitch Announcement." *MLB.com* Video, 1:19, posted by MLB FilmRoom, January 25, 2022, https://www.mlb.com/es/video/anuncio-de-rawitch.

Red, Christian. "Baseball's Recognition of Negro Leagues 'Long Overdue' to Heirs and Supporters." *NBCNews.com*, December 18, 2020. Retrieved December 21, 2023, from https://www.nbcnews.com/news/nbcblk/baseball-s-recognition-negro-leagues-long-overdue-heirs-supporters-n1251704.

"Roger Goodell Issues Statement on Death of George Floyd, Nationwide protests." *NFL.com*. Retrieved January 11, 2024, from https://www.nfl.com/news/roger-goodell-issues-statement-on-killing-of-george-floyd-nationwide-protests.

Salvatore, Victor. "The Man Who Didn't Invent Baseball." *American Heritage*, June/July 1983. Retrieved April 28, 2023, from https://www.americanheritage.com/man-who-didnt-invent-baseball.

Schlossberg, Dan. "Writers Remove J.G. Taylor Spink Name from Prestigious Award After Research Reveals Racist Tendencies." *Forbes*, February 5, 2021. Retrieved April 13, 2023, from https://www.forbes.com/sites/danschlossberg/2021/02/05/writers-remove-jg-taylor-spink-name-from-prestigious-award-after-research-reveals-racist-tendencies/?sh=2f17a44e1e17.

Scott, Nate. "A Night of Protest: Where NBA, WNBA, MLS, and MLB Stand After Players Boycott Games." *USA-Today.com*, August 27, 2020. Retrieved January 11, 2024, from https://ftw.usatoday.com/2020/08/nba-wnba-mls-mlb-protests.

Sherman, Joel. "Vets Vote Him In, But … No Way Maz Deserves Hall." *New York Post*, March 7, 2001. Retrieved December 14, 2023, from https://nypost.com/2001/03/07/vets-vote-him-in-but-no-way-maz-deserves-hall/.

Silva, Drew. "Throwback: Ted Williams' Hall of Fame Speech." *NBCSports.com*, July 27, 2014. Retrieved September 14, 2023, from https://www.nbcsports.com/mlb/news/throwback-ted-williams-hall-of-fame-speech.

Smith, Johnny "Jackie Robinson Was Asked to Denounce Paul Roberson. Instead, He Went After Jim Crow." *Andscape.com*, April 15, 2019. Retrieved September 5, 2023, from https://andscape.com/features/jackie-robinson-was-asked-to-denounce-paul-robeson-before-huac-instead-he-went-after-jim-crow/.

Smith, Tovia. "Boston Changes 'Yawkey Way' to 'Jersey Street' After Concerns Over Racist Legacy." *NPR.org*, April 26, 2018. Retrieved October 31, 2023, from https://www.npr.org/2018/04/26/605851052/boston-red-sox-want-to-strike-former-owners-name-off-street-sign.

Snyder, Brad. "When Segregation Doomed Baseball in Washington." *Washington Post*, February 16, 2003. Retrieved August 16, 2023, from https://www.washingtonpost.com/archive/sports/2003/02/16/when-segregation-doomed-baseball-in-washington/90dfcd24-7414-4de9-affd-518faba3cd87/.

Society for American Baseball Research. "10 Finalists Named for Baseball Hall of Fame's 2013 Pre-Integration Era Ballot." *SABR.org*, November 1, 2012. Retrieved December 6, 2023, from https://sabr.org/latest/10-finalists-named-for-baseball-hall-of-fames-2013-pre-integration-era-ballot/.

"The Souls of the Game: Voices of Black Baseball." *YawkeyFoundation.org*. Retrieved January 7, 2024, from https://yawkeyfoundation.org/the-souls-of-the-game-voices-of-black-baseball/.

Bibliography

"'The Splendid Splinter' is enshrined in Cooperstown." YouTube video, 3:00, posted by MLB, December 12, 2013, https://youtu.be/Yi8ukM_NCf4?si=O1GmTqqq9yup7mJ5.

Staff Report. "Hall of Fame Names New President." *AllOtsego.com*, June 28, 2021. Retrieved June 21, 2023, from https://www.allotsego.com/hall-of-fame-names-new-president/.

Storrs, Francis. "Boston's Best Feuds." *BostonMagazine.com*, December 28, 2009. Retrieved September 14, 2023, from https://www.bostonmagazine.com/2009/12/28/bostons-best-feuds/.

Stout, Glenn. "Tryout and Fallout: Race, Jackie Robinson, and the Red Sox." *Massachusetts Historical Review* 6 (2004): 11–37. *Glennstout.com*. Retrieved August 14, 2023, from https://glennstout.com/tryout-and-fallout-race-jackie-robinson-and-the-red-sox/.

Sun-Times Wire. "White Sox Legend Miñoso on Hall of Fame Ballot for 2012." *Chicago.suntimes.com*, November 3, 2011. Retrieved December 6, 2023, from https://chicago.suntimes.com/news/2011/11/3/18548047/white-sox-legend-minoso-on-hall-of-fame-ballot-for-2012.

Svrluga, Barry. "Baseball Is Finally Ending Its Racist Past, but Its Work Can't End There." *Washington Post*, December 16, 2020. Retrieved June 14, 2023, from https://www.washingtonpost.com/sports/2020/12/16/mlb-josh-gibson-satchel-paige-negro-leagues/.

"Ted Williams (part one of three)." YouTube video, 14:19, posted by MyyyClips, September 21, 2010, https://youtu.be/DeiNQqMyQ_k?si=-jOovhlRAp6t5Z-um.

Thorn, John. "The Letters of Abner Graves." *OurGame.mlblogs.com*, February 20, 2013. Retrieved May 1, 2023, from https://ourgame.mlblogs.com/the-letters-of-abner-graves-8fc6a4694419.

"Tipping Your Cap." *TippingYourCap.com*. Retrieved December 19, 2023, from https://www.tippingyourcap.com/.

"Voting Rules History." *Baseballhall.org*. Retrieved August 1, 2023, from https://baseballhall.org/hall-of-famers/rules/voting-rules-history.

Walker, Ben. "MVP Plaque Presenters to Discuss Landis' Name on MLB Trophy." *Associated Press*, July 2, 2020. Retrieved April 17, 2023, from https://apnews.com/article/82cdd84723ffb741e885d4795afc09f3.

Weinbaum, William. "50 Years Ago, Major League Baseball Stumbled Before Inducting Satchel Paige to the Hall of Fame." *Andscape.com*, August 9, 2021. Retrieved June 5, 2023, from https://andscape.com/features/50-years-ago-major-league-baseball-stumbled-before-inducting-satchel-paige-into-the-hall-of-fame/.

Whirty, Ryan. "HOF: No More Negro Leaguers, and No Changes to Policy." *Homeplatedontmove.wordpress.com*, January 14, 2016. Retrieved December 1, 2023, from https://homeplatedontmove.wordpress.com/2016/01/14/hof-no-more-negro-leaguers-and-no-changes-to-policy/.

Whirty, Ryan. "Posnanski: Hall of Fame Is 'Tone Deaf.'" *Homeplatedontmove.com*, February 3, 2016. Retrieved December 7, 2023, from https://homeplatedontmove.wordpress.com/2016/02/03/posnanski-hall-of-fame-is-tone-deaf/.

Yates, Clinton. "MLB Elevating the Status of the Negro Leagues Is the Problem, Not the Solution." *Andscape.com*, December 16, 2020. Retrieved December 20, 2023, from https://andscape.com/features/mlb-elevating-the-status-of-negro-leagues-is-the-problem-not-the-solution/.

Documentaries and Films

Baseball. Directed by Ken Burns. National Endowment for the Humanities, 1994.

Index

Aaron, Hank 23, 26, 117, 121, 163
Adams, Doc 181
Alexandra (LA) *News Leader* 78
Alfred Corning Clark Gymnasium 13
Ali, Muhammad 26, 92
All-American Girls Professional Baseball League 63
Allen, Dick 152–153
Allen, Newt 116, 142
Alston, Walter 111
Amateur Athletic Union 9
American Association 181
American League 19, 30, 47, 51, 53, 56, 68, 113, 136, 164, 181
American Library Association 151
American Negro League 165
Anson, Cap 32, 170
Aparicio, Luis 138
Arizona Diamondbacks 168, 170
Arizona Republic 129
Ashland, Kentucky 118, 120–123, 125, 127
Ashwill, Gary 165
Associated Press 39, 78, 95, 129
Atlanta Braves 85
Averill, Earl 107

Baltimore Afro-American 45
Baltimore Elite Giants 31, 40
Baltimore Orioles 27, 161
Baltimore Stars 80
Banks, Ernie 119, 121, 126, 143, 146
Barlick, Al 113
Barnes, Eppie 31, 94–95
Barnhill, Dave 39
barnstorming 2, 33–34, 63–64, 67–68, 166; outlawed by Landis 17
Baseball documentary 127–128, 130, 134, 143, 158
baseball, origins 6, 9, 11
Baseball-Reference.com 166, 185
Baseball Writers Association of America

3, 14, 23, 25, 28, 53–55, 59, 71, 73, 79, 85, 87, 90, 94, 124, 139, 153, 156; and Career Excellence Award 164; and Hall of Fame 28, 108; and Hall of Fame voting 54, 57–58, 69–70, 79, 82, 86–87, 100, 102, 106–107, 137, 140; and integration 51; leadership 86; and minstrel show 23; and MVP Award 163–164; segregated 23, 25, 57
Basie, Count 123
BBWAA *see* Baseball Writers Association of America
BBWAA Career Excellence Award 164
Beckwith, John 131, 142
beer industry 13
Bell, Cool Papa 1, 65, 67, 72, 81, 114, 116, 167; Hall of Fame election 104
Bell, William 142
Bender, Charles 76
Benswanger, William 39–40
The Bible of Baseball *see* *The Sporting News*
Black, Joe 114, 120
Black Baseball Initiative 175, 177–178, 185
Black Economic Union in Kansas City 123
Blackball Stars 134
Blaeholder, George 73
Blue, Vida 152
Bonds, Barry 76
Bonds, Bobby 152
Boston Bees *see* Boston Braves
Boston Braves 44–45, 55, 84
Boston Globe 45, 77, 99, 169
Boston Herald 77
Boston Record 36
Boston Record-American 86
Boston Red Caps 15
Boston Red Sox 44–46, 48, 53, 56–57, 68, 76–77, 110, 119
Boston Traveler 77

223

224   Index

Bottomley, Jim 107
Boudreau, Lou 78, 80, 92, 100
Bowie, Jim 88
Brands, Edgar G. 27–28
Breadon, Sam 47, 50
Bresnahan, Roger 30, 48
Brett, George 163
Brewer, Chet 67, 120, 142
Briggs, Walter 56
Brock, Lou 117, 143, 146
Broeg, Bob 89, 115
Brooklyn Dodgers 35, 38, 43, 46, 50–52, 55, 60–64, 67, 81, 84, 148, 170, 174
Brown, Barney 37
Brown, Jim 92
Brown, Joe L. 117, 137–138, 140
Brown, John Y. 120
Brown, Ray 142
Brown, Warren 36
Brown, Willard 57, 72, 106, 131, 142–143, 146
Buck O'Neil Education and Research Center 149
Buck O'Neil Lifetime Achievement Award 63, 149–150
Bulkeley, Morgan 8
Burgos, Adrian 142
Burlington (NC) *Daily Times-News* 80
Burns, Bud 78
Burns, Ken 127, 129–130, 134, 143, 158; and Buck O'Neil 128–129; and NLBM 129
Busch, August, Jr. 88
Bush, George W. 163
Byrd, Bill 142

Caldwell, Earl 53
Calloway, Cab 123
Camilli, Dolph 46
Campanella, Roy 39–40, 64, 76, 80, 86, 91, 95, 100, 103, 112; and Dick Young 83, 87, 91; and Hall of Fame 94, 103; Hall of Fame election 86; and Veterans Committee 108–109, 115
Carpenter, Bob 43
Carter, Jimmy 163
Carter, Joe 143
Cartwright, Alexander 25, 60
centennial celebration 14, 19, 25, 28
Centennial Commission 25, 28, 70
Central Press Association 72
Chadwick, Henry 6–7, 11, 30
Chance, Frank 48, 71
Chandler, Albert "Happy" 43–44, 48, 51, 58–60, 119; Hall of Fame election 111; resignation 59

Chapman, Ben 43, 51–52, 64
Charleston, Oscar 22, 81, 116; Hall of Fame election 104
Chicago American 36
Chicago American Giants 26, 111
Chicago Cubs 39, 47, 55, 117, 125
Chicago Defender 32, 81, 103, 105
Chicago Herald-Examiner 36
Chicago Tribune 72, 78–79
Chicago White Sox 40, 53, 55, 59
Chicago White Stockings 32
Cincinnati Reds 41, 56, 110, 161
Civil Rights movement 3, 92, 124, 158
The Civil War documentary 127–129
Claflin, Larry 86
Clark, Dick 141–142
Clark, Jane Forbes 139, 141, 145, 156, 162, 170
Clark, Stephen C. 13–14, 20, 23, 57–58, 79, 183
Clark Foundation 14, 79
Clark Sports Center 6
Classic Baseball Era Committee 174–175, 182
Cleland, Alexander 14, 16, 18, 23, 25, 183; and Landis 19
Clemente, Roberto 83
Cleveland Buckeyes 45
Cleveland Call and Post 81
Cleveland Indians 51–53, 55, 64, 68–69, 99
Cleveland *Plain Dealer* 38, 52
Clinton, Bill 163
Cobb, Ty 17, 30, 89; and Hall of Fame 31
Cobbledick, Gordon 38, 52–53
Collins, Eddie 44–46
Comiskey Park 47
Concepción, Dave 152
Condon, Dave 72, 78–80
Contemporary Era Committee 174–175, 182
Cooke, Bob 53–54
Cooper, Andy 142
Cooper, James Fenimore 6
Cooperstown, New York 1, 2, 5–6, 9–11, 13, 15–17, 19–20, 30, 32, 74, 79, 86, 98, 101, 104, 119, 120, 126, 170, 176, 178–179, 182; economy 13–15; tourism 13–14, 57–58
Costas, Bob 76
Covid-19 pandemic 159, 161–162, 167, 168
Cox, Bobby 152
Cox, William 42–43
Cronin, Joe 45–46, 56–57, 115
Crutchfield, Jimmie 120

Index 225

Cuban players 41
Cummings, Candy 29
Cy Young Award 55

Dahlen, Bill 181
Daily Worker 23, 36, 38–39
Daley, Arthur 54
Dandridge, Ray 106, 113, 116, 119, 132
Daniel, Dan 23, 102
Day, Leon 106, 131–133
Dean, Dizzy 30, 63
DePauw University 61
Des Moines Register 72
Detroit Free Press 97
Detroit Tigers 41, 56
Dihigo, Martin 22; Hall of Fame election 104–105
DiMaggio, Joe 30–31, 54
Dixon, Phil 126, 151, 171
Dixon, Rap 142
Doby, Larry 51, 52, 64, 68, 113, 132–133; on Bob Feller 68
Doerr, Bobby 112
Donaldson, John 22, 106, 142, 146
Doswell, Ray 145–146, 151
Double V Campaign 43
Doubleday, Abner 9–10, 16, 19, 25, 182; baseball origin myth 1–2, 11–12, 14, 117, 178; and omission from Hall of Fame 25
Doubleday Baseball 13–14, 176
Doubleday Field 14, 19
Doucet, Jacques 173
Doyle, Charles J. 28
Dreyfuss, Barney 151
Du Bois, W.E.B. 177
Duffy, Hugh 45, 48
Duncan, Frank, Jr. 155
Durocher, Leo 38, 41; Hall of Fame election 114
Dykes, Jimmy 40

Early, Gerald 177
Early Baseball Era Committee 156–157, 159, 161, 171, 175
East-West League 165
Eastern Colored League 165, 181
Eckert, William 74
Edwards, Bruce 64
Egan, Dave 36, 77
Elias Sports Bureau 165, 167
Eras Committees 148, 151–154, 156, 161–162, 171, 174, 182
ESPN 128–129
Evansville Press 101
Evers, Johnny 48, 71

Evers, Medgar 92
Executive Order 8802 41
exhibition games 2, 65
Expansion Era Committee 152

Fain, Ferris 55
Fangraphs.com 166
Farmers Museum 79
Feller, Bob 65, 69, 92, 100, 146, 177; on Black ballplayers 65–69, 72; and father 66–67; and Hall of Fame 69–70; and Jackie Robinson 67, 72, 86; and Larry Doby 68–69; and Negro Leagues reunion 119; opinionated 66, 73;and Satchel Paige 65–67, 71, 78, 124; and *Saturday Evening Post* article 71
Fenway Park 45–46, 48, 110, 119, 170, 186
Ferrell, Rick 112, 137, 138, 146
Flood, Curt 152
Floyd, George 3, 159–160, 167; protests 160
Fly Creek, New York 13
Foote, Shelby 127–128
Forbes, Frank 94–95
Forbes Field 39
Ford C. Frick Award 51, 63, 140, 155, 173
Foster, Andrew "Rube" 18, 22, 26, 30, 32, 80, 90, 106, 116, 129, 135, 154, 162; Hall of Fame election 111, 116–117
Foster, Willie 106, 116, 131–133
Fowler, Bud 2, 15, 30, 48, 131, 175, 178; baseball career 15; in Cooperstown 15; Hall of Fame election 171
Fox, Nellie 137
Foxx, Jimmie 70
Fredland, John 184
Frick, Ford 22, 32–34, 36–37, 41–43, 46–48, 50, 62, 78, 81, 92, 173, 177, 183; and asterisk 22; autobiography 20, 22, 24; and Babe Ruth 22–23; and BBWAA 23; as commissioner 59–62, 79; early years 20; as Hall of Fame chairman 79, 82, 88, 100; as Hall of Fame founder 20; and Hall of Fame opening 25; and integrating baseball 24; and minstrel show 23; as National League president 19; opposes Negro Leagues HOF eligiblity 90–91; portrait 20; public relations 19, 25; and segregation 21, 23, 33, 35; support of Hall of Fame 19
Frisch, Frankie 31, 39, 57; and Hall of Fame 102, 107

Gallagher, James 39
Gammons, Peter 164

226 Index

Garagiola, Joe 51, 63, 150, 177; and Jackie Robinson 51, 63
Gehrig, Lou 37, 66, 100
George, Steve 67
Gibson, Josh 1, 30, 32, 37, 39, 48, 75–76, 78–79, 81, 87, 89–90, 96, 116, 124, 166–167; Hall of Fame election 98, 104
Gila River Internment Camp 174
Giles, Warren 110
Gillick, Pat 151–152
Golden Days Era Committee 152, 156, 161
Goodale, George 76
Goodwin, Doris Kearns 129
Gordon, Joe 140, 148, 151
Gottlieb, Ed 95
Grant, Charlie 32
Grant, Frank 26–27, 142, 154
Graves, Abner 9–14, 182; inaccuracies 10; murder committed 12, 14; wife 12
Gray, Pete 41
Great Depression 13
Greater Ashland Foundation 122
Green, Pumpsie 56, 76
Green Light Letter 40
Greenup, Kentucky 118, 126
Greenup County Sentinel 118
Griffith, Calvin 49, 56
Griffith, Clark 48–49, 58
Griffith Stadium 48, 89
Guilfoyle, Bill 131, 133

Hafey, Chick 137
Hagen, Paul 164
Hairston, Jerry, Jr. 165
Hairston, Sam 165
Hall of Fame *see* National Baseball Hall of Fame and Museum
Hall of Fame for Great Americans 20
Harlem Globetrotters 42
Harridge, William 19–20, 47, 53
Harris, Vic 178
Harrison, Claude 81
Harvey, Doug 151
Heilmann, Harry 132
Henderson, Edwin 32, 103
Heritage Celebration 125
Herman, Billy 107
Herzog, Whitey 151
Heydler, John 19, 23
Heyman, Jon 139
Higbie, Kirby 50
Higgins, Pinky 56
Hill, Herman 40
Hill, Pete 142, 154
Hilldale Club 119
Hitler, Adolf 36, 56

Hodges, Gil 139, 172
Hogan, Larry 141–142
Holiday, Billie 123
Holtzman, Jerome 23, 25, 134–137
Holway, John 94–95, 104, 112, 116, 131–132, 134, 144
Homestead Grays 32, 39, 48, 89, 126
Honolulu Advertiser 97
Horgan, Tim 77
Horn, Brad 148–149
Hornsby, Rogers 40, 57; prejudices 40
Hostetler, Chuck 41
House of David 181
House Un-American Activities Committee 64
Houston Astros 161
Howard, Elston 57, 84
Hughes, Sammy T. 39, 65, 142
Hunt, Marshall 26
Hunter, Rose 165

Idelson, Jeff 149–150, 168
Indianapolis Clowns 80
Indianapolis Star 99
International Association 15
International League 67, 84
Irvin, Monte 90–91, 95, 97, 112, 116, 119–120, 132–133, 142; Hall of Fame election 104–105; and Special Committee on the Negro Leagues 104
Isaacs, Stan 79, 89

Jackie Robinson Day 161
Jackie Robinson Foundation 177
Jackie Robinson Museum 171, 174
Jackson, Reggie 163
Jackson, Sheep 81
Jackson, Travis 111
Jacobson, Steve 80
Jaffe, Jay 138, 153–154, 174
James, Bill 139
Jansen, Larry 55
Jarrín, Jaime 171
jazz 123, 125, 127
Jean Thomas Museum 122
Jenkins, Fats 31, 142
Jeter, Derek 163
Jethroe, Sam 45–46
J.G. Taylor Spink Award 140
Jim Crow laws 64, 97, 149
Johns, Walter L. 72
Johnson, Ban 30
Johnson, Home Run 142
Johnson, Jack 22, 26
Johnson, Judy 94–95, 113, 116, 119, 121; Hall of Fame election 104–106

Index

Johnson, Magic 163
Johnson, W. Lloyd 127
Johnson, Walter 89
Jolson, Al 22
Jones, Adam 161
Jones, Slim 81, 87
Joss, Addie 29, 77, 110; Hall of Fame rule 29
Judd, Naomi 118
Judd, Wynonna 118

Kaepernick, Colin 161
Kansas City, Missouri 33, 122–123, 125–127, 129, 141, 144, 149, 162, 171
Kansas City Monarchs 45, 115–117, 123, 125, 133, 155
Kansas City Royals 117, 125–126, 138, 173
Kansas City Star 143
Kansas City YMCA Building 122, 125, 162
Kauffman Stadium 173
Kay, Eric 167–168
Keane, Clif 45
Kell, George 111
Kellet, Red 31
Kelly, George "Highpockets" 137, 138
Kendrick, Bob 33, 144, 162, 164–165, 167, 171, 177
Kenosha, Wisconsin 161
Kerr, Paul 78–79, 82, 87–92, 100–101
Kessler, Gene 26
Killebrew, Harmon 138
King, Martin Luther, Jr. 92
Klein, Chuck 110, 116, 119, 146
Knickerbocker Base Ball Club of New York 10
Koppett, Leonard 81
Ku Klux Klan 21–22, 31–32, 40, 58
Kuhn, Bowie 87- 92, 96, 98–99, 101, 104; and Hall of Fame 89, 94–95, 100; Hall of Fame election 151; and Negro Leagues 89, 103, 124; and Negro Leagues Hall of History 120–121; and Negro Leagues reunions 119–120, 122; and Special Committee on the Negro Leagues 104, 106, 108

Lacy, Sam 45–46, 48, 95; and BBWAA membership 54; and Hall of Fame 94; and Special Committee on the Negro Leagues 103
Lake Otsego 13
Lanctot, Neil 115
Landis, Kenesaw Mountain 3, 16, 22, 28, 31–32, 36, 38–44, 46, 56, 58, 60, 163, 170, 173; death 43; elected to Hall of Fame 43, 57; and Hall of Fame 17, 19; name removed from MVP Award 163; opposing integration 3, 33; outlawed barnstorming 17; and segregation 23, 37–38, 40
Lang, Jack 90
Larkin, Barry 163
LaRussa, Tony 152
Lazzeri, Tony 113
Lee, Julia 123
Leonard, Buck 37, 48, 76, 95, 114, 116, 119, 122, 165; Hall of Fame election 104
Leonard, Dutch 53
Lester, Larry 126, 141–142, 144–147, 151, 169, 171, 177
Letterman, David 134
Lewis, Allen 117
Lewis, Ira 37
Leyland, Jim 175
Lieb, Fred 26, 102, 117
Lindstrom, Freddie 107, 137–138
Linn, Ed 71
Lloyd, John Henry "Pop" 30, 32, 87, 90, 135, 154; Hall of Fame election 104–105
Lombardi, Ernie 112
Long Island Press 90
Los Angeles Angels 76, 167–168
Los Angeles Dodgers *see* Brooklyn Dodgers
Louis, Joe 26, 51
Lundy, Dick 106, 142
Luque, Dolf 57, 84
Lynn Live Oaks 15

Mackey, Biz 32, 106, 112, 131, 142, 146
MacPhail, Larry 46–47, 110
Maglie, Sal 61
Major League Baseball 1, 5, 15–17, 76, 78, 86, 88, 141, 154, 160–163, 165, 168, 176–177; coordination with Hall of Fame 18; and Negro Leagues recognition 164, 166
Major League Baseball Advanced Media 170
Major League Baseball Player's Association 162, 177
Major League Committee on Baseball Integration 46
Malarcher, Dave 178
Malcolm X 65, 92
Manfred, Rob 160, 163–165, 168
Manley, Abe 105
Manley, Effa 96, 105, 120, 142, 146
Manson, Charles 118
Maranville, Rabbit 132, 138

228   Index

Marcelle, Oliver 142
Maris, Roger 22
Marshall University 118
Mary Imogene Bassett Hospital 13
Mathewson, Christy 32
Mays, Willie 75–76, 113, 121; on Hall of Fame 97
Mazeroski, Bill 137–140, 161–162
McCovey, Willie 138
McDonald, Webster 115
McGowan, Bill 113
McGraw, John 26, 32
McGriff, Fred 175
Mead, Tim 167, 168
Medwick, Joe 51, 63
Memphis Red Sox 117
Méndez, José 32, 106, 142, 154
Mexican League 40
Meyer, Russ 61
Mills, Abraham 8, 10–11, 12
Mills Commission 7–10, 14
Milwaukee Brewers 42, 161
Milwaukee Bucks 161
Minneapolis Millers 113
Minnesota Twins 49
Miñoso, Minnie 142–143, 146, 149, 152, 172; Hall of Fame election 171
Mize, Johnny 116, 137
Modern Baseball Era Committee 156
Montreal Expos 173
Montreal Royals 64, 67, 83–84
Moore, Al 31
Moore, Dobie 142
Moreland, Nate 40
Morgan, Bud 129
Morgan, Joe 139, 155
Most Valuable Player Award 55, 67
Motley, Bob 126, 178
Motley, Don 126, 129, 134, 144–146
Muchnick, Isadore 44, 45
Muckerman, Richard 55
Murphy, Bob 27
Murray, Jim 72, 97

Nashville Tennessean 78
Nason, Jerry 77
National Association 29, 103, 181
National Baseball Hall of Fame and Museum 3, 5, 6, 21, 29, 43, 46, 48–49, 51, 55, 57, 60, 63, 70, 73–74, 76, 78, 92, 96, 100–101, 111, 120, 124, 126, 132, 138–139, 141, 149–150, 161, 174, 179; artifact collection 18; and BBWAA 23, 28; changes to voting process 108, 130–131, 133, 135, 140, 155–156, 162, 172, 174; displays 3; election bodies

29; eligibility rules 29, 79–80, 82, 107, 140; first class 30; founding 16, 20, 28; grand opening 25; grounds 6; leadership 76, 78–79, 82, 90, 92, 99–100, 105–106, 115–116, 122, 124–125, 130, 137, 139, 141, 149, 154–155, 158, 167–168, 170, 174; location 6; and Negro Leagues 32, 69, 85, 88, 97–99, 102–104, 109–110, 114, 116–119, 121, 123–124, 130, 135, 148, 155, 158; Negro Leagues display 115, 120, 122, 125, 133, 141, 151, 167–169, 175–176, 178; and NLBM 171; origins 1, 2, 14; plaque gallery 20, 93, 95; and public opinion 159, 163; racial disparity of members 135–137, 153, 169, 180; and segregation 21, 40; study of Black baseball 141–142; 2006 Special Committee on African-American Baseball 144–148, 158
National Basketball Association 160, 161
National Football League 160
National Hockey League 160
National League 7, 8, 15, 19, 20, 23, 26, 28, 30, 34, 35, 42, 43, 47, 51, 60, 88, 110, 114, 132, 136, 164, 181
Neal, LaVelle E., III 25
Negro American League 117, 165, 181
The Negro in Sports 32
Negro Leagues 1, 21, 25, 27, 29–30, 32, 34, 39, 41–42, 45, 47–48, 58, 64, 69, 72–73, 76–79, 81, 83, 85, 87–91, 93, 96, 100, 102, 104–105, 108, 111, 115–116, 124, 126, 128–130, 134, 138, 164, 166; and Hall of Fame 2, 103, 106, 109, 110, 113, 114, 115, 116, 117, 118, 122, 124–125, 130, 135–137, 139, 142, 147–149, 151–156 158–159, 161, 168, 173–175, 179–180; Hall of Fame eligibility 89, 92, 94–95; 100 year anniversary 162, 167; recognized as major league 164–166; record against White major leagues 17; reunions 118, 119, 123; statistics 1; and 2006 Special Committee on African-American Baseball 146; and Veterans Committee 117
Negro Leagues Baseball Museum 33, 126–128, 134, 141, 143–147, 149, 151, 158, 162, 165, 167, 177; and *Baseball* documentary 129; founding 126; and Hall of Fame 171, 173; Tip Your Cap campaign 162
Negro Leagues Hall of History 120–123, 125–126
Negro National League 17, 18, 22, 30, 65, 90, 106, 111, 122, 125–126, 129, 153–154, 162, 165, 181

Index

Negro National League (II) 165
Negro Southern League 165
New York Black Yankees 31, 126
New York *Daily Mirror* 36, 79
New York Daily News 32, 36, 82–83, 106, 113
New York Giants 32, 55, 60–61, 90, 94
New York Herald Tribune 53
New York Post 78
New York Times 54, 99
New York Yankees 45–46, 51, 56–57, 59, 62, 84, 152, 160
Newark Eagles 96, 106, 120, 132–133, 146
Newcombe, Don 55, 64, 84, 120, 152
Newhouser, Hal 113
Newsday 79, 89, 134, 149
Nichols, Ed 72
Nightengale, Bob 164
Nixon, Richard 65
NLBM *see* Negro Leagues Baseball Museum
Norton, Pete 54
Nugent, Gerry 41–43
Nuxhall, Joe 41

Oakland Athletics 161
Oakland Oaks 46
Obama, Barack 163
Obenshain, Earl 28
Obermeyer, Jeff 47
O'Day, Hank 152
Odom, John "Blue Moon" 76
Oh, Sadaharu 178
Olbermann, Keith 128
Old Timers Committee 32, 57, 58, 69
Oliva, Tony 152, 172
Oliver, Al 152
O'Malley, Walter 148, 151
Oms, Alejandro 142
O'Neil, Buck 63, 68, 95, 98, 120, 125, 130, 134, 141–142, 149–151, 158, 162, 173–175, 180; and *Baseball* documentary 127–130; and Hall of Fame 117, 123, 125, 133, 155; Hall of Fame election 171–172; and Negro Leagues Baseball Museum 123, 127, 129, 145; statue 149, 168; and 2006 Special Committee on African-American Baseball 143–147; and Veterans Committee 117–118, 130–133, 137, 144
Only the Ball Was White 89, 95, 99, 102, 104, 124, 134, 145
Orlando Magic 161
Ortiz, David 138, 171
Otesaga Hotel 13

Ott, Mel 70
Overmyer, Jim 142

Pacific Coast League 46
Page, Ted 115
Page Fence Giants 176
Paige, Satchel 34, 37–38, 52–53, 65, 67–68, 71–73, 75–81, 85, 87, 90, 95–96, 113, 116–117, 134, 167, 169, 173, 178–179; barnstorming 30; and Bob Feller 68; with Cleveland Indians 68–69; Hall of Fame election 78, 96–101, 104, 106, 124; and Negro Leagues reunions 119; and Ted Williams 76
Parker, Dan 36
Parker, Dave 152
Parnell, Roy 142
Patterson, Pat 31
Paula, Carlos 49
Paxton, James 160
Pennock, Herb 43, 51, 57–58, 132
Pershing, John J. 28
Peterson, Robert 89–91, 95, 99, 102–104, 112, 124, 134; death 145; suggests Negro Leagues Hall of Fame eligibility 90
Petroskey, Dale 139, 141, 145, 149
Philadelphia Athletics 55
Philadelphia Phillies 41–43, 51–53, 56, 61, 64, 132
Philadelphia Stars 31, 45
Philadelphia Tribune 81
Pinson, Vada 152
Pittsburgh Courier 23, 25, 32–33, 37, 39, 43–44, 78, 80
Pittsburgh Crawfords 39, 65, 129
Pittsburgh Pirates 34, 39–40, 53, 56–57, 94, 137, 151
Poles, Spottswood 32, 142
Polo Grounds 47, 60
Pompez, Alex 94, 95, 142
Posey, Cumberland 32, 39, 142
Posnanski, Joe 67, 143, 148–149, 154–155, 173, 177, 184
Povich, Shirley 36, 78
Powell, Richard 104
Powers, Jimmy 32, 36, 103
Pre-Integration Committee 148, 152–153, 155, 156
Public Broadcasting Service 127–128
public opinion 3, 35, 100–101, 124, 129, 158
Putnam, Mary Lou 122

Radcliffe, Ted "Double Duty" 76
Rainey, Joseph H. 46

230 Index

Rawitch, Josh 168, 170–176
Reach, Al 8
Redding, Dick "Cannonball" 22, 30, 32, 35, 106, 113, 131–132, 142, 146
Reese, Pee Wee 112
Reichler, Joe 92, 94, 96, 98, 101, 105; and Special Committee on the Negro Leagues 104
Reliford, Charlie 118
Renfro, Othello "Chico" 115, 120, 122
Retrosheet 166
Reynolds, Allie 152
Rickey, Branch 28, 46–47, 50–52, 62, 64, 67, 80–81, 132, 148
Rizzuto, Phil 114
Roberts, Ric 44, 78
Robeson, Paul 32, 37, 64
Robinson, Alan 129
Robinson, Bill "Bojangles" 123
Robinson, Don 118
Robinson, Frank 155
Robinson, Jackie 35, 40, 43, 45–46, 48, 50–56, 59–65, 67, 69, 71–72, 76, 80–81, 92, 100, 103, 110, 112, 114, 132–133, 148, 150–151, 155, 164, 174, 183; autobiography 83; and Bob Feller 86; and Casey Stengel 84; and Dick Young 83–84, 87; and Hall of Fame 70, 72, 95, 97, 99, 150
Robinson, Rachel 133, 150
Rodney, Lester 36–37, 40
Rogan, Charles "Bullet" 81, 106, 115, 131–133
Rookie of the Year Award 50, 55
Roosevelt, Franklin Delano 40–41, 43, 45
Rosecrans, C. Trent 164
Rosenthal, Ken 163
rounders 6–7
Rudd, Paul 163
Ruppert, Jacob 152
Rusie, Amos 107
Russell, Bill 92
Russell, Fred 26
Ruth, Babe 17, 26, 89, 100, 117, 176; barnstorming 17; and Ford Frick 20, 22; praise of Black players 30, 33–34; suspected Black ancestry 17, 26; suspension 17

St. Louis Browns 41, 55, 57
St. Louis Cardinals 47, 50–51, 54, 56, 61, 63, 88, 112, 155, 160
St. Louis Post-Dispatch 89, 115
Salisbury (MD) *Daily Times* 72
San Diego Padres 155
San Francisco 49ers 161

Santo, Ron 141, 152
Santop, Louis 142, 145, 154
Saperstein, Abe 42
Saturday Evening Post 71
Scales, George 142
Schalk, Ray 138
Schlemmer, Jim 26
Schmidt, Mike 163
Schoendienst, Red 113
Scully, Vin 173
Seager, Corey 163
Seamheads Negro Leagues Database 165–166
Seattle Mariners 171
Seay, Dick 120
Selig, Bud 146
Sewell, Joe 107
Sewell, Rip 53
Shaughnessy, Dan 169
Shepard, Bert 41
Shestakofsky, Jon 174, 184
Shieber, Tom 168–169
Simmons, Al 57
Singer Sewing Machine Company 13
Sissle, Noble 61
Skaggs, Tyler 167–168
Slaughter, Enos 51, 112
Smith, Hilton 106, 133–134, 137, 141
Smith, Ken 79, 100
Smith, Lee 143
Smith, Ozzie 155, 163
Smith, Wendell 23, 33–37, 39, 40, 44–45, 50, 56, 61, 78, 84, 95–96; and BBWAA membership 23, 54; and Hall of Fame 94; and Special Committee on the Negro Leagues 103
Society for American Baseball Research 47, 112, 141, 145, 181, 184
Southworth, Billy 148, 151
Spalding, Albert 6–7, 9, 10–12, 29, 30; and baseball origins 8
Spalding Base Ball Guides 7
Speaker, Tris 30–31
Special Committee on the Negro Leagues 92, 99, 102–103, 105, 108, 113–117, 142, 169, 180; disbanded 105–109
Special Early Baseball Overview Committee 171
Spencer, Ted 133
Spink, C.C. Johnson 81, 107
Spink, J.G. Taylor 26, 28, 36, 43, 164, 173; death 81; and Landis 28; named removed from Career Excellence Award 164; and Negro Leagues 26; and segregation 38, 51–53

Index 231

The Sporting News 3, 23, 26, 38, 51–53, 61, 67, 78, 81, 107, 164; coverage of Negro Leagues 26; and racist stereotypes 27–28
Sports Illustrated 98
Stack, Ed 104, 116, 130, 141
Stearnes, Turkey 106, 119, 131, 133
Stengel, Casey 35, 57, 78–80, 82; and Dick Young 85; Hall of Fame election 82–83; racism accusations 84
Stephens, Jake 119
Stephens, Vern 68
Stockton, Roy 102
Stoneham, Horace 55
Streets Hotel 123
Stroman, Marcus 160
Strong, Ted 123
Strouse, Charles 129
Stultz, Tom 118–120, 126
Sullivan, James 9
Sullivan, Paul 163
Surface, Bill 40
Suttles, Mule 106, 131, 142, 146
Suzuki, Ichiro 171

Talbot, Howard 100, 122
Tampa Black Smokers 117
Tampa Tribune 54, 128
Taylor, Ben 142, 154
Taylor, Breonna 159–160
Taylor, Candy Jim 142
Taylor, C.I. 142
Taylor, Willis "Sec" 72
Tebbets, Birdie 117
Terry, Bill 102
Thomas, Clint 118–119
Thompson, Hank 68
Thorn, John 167
Tiant, Luis 152–153
Tiant, Luis, Sr. 116
Tinker, Joe 48, 71
Today's Game Era Committee 156
Toronto Blue Jays 173
Torre, Joe 152
Torriente, Cristóbal 106, 115, 131, 142
Traynor, Pie 34
Tri-State Fair and Regatta Organization 121
Trout, Mike 163

USA Today 164

Vaughan, Arky 112, 137
Veeck, Bill 41–42, 51–53, 55, 72; on Hall of Fame 97; Hall of Fame election 113
Veeck, Bill, Sr. 42

Veterans Committee 82, 85–88, 91, 102, 105–108, 110, 112, 114, 119, 123, 125–126, 130–141, 143–144, 148, 151–153, 156, 158, 162, 174, 180; expansion 108; and Negro Leagues 108–109, 111–118, 133, 146
Vincent, Fay 145

Wagner, Honus 30, 89
Wainwright, Adam 160
Wakefield, Dick 59
Walker, Dixie 52, 64
Walker, Moses Fleetwood 27
Ward, Geoffrey C. 128
Washington Elite Giants 65
Washington Post 36, 78
Washington Senators 41, 48–49, 56, 59
Washington Tribune 48
Wawaka, Indiana 20
Webb, Brandon 118
Weiss, George 56
Wells, Willie 106, 114–116, 120, 131–133
West Point 9, 11
White, Frank 126, 138–139
White, James "Deacon" 141, 149, 152
White, Sol 30, 142, 154
Wilkinson, J.L. 131, 142
Will, George 129
Williams, Billy 117
Williams, Dick 151
Williams, Marvin 45–46
Williams, "Smokey" Joe 32, 81, 87, 106, 113, 115, 132–133
Williams, Ted 73, 82, 85, 92, 100, 158, 161, 162; and Boston media 77; and Dave Egan 77; Hall of Fame speech 74–75, 78–79, 81, 124; praised by media 78; and Satchel Paige 75–76; and Veterans Committee 139
Wills, Maury 152–153
Wilson, Hack 110, 116, 146
Wilson, Jud 131, 142
Wood, Hal 97
Woodall, Larry 45
Woolery, Chuck 118
World Baseball Classic 170
World War II 3, 37, 40, 57, 108, 113, 124, 138
Wright, Bill 31, 87
Wright, George 8, 29
Wright, Glenn 119
Wrigley, Phil 47
Wynn, Early 99

Yancey, Bill 94
Yankee Stadium 47

Yates, Clinton 165
Yawkey, Jean 177
Yawkey, Tom 45–47, 56, 77, 169, 177; Hall of Fame election 110, 119; named removed from street 170
Yawkey Foundation 177
York, Rudy 88
Young, A.S. "Doc" 42, 81, 88, 104–105
Young, Dick 78, 86, 90, 158; advocates for Negro Leagues 87, 91, 96, 99; and Casey Stengel 82–85; and Hall of Fame 94; and Jackie Robinson 83–84; and Negro Leagues 81–82, 85, 90; and Roy Campanella 83, 86–87, 91; and Special Committee on the Negro Leagues 103–104, 106
Young, Fay 42
Young, Nicholas 8